1. Myths
2. Poor Use of Research
3. Organization
4. Poor editing - references not found in reference list
   spelling of author's name
5. Different forms of violence
   Chpt 10 on mental disturbance

Chpt 10 pretty good

6. Deficit individual model

I. Introduction
   1. Purpose of Book
   2. Overview of Materials Covered

II Strengths
   1. various forms + settings for violence
   2. Chapter 10
   3. Chapter on Trauma

Overall - nothing really new or provided in enough detail to be useful.

III. Weaknesses
   1. Poor Organization - odd opening chapter
      no adequate intro
      no sections
      no bridges

ex. is chpt 10.

   2. Poor use of research
      1. Myths - drugs, alcohol, psychopathology
         P. 70 esp
      2. Inaccurate use of research. Chpt 2
         p. 41.
      3. Deficit Model - Bad people
      2. Case ex. don't always fit Chpt 1

No real evidence any of the intervention works (Stereometry)

p. 87. focus on small violence

p. 88 - poor

VIOLENT INDIVIDUALS AND FAMILIES

VIOLENT INDIVIDUALS AND FAMILIES

A Handbook for Practitioners

Edited by

SUSAN SAUNDERS, A.C.S.W.

ANN M. ANDERSON, A.C.S.W.

CYNTHIA ALLEN HART, M.S., R.N.

and

GERALD M. RUBENSTEIN, Ed.D.

CHARLES C THOMAS • PUBLISHER

Springfield • Illinois • U.S.A.

Published and Distributed Throughout the World by

CHARLES C THOMAS • PUBLISHER
2600 South First Street
Springfield, Illinois 62717

ISBN 0-398-04833-9

Library of Congress Catalog Card Number: 83-366

With THOMAS BOOKS *careful attention is given to all details of manufacturing and design. It is the Publisher's desire to present books that are satisfactory as to their physical qualities and artistic possibilities and appropriate for their particular use.* THOMAS BOOKS *will be true to those laws of quality that assure a good name and good will.*

Library of Congress Cataloging in Publication Data

Main entry under title:

Violent individuals and families.

Bibliography:p.
Includes index.
1. Violence--Psychological aspects--Handbooks, manuals, etc. 2. Violence--Treatment--Handbooks, manuals, etc. 3. Family violence--Treatment--Handbooks, manuals etc. I. Saunders, Susan, A.C.S.W. [DNLM: 1. Violence. 2. Family. 3. Crisis intervention. 4. Psychotherapy. WM 401 V795]
RC569.5.V55V58 1983 616.85'82 83-366
ISBN 0-398-04833-9

Printed in the United States of America
Q-R-1

CONTRIBUTORS

PATRICIA L. AMISH, B.S., received her degree from Cornell University in human development and family studies in 1981. Since her graduation, she has worked in the area of child abuse at the Mt. Hope Family Center sponsored by the University of Rochester Psychology Department. She has published several articles on child abuse.

ANN M. ANDERSON, C.S.W., A.C.S.W., received her MSW from Simmons College School of Social Work. She is currently a chief social worker of psychiatry at the University of Rochester School of Medicine and Dentistry. She is also a doctoral student in child and family studies at Syracuse University. In addition to her clinical experience, Mrs. Anderson has taught and conducted research in the area of child abuse.

CAROLE A. ANDERSON, R.N., Ph.D., F.A.A.N., is an associate dean for undergraduate and graduate studies at the University of Rochester School of Nursing. She is a primary therapist in her psychiatric nursing practice. Her research interests include women, substance abuse, and family violence.

DAVID J. BARRY, M.D., is a clinical associate professor of psychiatry at he University of Rochester School of Medicine and Dentistry. His teaching and research interests include pharmacology and treatment of mentally ill persons within the criminal justice system. He directs the Court Clinic, which provides mental health services for sentenced and unsentenced prisoners in Monroe County.

JUDITH BROAD, R.N., M.S.N., is an associate professor, clinical chief, and chairperson for psychiatric mental health nursing at the University of Rochester School of Nursing. She is a part-time doctoral student in nursing. Her interests include assaultive behavior in acute care inpatient psychiatric settings.

VIVIAN B. BROWN, Ph.D., is senior deputy director of the Didi Hirsch Community Mental Health Center, director of the Consultation, Education and Preventive Division, director of the Southern California Rape Prevention Study Center, and director of the Substance Abuse Division. She is a consultant to numerous community, health, governmental, educational, and international organizations. Her interests include crisis intervention and the application of research findings to the prevention of victimization and other societal problems.

CYNTHIA HART, R.N., M.S., is an assistant professor of the psychiatric mental health nursing faculty at the University of Rochester School of Nursing. She practices as a psychiatric mental health nurse specialist and consultant to medical nursing at the University of Rochester Medical Center. Ms. Hart is a co-author of *Introduction to Psychotropic Drugs* (1981). She also is a doctoral student in the Graduate School of Education and Human Services at the University of Rochester.

TYRONE C. HOLLERAUER, Psy. D., received his doctoral degree from the Illinois School of Professional Psychology. For more than five years he was supervisor of a residential treatment program for aggressive mentally ill or mentally retarded individuals. Since 1980 he has been primarily engaged in the practice of private psychotherapy.

DENNIS KUTZER, M.D., is clinical director of Spring Grove Hospital Center in Catonsville, Maryland. During his residency program at the University of Maryland's Institute of Psychiatry and Human Behavior, Dr. Kutzer was coleader of a "violence group" under the supervision of John R. Lion, M.D. Dr. Kutzer maintains a part-time private practice and remains active in teaching at the University of Maryland Department of Psychiatry.

BARRIE LEVY, L.C.S.W., teaches at the UCLA School of Social Welfare and the University of Southern California School of Social Work. She is the founder and former director of the Southern California Coalition for Battered Women. She was also program coordinator for the Southern California Rape Prevention Study Center, a division of the Didi Hirsch Community Mental Health Center, and is currently consultant on a child sexual assault prevention project at the Center. She has had years of experience, with the Los Angeles Commission on Assaults Against Women, counseling sexual assault victims. Ms. Levy is in private practice as a therapist and consultant specializing in prevention.

JOHN R. LION, M.D., is a professor of psychiatry at the University of Maryland School of Medicine. His main academic interests have been the study of violence and aggression in man, the management of personality disorders, and clinical psychopharmacology. He has authored and edited five books on these topics and has contributed to numerous scientific publications. Dr. Lion has consulted with many government agencies including the National Academy of Science, National Institute of Health, FDS, and the American Psychiatric Association, where he has served on committees to study terrorism, restraint and seclusion of psychiatric patients, and clinical nomenclature. Dr. Lion administers a forty-five–bed inpatient service and maintains a small private practice in Baltimore, Maryland.

JOSEPH MEHR, Ph.D., received his doctoral degree from the Illinois Institute of Technology. He was associated with a residential treatment program for the aggressive mentally ill or mentally retarded from 1973 to 1980. He was the program's administrator from 1976 to 1980. Since 1976 he has also been the chief psychologist at Elgin Mental Health Center. Dr. Mehr has authored several textbooks including a college text in abnormal psychology.

CYNTHIA ROHRBECK, B.A., graduated *magna cum laude* from Cornell University with a bachelor's in psychology. She is currently a doctoral student in clinical psychology at the University of Rochester. She has published in the area of child abuse.

GERALD RUBENSTEIN, Ed.D., is a psychologist in private practice and a clinical assistant professor of psychiatry and psychology at the University of Rochester Medical School. He has worked in correctional facilities and probation departments and was a consultant to the Rochester Police Department.

SUSAN SAUNDERS, M.S.W., C.S.W., is an assistant professor of psychiatry (social work) and nursing at the University of Rochester

School of Medicine and Dentistry. She is associate director of social work at Strong Memorial Hospital and director of community and preventive psychiatry. Her interests include authority, power, and change in complex organizations, group dynamics, and the prevention and community treatment of mental and emotional problems.

RODNEY SHAPIRO, Ph.D., is the director of the family therapy program, San Francisco Veterans Administration Medical Center, and a clinical associate professor, department of psychiatry, University of California Medical School. Dr. Shapiro is also a faculty member of the Pacific Graduate School of Marital and Family Therapy. He has published extensively and is on the editorial board of two family therapy journals. Dr. Shapiro's interests include family violence, alcoholism, and treatment outcome research.

ROGER C. SIDER, M.D., is an associate professor of psychiatry, director of adult ambulatory services, and codirector of the program in psychiatric ethics in the Department of Psychiatry at the University of Rochester School of Medicine and Dentistry. He is a clinician with broad interests and has published mainly in the areas of psychiatric education and psychiatric ethics.

SUZANNE K. STEINMETZ, Ph.D., is a professor of individual and family studies at the University of Delaware. She is the author of "Cycle of Violence: Assertive, Aggressive and Abusive Family Interactions" (1977). She co-authored, with M. Strauss and R. Gelles, *Behind Closed Doors: Violence in the American Family* (1980). Dr. Steinmetz is currently completing a study of elder abuse in generationally inverted families.

SHARON TRIMBORN, B.S.N., M.S.N., is an assistant professor of nursing at the University of Rochester and associate clinical chief of psychiatric mental health nursing and director of the general psychiatry inpatient subprogram, Strong Memorial Hospital. She is a part-time doctoral student at the University School of Nursing. Her special interests include violence of psychiatric inpatients: determinants, prevention, and intervention. She is completing data collection on a research project exploring the perceptions of staff and patients regarding patient symptomatology immediately prior to seclusion.

CRAIG T. TWENTYMAN, Ph.D., is a faculty member in the department of psychology of the University of Rochester. He is also founder and director of the Mt. Hope Family Center, which includes a day service program for abused and emotionally disturbed children as well as an adult outpatient clinic for their parents. He is the author of numerous journal articles on behavior therapy and child abuse.

DEWITT L. WEATHERLY, M.D., is assistant chief medical officer of the Circuit Court for Baltimore City, Maryland. He has evaluated approximately 2,000 people in various stages of criminal proceedings. He has subspecialized in forensic psychiatry since 1972 and has directed his attention to the issue of dangerousness through his work with pre- and postsentence cases. Dr. Weatherly is also a clinical associate professor in psychiatry at the University of Maryland School of Medicine.

LYMAN WYNNE, M.D., Ph.D., received his professional training in psychiatry and social psychology from Harvard University. He has been interested in issues of family theory and the family's role in mental illness and healthy family development for the past thirty years. In the mid 1950s he contributed to the beginning of family therapy as an approach to treatment. Many of the families in his therapeutic and research work have been disturbed by violent feelings and behavior.

INTRODUCTION

VIOLENCE and its generational ripple effects are corrosive and nagging undercurrents in contemporary society. Interpersonal and family life is marred routinely by outbusts of physical violence. Many individuals trapped in cyclical violence emerge as labeled, social casualties: battered women, abused children, suicides, homicides, rape victims, and felons. Many more remain undetected, physically brutalized, yet not propelled by circumstance toward institutional support. Beyond the victims of overt violence are countless people caught up in the chronic, verbal violence characteristic of many relationships, families, and work settings. These are the victims of exclusion, denigration, and emotional alienation.

The growing, near normative occurrence of violence has placed increasing demands on community institutions throughout the country. Media are lobbied to reprogram the American ego ideal toward a less violent, more nurturant prototype. Academic and research groups are pressed to discover the etiology of violence and to develop more reliable methods for its prediction and prevention. Law enforcement and judicial institutions are confronted with demands for more rapid and equitable apprehension and prosecution of the perpetrators of violence. Legislatures and correctional institutions are pressured to find more effective and secure means for cloistering the chronically violent. Health and human service agencies are expected to treat the violence-prone, rescue the victimized, and mend the physical and psychological wounds of violence.

Professionals practicing within the institutional network—police officers, health and mental health practitioners, child protective workers, educators, clergy, and victim assistance personnel—execute a variety of critical tasks in society's overall effort to contain and treat violence. They assess dangerousness, provide testimony, restrain violent individuals, provide emergency medical treatment, collect evidence of abuse and rape, perform psychological testing, administer drugs, offer psychotherapy, and shelter victims. It is the quality of these professional interventions, carried out daily, which determines the ultimate effectiveness of a community's response to violence.

Quality interventions in situations characterized by violence cannot be based solely on general knowledge and intuition gained in professional training and practice. Such interventions must be based on knowledge of the social and psychodynamic underpinnings of violence and victim psychology. They must proceed from a sophisticated skill repertoire that enables practitioners to confront and restrain violent individuals, subdue potentially explosive situations, ease the victim's trauma and rage, and predict and prevent future violence. Also, quality interventions can emanate only from practitioners who are self-aware, in control of their actions and behavior, and able to move beyond judgment and anger in their response to the perpetrators and victims of violence.

This handbook has been created for professionals who work with violence-prone individuals and families and with the victims of violence. It contains methods for assessing and predicting violence; cognitive and psychodynamic formulations about the origins of violence; behavioral, psychopharmacologic, and psychological treatment approaches to violence; and a range of intervention skills useful in managing violent behavior and stabilizing victims in crisis. The handbook is designed to enhance professional skill and knowledge and enrich the resources available for use in the supervision and evaluation of work with violent individuals and families. It is hoped that the handbook will serve as a stimulus for dialogue among professionals about the particular difficulties and dynamics associated with working with the violent. As well, we hope that the handbook will enhance the self-awareness of professionals and stimulate them to develop more formal models, theories, and methods for work with violent individuals and families.

CONTENTS

Page

Introduction xi

Chapter

1. DEVELOPMENTAL AND FAMILY ORIGINS OF VENGEANCE AND VIOLENCE 3
   Lyman C. Wynne
2. METHODS FOR ASSESSING POTENTIAL FOR VIOLENCE IN CLIENTS 19
   DeWitt L. Weatherly
3. THE PRACTITIONER'S INITIAL RESPONSE TO VICTIMS OF VIOLENCE 35
   Carole A. Anderson
4. STRATEGIES FOR CRISIS INTERVENTION WITH VICTIMS OF VIOLENCE 57
   Barrie Levy and Vivian Brown
5. THE VIOLENT PATIENT: ASSESSMENT AND INTERVENTION 69
   Dennis J. Kutzer and John R. Lion
6. A COGNITIVE-BEHAVIORAL APPROACH TO CHILD ABUSE: IMPLICATIONS FOR TREATMENT 87
   Craig T. Twentyman, Cynthia A. Rohrbeck, and Patricia L. Amish
7. THERAPY WITH VIOLENT FAMILIES 112
   Rodney J. Shapiro
8. FAMILY VIOLENCE TOWARD ELDERS 137
   Suzanne K. Steinmetz
9. MANAGING VIOLENCE IN AN INPATIENT SETTING 164
   Cynthia Allen Hart, Judith Broad, and Sharon Trimborn

Chapter *Page*

10. Behavioral Treatment for Aggression in Residents of Institutions for the Emotionally Disturbed and the Mentally Retarded 198
Joseph J. Mehr and Tyrone C. Hollerauer

11. Pharmacotherapy in Violent Behavior 226
David Barry

12. Training Mental Health Providers to Work With Violence-prone Patients 243
Roger C. Sider

Name Index 253

Subject Index 259

VIOLENT INDIVIDUALS AND FAMILIES

Chapter 1

DEVELOPMENTAL AND FAMILY ORIGINS OF VENGEANCE AND VIOLENCE*

LYMAN C. WYNNE

VENGEANCE and violence are closely linked. Shakespeare characterized the connection metaphorically in *Titus Andronicus*: "Vengeance is in my heart, death in my hand. Blood and revenge are hammering in my head." This linkage is also familiar to mental health clinicians. As my starting point in this chapter, I shall make a distinction between *feelings* of vengeance and *acts* of violence that may stem from these feelings. My concern will be with the precursors and the underlying factors related to violent acts and to those immoderate feelings, passions, and emotions that often are subsumed under the title of vengeance. The precursors to which I shall give special attention are those that generate vengeance in individual psychological development within the family context and lead to individual violence. A few comments on implications for treatment approaches with individuals and families will follow.

Collective Violence

Dramatically contrasted with violence of individuals is the collective violence of warfare and of some terrorist and cult groups. The intensity and destructiveness of collective violence is often detached

*Presented at the Conference on Violence, Rochester, N.Y., June 2, 1979.

from or disproportionately exceeds the intensity of individual vengeance. Individuals often become participants in collective violence as a function of group dynamics, especially what Bion (1959) called the basic assumption of "fight or flight." Hence, the psychological background of followers in group violence probably differs, at least in earlier development, from that of cult leaders, such as James Jones, and political leaders, such as Hitler. Nevertheless, such group leaders have certain qualities related to their feelings of vengeance in which we all share to some degree, whether or not we engage in individual or collective violence, and whether or not we are diagnosed as mentally disordered or caught up in cults or in military combat.

Biological Contributions to Violence

Just as some group participants may take part in collective violence with relatively low levels of vengeance, there are forms of individual violence that are relatively passionless and lacking in the felt experience of vengefulness. Such instances are most clearly recognized when individuals suffer from organic brain syndromes that produce episodic dyscontrol (Monroe, 1970). For example certain forms of psychomotor epilepsy lead to episodic violence, homicidal and/or suicidal. Most of these patients have treatable electroencephalographic abnormalities (6-14/second spikes and temporal lobe spikes) and soft neurological signs. Other instances of seemingly senseless violence are associated with ingestion of street drugs, especially amphetamines ("speed") and phencyclidine (PCP or "angel dust").

Clinicians need to be alert to the possibility of these somatic disorders but at the same time recognize that violent behavior in most instances cannot be accounted for by a brain syndrome. In addition, as Harbin (1980) has shown, organic instability increases an individual's vulnerability to a multiplicity of developmental, family, and peer pressures leading to violent episodes that may occur only when some of these potent stressors have been present. Then, when several such episodes have occurred, a cyclical pattern of violence and retrenchment may be woven into family interaction patterns and be sustained without much continuing organic dysfunction. Such patterns are especially common in families of alcoholics. In alcoholism, an organic syndrome is a common ingredient but provides an incomplete explanation.

Vengeance Transformed to Violence: An Example

As a prelude to discussing psychological and family aspects of violence, let me recall a recent news report of an eighteen-year-old boy who had murdered his entire family. Reporters uncovered a tragic story of a boy who had been generally regarded as the model child of a seemingly model, upper middle-class family. He had been a good child, never violent as he was growing up, but rather shy, as his schoolmates recalled, and a scapegoated object of ridicule in his classrooms. Further details revealed that he also had been the object of humiliation within his family, by his father, who had been deeply disappointed in this quiet kid who did not take on the athletic, aggressive, and, in a real sense, violent characteristics of the father. The father wanted this son to straighten up, to learn how to be tough, and, hence, sent him to a very tough military academy in the South. There his experience again was one of humiliation, of being cracked down upon, particularly during his first year, when there was an inordinate amount of hazing. He wanted to return home; his father refused to let him leave school. It was with this history, in the context of this family and schooling, that this boy became vengeful. He ran away from school, went home, and deliberately murdered his entire family.

This is an extreme example of vengeance leading to violence that apparently began in a family context and then became replicated in other spheres of the boy's life. Perhaps in this vivid example we can identify some general principles that apply in other instances and also may be relevant to differences between individuals growing up in diverse social class and ethnic/cultural settings.

THE PSYCHOLOGY OF VENGEANCE

The psychology of vengeance that is associated with interpersonal violence involves three features that are especially noteworthy. First, the feeling state itself, the emotional, gut-level state, is a *persisting retaliatory rage*. Second, in order for the rage to be persisting, it ordinarily needs to be *structured* into a *belief system*, sometimes paranoid, but not necessarily. This might be called the cognitive aspect of vengeance. Third, and this aspect is most often overlooked, vengeance occurs in the context of a disappointment, loss, or failure in a *relationship* with another person or a group, organization, or ideology. Typically, there has been a failure of relational reciprocity.

Persisting Retaliatory Rage

Vengeance and vengefulness, by definition, involve the desire to return an injury for an injury, with force or fury as punishment, retribution, or retaliation. The wish or the intent to return injury for injury that is involved in vengeance may or may not be converted into an actual act of violence. The retaliatory aspect of the vengeance is ancient and is repeatedly cited in the Bible, for example, in Deuteronomy: "To me belongeth the vengeance and recompense," that is, to return in kind. Functionally, vengeance is thus a coping mechanism, an attempt to exact reparations or to redress a wrong or a hurtful experience.

Still another related term is *avenge*, which implies inflicting just punishment, usually on someone other than oneself. For example, in many parts of the world there are well-established customs whereby members of a family or organization incur an obligation to avenge whatever is deemed an injury to a member of the family or organization.

In addition, vengeance differs from sporadic angry outbursts by being persistent. It constitutes an abiding fury or bitterness that continues until redress has occurred. However, since vengeful feelings over a long period of time tend to be self-sustaining, especially with reciprocal escalation of injuries, simple and clear reparations and justice may be difficult to recognize.

The Belief Systems of Vengeance

Although the words *vengeance* and *vindication* have the same Latin root (*vindicare*), vengeance connotes the desire for retaliatory injury while vindication emphasizes exoneration and the achievement of justice. The rage of vengeance is on a continuum with beliefs about righteousness. Righteous indignation toward others is a central ingredient in most group causes that lead to collective violence. Such violence is typically justified in an elaborate belief system, for example in the ideology of Naziism.

Similarly, individuals, families, and small groups also construct belief systems that support vengefulness. Best known are family feuds, such as the Hatfields and the McCoys. Vengeful family beliefs are but one variety of family myths that may orient and structure family patterns for generations. With individuals, vengeful beliefs are usually labeled as paranoid. At any level of personal or social organization, vengeance is experienced as an effort and need to correct injustice; others usually view the same intentions as potential corruptions of justice.

Issues of fairness and justification involve cognitive beliefs that help perpetuate vengeance and are intrinsically bonded to the affective component of vengeance. If one looks at these issues from the standpoint of religion, many of us have been impressed by the teaching we received as children after an event has occurred that seems unfair and unjustified—a loss, death, illness, tragedy, etc. God is then brought in, and His benevolence and fairness are introduced to restore a sense of justice. We ask in what sense can there be a balance, an accounting when there is "senseless" death, pestilence, and tragedy. Alexander Pope succinctly commented on this difficult question: "Laugh where we lack;/ Be candid where we can;/ Vindicate the ways of God to Men." The bottom line seems to be that when we cannot find any other way of balancing the books, in effect, we turn to God to buttress our belief system. The redress is mysterious and remotely in the future, usually after death, but with the recompense in most religious systems thought to be assured for believers. From a cross-cultural standpoint, the universal recourse to religion has been described at length by anthropologists.

In adolescence, the cognitive structuring of beliefs about what constitutes fairness becomes prominent as a developmental process. When a person's beliefs about fairness are especially rigid, the likelihood increases that the individual will later experience violations of this code with righteous indignation and vengeance. The cognitive aspects of moral judgments have been studied at length by Kohlberg (1976). Piaget was one of the first to describe the changes in the cognitive functioning of the adolescent, usually around age thirteen or fourteen, varying of course from culture to culture and family and from child to child. Piaget showed that somewhere in that age range the adolescent develops the capacity for formal operational reasoning (Inhelder and Piaget, 1958). This ability to reason and to make cognitive discriminations also heightens the adolescent's ability to make discriminations between right and wrong and to assess the balance of fairness.

Indeed, many adolescents become preoccupied with fairness. Those who remember their adolescence or work with adolescents will be aware of the marked rise in the concern for fairness, rightness, and justice that adolescents experience in many forms. A minor but typical example is that they often become quite indignant with their parents' infringements of the letter of the law, such as going 40 miles an hour in a 35 mph speed zone. Also, their sense of fairness about what is due themselves and their siblings is heightened. Such feelings have been there all along, but now they become finely honed with their new cognitive capacities. At the same time, these beliefs support emotional protest and passion about any kind of social unfairness. Thus, it is no accident that by late adolescence there is a combination of sharp cognitive alertness and intense feeling about issues of fairness, justice, and the balance of merits and obligations. At home, this may involve such mundane questions as to who is fairly asked to take out the garbage or who is to mow the lawn. At the same time, when adolescents are accused on grounds that they believe to be unjust, this typically provokes open fury or sullen bitterness.

Adults are fond of pointing out that adolescents do not have sufficient life experience to "understand" that such concerns and passions are pointless. Most adults have learned to slide over the niceties of fairness and injustice in order to survive in a world of much injustice. Doing so also reduces the likelihood that they will become vengeful. At the same time, the blurring of feelings of righteous indignation may blunt participation in socially valuable, angry movements, such as the anti-Vietnam war and the civil rights protest movements.

Although adolescents and young adults often are more vehemently involved than their elders in such movements, they also are more vulnerable to being caught up in cults. These totalistic groups with a pseudo-religious ideology usually make a strong appeal to young people who are turned off by the larger society's cynicism, callousness, and lack of caring and justice. Once in the cults, their perceptions are systematically blocked and warped with respect to the exploitative aspects of the group. As the world vividly saw in Jonestown, preservation of the cult beliefs led to brutal and tragic violence. More favorably, deprogramming from a cult includes a major emphasis on cognitive corrections and restructuring of what has taken place.

Failures of Relational Reciprocity

Most often, violence occurs between people who are well known to one another, in the primary group of the family, of a peer group, of children, or of people with fundamental relationships. It is in these relationships in which we have a long-standing expectation of reciprocity, of give and take, of *quid pro quo*, that vengeance and violence have their seeds. Here we need to understand how the social structure surrounding the individual's feelings and beliefs functions. Alvin Gouldner has written a classic paper on this topic entitled "The Norm of Reciprocity" (1960). Defining reciprocity as a pattern of equivalent exchange in which each party has rights and duties, he concluded from the anthropologic evidence that reciprocity is universal in all cultures and is an essential factor in maintaining social systems. On the positive side, reciprocity involves the minimal positive demands that people should help those who have helped them and that people should not injure those who have helped them. The negative norm is expressed in the talon principle, an eye for eye. Long ago, Cicero commented that there is "no duty more indispensable than that of returning a kindness, and that all men distrust one forgetful of a benefit." The social scientist Howard Becker went so far as to describe this idea of reciprocity as perhaps the most destructive characteristic of human beings. Somewhat facetiously perhaps, instead of calling man *homo sapiens*, he calls man *homo reciprocus*.

The concept of exploitation may be looked upon as a failure of reciprocity relevant to whole groups, such as blacks in America. One claim now is that there needs to be reciprocity and a redressing of the balance by overcorrecting in the short-term for centuries of exploitation. How to achieve a balance in the short run versus the long run is a very complicated legal and ethical question. This is also a problem in families. But if there is no redress at *some* point, then the persons who experience exploitation become characteristically vengeful in a manner that is supported by the norm of reciprocity.

Reciprocity and the related concept of complementarity are more complex than may be apparent at first glance. The response to a kindness does not need to be the same kind of kindness. A mother who gives her baby milk and receives in return a smile is involved in an exchange and balance that is rewarding and meaningful to both. Similarly, a marriage where one spouse contributes by breadwinning outside of the home while the other spouse contributes inside the home involves traditional complementarity, but now, often, it is no longer experienced as equivalent.

Another way to describe this interchange is in terms of the building up of merits. This is a topic that Boszormenyi-Nagy and Spark have discussed in their book *Invisible Loyalties* (1973). They speak of a "ledger" of merits and obligations that may build up over generations and that needs to be balanced and reconciled. What they call invisible loyalties often involve obligations that incur because of what has been done in the past, what may have been done for or to one's parents, and what now needs to be balanced. Things have to be "given back" in order to balance the ledger.

Such reciprocity is far more complicated than simply the eye for an eye, tooth for a tooth of the Mosaic Law and of other moral codes that take reciprocity at a primitive level. Biblical approaches in their entirety are more difficult to follow and difficult to work with clinically. Not only should people help those who help them and not injure those who have helped them, but there is the contradiction between the Old Testament law of vengeance and the New Testament injunction that one should turn the other cheek. This may take more subtle forms such as the disguised retaliation when one person shames another through exhibiting superior morality, through deliberately sustaining insults or blows from an angry opponent. Accepting injury to oneself then becomes a form of one-upmanship and aims not at balance but at gaining the advantage in an imbalance. St. Paul (Romans) gives the reciprocity principle still another twist: "Vengeance is mine. I will repay, saith the Lord. Therefore, if thine enemy hungers, feed him; if he thirsts, give him drink, for in so doing thou shalt heap coals of fire on his head."

In addition to exploitation, injury, and humiliation, the experiences of disappointment, grief, separation anxiety, and humiliation represent other forms of failure of relational reciprocity. These and underlying emotions and experiences from which vengeance, and ultimately violence, often build up in interpersonal settings. The family provides a setting for the development of a sense of fairness, but also for experiences of injustices. In the earliest family relationships, mother, father, and infant balance in a triangle. The balance often is jeopardized when the mother is physically the giving one too exclusively and the baby is the receiving one. Unless there is a trade-off along other lines, the mother is apt to feel drained and worn out psychologically and physically. If her husband or someone else is not available to help, she is under a burden and is likely to develop an angry sense of unfairness, sometimes with vengefulness manifest in child abuse, and this is likely to set in motion a family pattern that may continue indefinitely. Such experiences are especially common among single, teenage mothers without supports from husband or their own parents. These are the persons with the highest incidence of child abuse. In terms of the concept of reciprocity, single teenage mothers have the least experience with reciprocity in the family. Their vengeance and rage get heaped upon the child who is perceived by the mother to have caused the unfairness. Part of the corrective process is to provide support for such persons so that the experience is less ungratifying. When the mother can experience something gratifying as coming from the child, such as smiling or cooing, the likelihood of rage and abuse is reduced.

Optimally, there has to be a give and take in each direction within the family. In present-day concepts of child rearing, the participation of the father both with the mother and with the baby, preferably from the earliest stage, will enhance the development of reciprocity in all relationships within the growing family from the outset. The addition of a baby to the family adds to the problem for siblings who feel unfairly cut off from previous parental relationships and who may develop vengeful feelings against the new baby.

One of the problems about vengeance and violence that is especially troublesome for the legal system, for the educational system, and for clinicians as well, is that violence and rage are so visible and often so far-reaching in their impact that it is very difficult to attend to other psychological and social problems that might be important. Not only families but also social institutions such as the law become caught up in retaliatory vengeance. Issues such as the prevention of future violence are then commonly brushed aside.

In addition, vengeance and violence in one setting are apt to be repeated in other settings. For example, when we assess adolescents who themselves are violent or are the target of violence as scapegoats, it is important to evaluate how they behave and what happens to them in more than one situation. Quitkin, Rifkin, McKay, and Klein (1973) identified adolescent boys who were extensively scapegoated on a psychiatric ward. These boys were found to have been significantly more scapegoated earlier in their childhood history and in other settings than other boys on the same ward who were not scapegoated.

Such problems go beyond the psychology of any individual. They include the unfairness associated with minority status, racial, ethnic, or religious, and with being physically clumsy or mentally handicapped. In each of these situations there is a failure of reciprocity that is difficult to redress. How can compensatory reciprocity be achieved for those disadvantaged by a crippling lifelong injury, cerebral palsy, blindness, developmental disorder, or the "wrong" skin color? Compensatory adjustments to a limited degree do sometimes occur, to be sure, but the realistic potential for having an experience of unfairness is so great that other alternatives, such as protective apathy and passivity, are common and have widespread social support. In many such circumstances, apathy and vengeance are the two sides of one coin.

In terms of the reciprocity principle, similar feeling states arise with much the same dynamics out of unresolved and intolerable experiences of personal loss. The impact of long-threatened and traumatic loss of a parent is, from the standpoint of the child and the later adult, difficult, if not impossible, to undo, even with prolonged therapy. Such experiences are the precursor, far more than is generally appreciated, for vengeful and angry feelings in later life, often rather diffusely directed. Expressing the vengeance then becomes a defense against reexperiencing the anxiety, disappointment, and painfulness of the original loss that is symbolically reactivated again and again in the inevitable separations and losses of daily life.

A Clinical Example

A relevant example that brings out many of these points has been described in a paper by Harold Searles on the "Psychodynamics of Vengefulness" (1956). In this case a thirty-two-year-old man came to treatment because of a persistent backache. But as exploration began, it became clear that during his upbringing he had been given to feel that his life was to be devoted fully to the welfare of his parents and other family members. To this he had acquiesced wholeheartedly on a conscious level. In the course of therapy he realized that the expectation had been building up within him all along that he eventually would be rewarded for all the devotion that he had given and that a balance, in other words, would eventually be achieved. When he married, one of his expectations was that the marriage and his new family would redress the balance never achieved in his family of origin. However, his needs were not at all satisfactorily met by his wife, whom he had tried to force to be caring, attentive, and affectionate. At that point he developed a backache and at the same time shifted from acquiescence to open reproachfulness. This was further complicated by the fact that his parents were still reproaching him and demanding that he give up his wife and come home to take care of his aging mother. During therapy, he became aware that he was tired of *giving* and realized that now "I just want to *take*." He said this with angry, passionate feeling. At the same time, when he realized he was expressing these feelings, he was filled with guilt and self-reproach. It gradually became clear that he was caught in a dilemma; his intense feelings of vengefulness were matched by self-reproach for not feeling more compassionate and not wanting to keep on giving. Having grown up in a family in which there was great importance attached to the acquisition of money, he now vengefully relished using up family money for his expensive psychiatric treatment. Only later during the treatment was he able to grieve about his disappointment over earlier losses and over how little he had received while he was looking after his family. His vengefulness gradually resolved as these underlying feelings of loss and grieving were reexperienced and became manageable.

GUIDELINES FOR THE TREATMENT OF VENGEANCE AND VIOLENCE

The principles outlined above quite clearly imply that the current and historical context is crucial in considering the treatment of vengefulness. The rules or guidelines for the relationship between clinician-therapist and the patient or family need to be considered carefully as part of that context. With patients who are angry and vengeful, there needs to be a much more clear-cut treatment structure than with most other patients. Guidelines for what is tolerable as the overt or violent expression of vengeance and the realistic limitations under which the therapist is willing to work should be spelled out. I and others have found that it is quite reassuring and facilitatory in therapy to have the therapist make it quite clear when he or she is afraid or feels threatened, and not to equivocate or pretend not to be. To do so will only stimulate and aggravate the patient's tendency to be vengeful, to be angry, and to force the other person to acknowledge that he or she is afraid. Only when limits are clearly and effectively established, but not punitively, can the vengeful person experience the treatment situation as safely free of reciprocally escalating vengeance and violence. Then corrective new emotional experiences and problem solving about new ways of coping can start to take place and eventually reduce the pressure for violent solutions.

Thus, the therapist needs to start by setting up the therapy in such a way that he or she can be at least reasonably comfortable. For example, if I feel threatened by a patient physically and fear that I might be assaulted, I say openly that this is not a condition under which I can work. I may insist that the gun the patient has brought along be removed. I may ask that one or two colleagues remain in the room with me. I tell the patient that these must be the conditions for our work until I am comfortable enough to think about what is being said in the interview. Some years ago, I observed Harold Searles with a violent patient with whom everyone else had failed to make any contact at all. The patient was throwing chairs and breaking down doors and security windows. People tried to have interviews with him through a door. Searles insisted that the patient be put in wet packs. They then had an interview in which he could talk with the patient and feel safe enough to relate to him. Under these circumstances, the patient started to relax and was able to start to deal with his grievances, which were not accessible when he had been caught up in vengeance and fury.

In addition to setting physical limits for the relationship, another limit that needs to be recognized is how much giving and caring can be expected from the therapist. Once vengeful patients begin to have positive expectations of the therapist, then their demands are apt to be rapidly inflated beyond the bounds of what the therapist can provide. Hence, the therapist needs to think through in advance what is possible and appropriate. Clarification about how much time the therapist is willing to give is of primary importance. It also is essential to have personal guidelines about being responsive to phone calls and being available when the law has become involved, when hospitalization or jailing has occurred, and when the patient has become surprisingly generous and friendly. It should be kept in mind that these patients will be expecting fraud and inconsistency and have high skill in evoking them.

These principles apply in both individual and family therapy. Working with couples and families in which one or more (usually more than one) person is vengeful and violent, the therapist needs to help them set realistic limits with one another, step by step, in one area of life after another. Indeed, this may be the most useful procedure of all in therapy with these problems.

Another condition of therapy is to limit the encouragement of catharsis and the expression of hostility. In the early days in psychotherapy, therapists believed that it was therapeutic to express feelings openly, including anger and vengefulness. We now know that such expressiveness needs to be within a structural, limit-setting context, even for inhibited patients. For those patients who come to therapy spewing hateful and vengeful feelings, we now know that to permit such expression is antitherapeutic if it continues after the problem is identified. This point about limiting expressions of hate and anger applies to individual therapy and group therapy, but it is not as well recognized with these latter approaches as it should be, because the immediate consequence often is merely that no real progress occurs. In marital and family therapy, the necessity for active intervention by the therapist is now almost universally recognized. Family relationships are likely to deteriorate with a passive family therapist. Chaotically escalating attacks ensue when persons who are vengeful toward one another meet in family therapy, or otherwise, and are allowed to ventilate. Milton understood this well: "Revenge, at first though sweet,/ Bitter ere long back on itself recoils" (*Paradise Lost*). In my recent clinical experience with vengeful couples embroiled in vitriolic custody disputes, I have been impressed again and again with the merit of this principle.

Far more effective than encouraging catharsis is to define the conditions and context of the work, and then to start slowly but firmly to identify the circumstances in which the rage, violence, and related problems occur. Typically, vengefulness is embedded in settings of sorrow and disappointment, of unresolved grieving, and of anxiety about repeated or impending loss or separation. It is when these losses and experiences of injustice are identified that an angry, exploitative, suspicious kind of person often turns, in a startling change, into a sobbing individual who yearns to be cared for and to be treated compassionately. In addition, a problem-solving approach directed toward present life circumstances is usually helpful, especially with couples and families. This approach, only roughly outlined here, can be surprisingly effective in a portion of cases in reducing the pressure of vengeance and ultimately beyond that, the likelihood of violence.

However, such therapy is far from simple, and special caution should be taken not to be too optimistic or too empathic. Expressions of caring are easily misunderstood, especially by deprived persons who will be skeptical, challenging, and suspicious. Therapists need to spell out the possibilities that therapy may result in no change or even make matters worse. It is essential not to generate expectations that may well lead to another disappointment and another round of bitterness. Thus, a matter-of-fact exploration of the sorrow, of the grieving, of disappointments, and so on, is usually most effective with these patients and their families. Here again, the omnipresent issue of reciprocity comes into the picture. The patient and family may feel that for the first time they have been given support in dealing with painful experiences, current or remote, but the therapist should be cautious in expecting or predicting how long the scales will remain balanced when profound injustices have been experienced.

Another aspect of vengeance that needs attention in treatment is that vengeance as a persisting emotion actually *holds* the other person in the relationship. Ordinarily, the other person is not actually being destroyed. Most violence does not reach the point of actual physical murder, even though for a long time it may fall just short of that. The other person may be injured and threatened with death but is, nevertheless, carefully saved from being killed. The vengeful person needs to save the other to be the future object of anger. Also, if actually killed, the loss incurred would repeat a painful loss of earlier life. To be sure, violent persons do not consciously think these matters through, but it is surprising how frequently threats, battering, and abuse occur at a fixed, severe level of intensity. This pattern helps explain why vengeance, and the paranoia often associated with it, may go on and on throughout life.

A final caution for therapists: Often the relationships of vengeful people become collusive with others, sometimes with therapists, and quite regularly with members of their families. Such relationships become reciprocally hateful, with each person feeling he or she is being held in a bind. Sometimes the bind is maintained through intimidation, as with a wife who fears she will be killed if she leaves a paranoid husband, or through dependency, as with the husband who may believe that his psychological survival depends on his wife's presence. Therapists may be held in a treatment relationship by their sense of therapeutic responsibility, meanwhile becoming more hateful toward the patient than they can readily acknowledge.

As a general principle, impasses of this order often become manageable by enlarging the treatment context: to see a couple together instead of an individual patient, to meet with a family system rather than only a couple, and to bring in a consultant to expand the therapeutic system. The goal is to modify the context of the treatment and thereby throw into imbalance the fixed reciprocal expectations that have nourished mutual hatred and sometimes vengeance. Vengeance and violence are indeed frighteningly difficult clinical problems and they deserve our most resourceful and thoughtful study, just as they challenge and stretch our therapeutic resources to the maximum.

REFERENCES

PressBion, W.R.: *Experiences in Groups*. New York, Basic Books, 1959.

Boszormenyi-Nagy, I., and Spark, G.M.: *Invisible Loyalties: Reciprocity in Intergenerational Family Therapy*. New York, Harper and Row, 1973.

Gouldner, A.W.: The norm of reciprocity: A preliminary statement. *American Sociological Review, 25*:161-178, 1960.

Harbin, H.T.: Episodic dyscontrol and family dynamics. In Howells, J.G. (Ed.): *Advances in Family Psychiatry*, Vol. II. New York, International Universities Press, 1980, pp. 163-170.

Inhelder, B., and Piaget, J.: *The Growth of Logical Thinking from Childhood to Adolescence*. New York, Basic Books, 1958.

Kohlberg, L.: Moral stages and moralization: The cognitive-developmental approach. In Likona, T. (Ed.): *Moral Development and Behavior*. New York, Holt, 1976.

Monroe, R.R.: *Episodic Behavioral Disorders*. Cambridge, Mass., Harvard University Press, 1970.

Quitkin, F., Rifkin, A., McKay, L., and Klein, D.F.: Scapegoating in hospital adolescents. *Archives of General Psychiatry, 28*:680-682, 1973.

Searles, H.F.: The psychodynamics of vengefulness. *Psychiatry, 19*:31-39, 1956.

Chapter 2

METHODS FOR ASSESSING POTENTIAL FOR VIOLENCE IN CLIENTS

DEWITT L. WEATHERLY

IN this chapter, I intend to present a sampling of methods for the practitioner to assess the potential for violence. Methods of assessing violence potential generally fall into two types. The statistical approach emphasizes rather irrefutable data, such as age, sex, education, and prior criminal convictions. The clinical approach accepts much subjective material. Some investigators use varying combinations of statistical and clinical methods.

Justice and Birkman (1972) report the use of a psychological instrument called the Birkman Method. They used a battery of tests consisting of a self-image and social perception scale plus an interest survey and an intelligence test. The self-image and social perception scale consisted of 234 true or false statements, half of which dealt with what the client perceived other people to feel or believe. The other 117 statements comprised the self-image section where the client responded in terms of what he or she felt and believed. Trait clusters of self-consciousness, dominance, materialism, tenacity, depressiveness, sociableness, restlessness, energy, and indecisiveness were scored. Twenty-four occupations were listed in clusters of four, and the client was asked which of the four occupations in each cluster appealed to him or her most and which occupation was second most appealing.

The authors claim that factor analysis of the trait clusters revealed a specific factor for violence. An equation was then derived and was used to predict which of the prisoners belonged to the violent group and which to the nonviolent group on the basis of their individual test scores. Those clients with violent backgrounds differed more in terms of intensity, rather than in trait, from those with nonviolent criminal records. When compared to a sample of nonincarcerated workers, both groups of inmates differed substantially, both in intensity and trait. Both the nonviolent and violent offenders were found to have strong negative self-images. The nonviolent clients seemed able to express hostile feelings by working with their hands. The violent group directed their hostility more towards people.

This study made use of the fact that some of their clients had already demonstrated violent behavior. The test proposed to be able to identify those violent clients and to separate the two groups of inmates by use of this test. The results reportedly correctly identified sixty out of the seventy-eight nonviolent inmates and seventy-three out of the ninety-five violent inmates. The authors believed that the method they used offered "promise for identifying the potentially violent and for being of assistance in rehabilitation efforts." They further stated that "the Birkman Method should also help officials in making judgments as to which inmates appeared to be the most employable in the free world. Outside the prison system the method should be of use in establishing programs that best fit young people who appear to be headed for serious trouble if appropriate intervention is not taken."

Wenk (1972) evaluated 4,146 clients who were wards of the California Youth Authority in order to develop a classification device for estimating assaultive potential. The assessment directed attention to past violence, primarily assault. Information used in the assessment included the client's record of violence in the past and the client's violent behavior, or lack of it, during a fifteen-month exposure period while on parole following the client's release from the institution. The client's background was explored extensively including elaborate case histories with emphasis on use of alcohol, drugs, suicide attempts, homosexuality, escape, and weapon carrying.

Attention was given to the past or present psychiatric diagnoses applied to the client, and there were current measures of mental and emotional functioning. The latter included testing for intelligence, maturity level, grade achievement, MMPI, and CPI. Comments from the client's counselors were also solicited in the form of prognostic judgments and the counselor's rating of the client's academic and vocational potential. The counselor was also asked to make recommendations for any specific type of training.

Justice, Justice, and Kraft (1974) did an extensive review of the literature with regard to the topic of individual violence, conducted 779 tape-recorded interviews with people in twenty-nine different professions having contact with troubled youth, reviewed 1,050 case studies of school children performed between 1955 and 1958, and then checked the names of those 1,050 clients against the files of the Texas Department of Correction, locating fifty-seven of those clients. Of the fifty-seven located in the correctional files, eight clients were found to have been convicted of violent offenses. The investigators then conducted an in-depth interview with those eight clients to assess the presence or absence of early indicators of violent behavior.

The method aplied by Justice, Justice, and Kraft appears to have a distinctly clinical orientation. The results of their investigation produced four early warning signs or behavior patterns that were considered important, early predictors of potential for violent behavior. Those four items incuded the presence in the client's childhood history of (1) fighting, (2) temper tantrums, (3) inability to get along with others, and (4) school problems and truancy. Other indicators from .childhood history, such as bed-wetting, cruelty to animals, and fire setting, were not found with the same frequency as the above-mentioned four items.

Cocozza and Steadman (1974) proposed a distinctly statistical method as opposed to a clinical method of assessing dangerousness. They devised a summary measure, which was referred to as the Legal Dangerousness Scale (LDS). This scale consisted of four aspects of previous criminal activity. Those aspects were presence of juvenile record, number of previous arrests, presence of convictions for violent crimes, and the severity of the original offense. The clients evaluated were clients released from New York Security Hospitals for the Criminally Insane as a result of the *Baxstrom v. Herold* court decision.

Although separate from the LDS scale, the investigators also included social and demographic factors, finding that only one variable appeared to be significantly related to subsequent criminal activity. That variable was age. The largest difference in subsequent criminal activity by age was found between those clients under age fifty and those clients age fifty or older. Thus it appears the Cocozza and Steadman method is a statistical method suggesting that the client's dangerousness increases with his LDS score and declines with his increasing age, especially after age fifty.

Kozol (1972) reported a ten-year study of 592 convicted offenders. The 592 clients had been screened by other psychiatrists from an original total population of 2,000 inmates. Most of the 592 had been convicted of sexual offenses. Several of the sexual offenses were compounded by other forms of extreme violence, including murder. The assessment of each client's potential for violence was based on clinical examinations, psychological tests, and a meticulous reconstruction of the life history enlisted from multiple sources. Those sources included the client, his family, friends, neighbors, teachers, and employers. Documentary records from the court, correctional facilities, and mental hospitals were also used. The clinical examination was made independently by at least two psychiatrists, two psychologists, a social worker, and others. The interviews were conducted in a fashion to encourage free communication by the client. The interview was neither confrontational nor inquisitional but rather unstructured and informal. Of paramount importance was a meticulous description of the actual assault. The investigators felt that a detailed description of the client as an aggressor in action was often the most valuable single source of information. The client's version of the actual assault was compared with the victim's version. During the study of each client, information on themes and experiences in the client's history was sought in hopes of revealing the structure and dynamic potential of the client's personality. This 1972 paper presents many examples of the kinds of questions and issues investigated during the interview process. The assessors were interested in the client's general life-style concerning such issues as social conformity, responsibility, and the type and amount of control the client asserted in his life pattern of behavior.

Psychological testing was used to supplement the above process. There was no routine test battery, but the tests principally used included the Rorschach, the Wechsler Adult Intelligence Scale, the Thematic Apperception Test, the Draw-a-Person Test and the Bender-Gestalt Test. Occasional supplementary tests included the MMPI, Holtzman Ink Blot Test, and the Wechsler Memory Scale.

Kozol defined dangerousness as "a potential for inflicting serious bodily harm on another." In applying the above methodology, the investigators asserted that "dangerousness in criminal offenders can be reliably diagnosed and effectively treated with a recidivism rate of 6.1%."

Breiner (1978) used a clinical methodology and concluded that the best predictors of severe violence would include a history of past violence, threats of violence, parental deprivation, enuresis past childhood, fire setting in childhood, cruelty to animals or other children in childhood, barbiturate and/or alcohol abuse, the threat of loss of self-esteem and/or love object, and the presence of an available gun.

Monahan developed a methodology for assessing and identifying violence-eliciting situations rather than identifying violence-prone persons. The major goal of his assessment process was to establish measures that would prevent violence from occurring. For example, in order to prevent rape from occurring, data concerning the episodes within the community might reveal that a sizable number of previous rapes had occurred in certain areas of the community with poorly lit streets at a time of day when women would be walking home after bus service had discontinued or when hitchhiking. Situational analysis of violence on policemen might demonstrate that many policemen are killed or injured when intervening in family disputes. Thus the focus of attention would be the dangerousness of family disputes.

Marcus and Conway (1969) examined dangerous sexual offenders within the Canadian Correction System. Their methodology resulted in focus on a cluster of developmental behavior deviances and unfavorable child environmental events as indicative warning signs of possible sexual offenses during adult life. The familiar triad of enuresis, fire setting, and cruelty to animals was found in combination with other predictors such as brutality from the father, delinquency as an adolescent, and a past criminal record of increasing sexual offenses with age and conjointly with other crimes. Other predictors included sustained excitement and/or bizarre fantasy preceeding and during the offense, lack of human warmth, indifference toward the victim, explosive outbursts, and the presence of a high IQ in connection with a lack of social skills. Absence of psychosis and absence of alcoholic intake were also considered to be predictive factors.

Smith (1965) performed clinical evaluations on eight adolescent clients who had committed murder. The orientation was psychoanalytic. His clients were found to show signs of early oral deprivation and infantile clinging to love objects, intense ambivalence of feelings, primitive, orally incorporative fantasies, and weak ego boundaries. Depersonalization or ego splitting were other psychoanalytic concepts found to be present in certain cases of extreme brutality in murder.

Satten examined three convicted murders using the Rorschach and the TAT Psychological Test. He noted an absence of guilt, depression, and remorse. The Rorschach protocols were brief and constricted. TAT stories were often meager and frequently autobiographical. Disturbances in dealing with color in Rorschach items was also characteristic. This investigator and his coworkers proposed a syndrome common to murderers who had committed impulsive and senseless murders. The syndrome included predisposition to severe lapses of ego control, feelings of inadequacy, physical inferiority, and severe sexual inhibitions.

We have now considered the methods or approaches of eleven investigators. Obviously the methods vary greatly. Some are quite cumbersome. Let me now propose what I hope will be a reasonably practical way of deriving a sensible opinion regarding the assessment of dangerousness and the prediction of violence.

1. DEFINE THE KEY WORDS. Consider these definitions of key words. What are *violent acts*? Examples that readily come to mind include suicide, attempted suicide, assault, homicide, physical child abuse, wife beating, rape, and a multitude of injuries to people occurring in the commission of violent crimes. Rubin (1972) defines violence as acts that produce injury or death to persons. Monahan (1974) notes that in 1969 the National Commission on Causes and Prevention of Violence included the destruction of property in the definition of violence and that in the District of Columbia (Comment, 1965) acts that "cause trouble or inconvenience to others" were included in the definition of violence. A current dic-

tionary defines violence as "exertion of physical force so as to injure."

Violence is a word from the common language, not the legal or social science arena. It appears that when professionals begin using the word in a legal or scientific way, the meaning begins to blur to include "inconvenience" or damage to things as well as people. This blurring is an important dynamic with impact on the validity of our assessment. If the event to be predicted is vague and ill-defined, the method of predicting will become equally vague and ill-defined with results approaching mere chance as Steadman has described. As Shah (1978) notes, "As the definition (of violent acts) is broadened, general agreement tends to decrease and problems of unreliability and vagueness increase."

The next key word is *danger* or dangerous or dangerousness. Dangerousness is also a word rooted in the common language. The dictionary defines dangerous as "able or likely to inflict injury." A dangerous person would be one who is able or likely to perform violence. Facile transposition of danger and violence seems to occur regularly in the literature. "Dangerousness is by its nature a prediction," Steadman says. He further states that "clearly dangerous behavior includes murder and assault and probably rape." It seems to me that murder is a violent, not a dangerous, act. Violence is the commission of an injurious act. Tanay (1975) states that "danger connotes harm that *might* occur . . . . It is not a clinical state in itself . . . dangerous is just another adjective like precarious, careless, or risky." Thus precise definition clearly shows that dangerous and violent are not synonymous.

A person can be dangerous and yet not act violently. An angry person pointing a loaded revolver at another person is clearly dangerous, but precise definition would exclude the presence of violence until there is bodily harm done to a human being. Assessing dangerousness is distinctly different from predicting a violent event.

The distinction between dangerousness and violence is something for the examiner to have in mind as the assessment of the specific client begins. At the point when the opinion or conclusion is rendered, the definition you used should be made explicit.

2. Define and Re-state the Question Being Addressed. *Precisely what are we being asked?* If you do not know the question,

how valid can you expect your answer to be? Are we being asked to assess current dangerousness or to predict a future violent act? If so, against whom? In what time frame?

Perhaps the best way to generate a clear understanding of the central question is to explore the dynamics that brought about the referral. What did the client do to raise the question? Who is making the referral? What is the referring agent likely to do to or with the client as a result of your evaluation?

Here is an example of an explicit statement that might be used to begin a report in a hypothetical case:

> Three days ago, Mr. Johnson struck his wife, Betty, in the face with his fist, fracturing her jaw. Mrs. Johnson called the police and filed charges of assault. Mr. Johnson's defense attorney, Mr. Brown, has referred his client to me for my opinion as to whether Mrs. Johnson is presently in danger from her husband and whether it is likely that Mr. Johnson will physically harm Mrs. Johnson in the future. After being advised that the purpose of my examination is to prepare a written report concerning his dangerousness and potential to act violently toward his wife, Mr. Johnson agreed to proceed with the examination.

Who asks the question? How is this question put to us? Sometimes we stumble upon a question of dangerousness. We might be asked to counsel a couple in marital distress and find ourselves worried about violence. In that case we end up putting the question to ourselves. More often someone else has sensed the question and asks it specifically of us, for example when we are called in to evaluate a client after they have overdosed or after a child-battering episode. The question may be presented from an institutional concern. Is this convicted arsonist going to pose a danger to the public if paroled? Should this person be charged with murder or have high bail, low bail, or no bail? Should this alcoholic person retain his driver's license? Should this person be involuntarily committed to a mental hospital because he is likely to harm himself or someone else? Is this chronically psychotic, paranoid person going to pose a danger to society if released from the hospital after years of inpatient stay? The client will seldom be the referring person. The more common exception is the suicidal person who does not want suicide or the person who is feeling irritable or depressed and fears that he might commit a violent act that he would come to regret. Far more often the client "submits" to the evaluation as ordered by the referring person, possibly a judge or a demanding spouse. Thus it is important to realize that we usually have a guarded client with a strong vested interest in convincing us that he or she is not dangerous. It would be reasonable to expect that the client will conceal facts and the simple truth from us. The accuracy of the information given to us by such a client should be viewed with skepticism until other information from other persons or sources is obtained.

Why are we being asked? Common sense, not science, dictates that we take action to diminish the perceived level of danger. Thus the purpose of assessing dangerousness is to decide what course of action is to be taken to deal with the possibility of a violent event. The quantification of dangerousness is made significantly more difficult by the concurrent interplay of social, humanitarian, political, economic, and legal forces. It is not nearly acceptable enough to declare that someone or some situation is or is not dangerous. As Tanay notes, dangerousness is not like pregnancy. People either are pregnant or they are not. It is more like obesity. Some overweight people are mildly obese, others are moderately obese, and still others are markedly obese. Perhaps our best hope of defining the extent of the danger is simply to say as much as we can about that current state of being that we are examining.

Who is the victim and when might violence occur? The above questions suggest that the contemplated future violent act is rather specific. Will this person commit murder or suicide or set another fire? Will he or she injure someone in an auto wreck? Sometimes the possible victim is fairly specified. In other instances, the possible victim is society or the general public.

The time frame for this specific event possibly to be committed by this specific client may range from the immediate future to the remainder of that client's lifetime. As might be expected, the longer the time of assessment is expected to be valid, the more difficult the answer is to compose with validity.

3. PRESENT THE RELEVANT PAST HISTORY, INCLUDING DEMOGRAPHIC DATA. In developing an assessment of violence potential, cull out aspects of the person's history that are statistically associated with violence. Monahan (1974) reports the following factors that make future violence more likely to occur:

1. Being a male,
2. Being between the ages of 16 and 30,
3. Being non-white, particularly black,
4. Being from a lower socio-economic group,
5. Being an abuser of alcohol or opiates,
6. Being unstable in employment and place of residence,
7. Being poorly educated,
8. Being of low intelligence,
9. Having been arrested or convicted in juvenile court or adult criminal court for past violent crimes, and
10. Having a history of reported violent behavior never brought to court.

It should be noted that a history of psychosis or neurosis does not correlate with violent behavior and in fact lowers the statistical likelihood of violent behavior.

4. FULLY DESCRIBE THE EPISODE LEADING TO THE REFFERAL. The assessor's description of the episode should incorporate not only a description of the client, but also of the victim or potential victim *and* what was going on between them. Who said what? Why did they do that? What were they thinking and feeling? What did they want to accomplish? What means (weapons) were used during the episode? What was the relationship between them? Was the episode sudden in onset or did it build over time? Were the client's actions in the episode reactive to the victim or did they seem to be idiosyncratic? What did the client do after the crest of danger or violence?

Let us go back to the hypothetical Johnson case. It matters whether Mr. Johnson slugged his wife because she told him dinner was not ready or because she berated him for an hour about his lack of income and poor performance in bed. It matters whether she threatened him. It matters that they knew each other and were not strangers fighting in the aisle of a grocery store. The willingness to act dangerously or violently toward a stranger or near stranger heightens the likelihood of subsequent diffuse aggression.

A sudden onset episode between strangers with little victim provocation, accomplished with the use of a lethal instrument, followed by remorseless pursuit strongly suggests the potential for future violence is quite high.

The client is certainly not the only informant. Other informants are any available people with knowledge of the client. Of paramount importance in this possibly large group of people is the potential victim. It is important to hear what he or she has to say about the client, but it is of equal importance to gather information about the victim's personality, attitudes, and actions toward the client. If there have been prior violent episodes between these same two people, the details of those episodes should be explored as carefully as possible. Unfortunately, the victim is often absent from the group of other informants, as in rape, other crimes, or concerns about the public or society.

If the client and victim are both available for interview, they may each tell substantially different stories, in effect accusing each other of lying. It may be necessary to choose which version to believe if the stories are markedly different. It may be useful to give great weight to the details of the extent of the physical damage to the victim. When the victim is not available, police reports and medical reports may be all we have.

The orientation of the assessor is significantly important to the process of assessing dangerousness. As with beauty, dangerousness is something that seems to lie in the eye of the beholder to some degree.

Whether the assessor is trained as a behaviorist or as a psychoanalytically oriented therapist will color the assessor's view. In psychoanalytic theory personality is viewed as a formed entity that gives rise to behavior patterns that may not be understood by the behaving client. Whether the client behaves in a friendly, constructive, antisocial, or dangerous way, his behavior is viewed as being produced by his formed personality. The assumption is then made that the client's personality will cause him or her to behave in a similar way in other situations as well. The *hysterical female*, the *passive-aggressive male*, the *borderline personality*, and the *paranoid personality* are terms commonly used to convey notions of how the person in question generally behaves in their everyday life.

While it is useful to understand the client's tendencies and orientation toward the world, it is equally important to understand the interaction between situational factors or setting and the client's personality. Personality can be seen as the currently prevailing style of the client. The client's personality of today may show changes from his or her past style while continuing unchanged with regard to some traits. When assessing the impact of the client's personality on his or her behavior, also bear in mind that the client's behavior is also a function of the situation.

5. DESCRIBE THE STRESSES IN THE CLIENT'S CURRENT ENVIRONMENT. Consider the extent to which the demands of the client's social and physical environment strain his ability to cope. General sources of stress include the family, the work place, the neighborhood, and the client's friends or associates. Identify specific problem areas and fully describe how the client is presently dealing with his tension. Is he coping well by use of nonviolent action or is he feeling worse? Is the current stress similar to past stresses that have caused him to act violently? Beware when the client says there are no stresses in his life or professes he feels fine, especially when you know his circumstances clearly contain factors that would stress you.

In describing the client's current environment, special attention should be given to two specific items. The first is the availability of the past victim or people of similar position in the client's life. If the client's past violence took the form of mugging elderly pedestrians, it can be assumed that plenty of potential victims remain available, depending on whether the client is incarcerated or not. If the past victim was a spouse who has since divorced and moved away, that may lower the likelihood of violence, unless the client now has a new relationship.

The second special item in the current environment is the matter of whether the client possesses an instrument—a gun, knife, or martial art skill—with which to inflict bodily harm on a person. The present weapon availability should be correlated with whether the client had used a weapon in past episodes of violence.

6. POSTULATE WHAT THE FUTURE ENVIRONMENT WILL BE. The emphasis in this speculation should be on the following three questions:

1. What *stresses* is the client likely to encounter? Of what magnitude are they likely to be? How successful is he likely to be in coping with them?
2. Will the future environment include a likely *victim* or persons of similar profile as the actual victims in the client's past, assuming a history of actual violence? The profile of past actual victims should include a demographic description of the victim and comments concerning the interaction between the client and victim at the time of the past violent episode.
3. Is the future *combination* of stress level and victim availability likely to be similar to the combination found in past episodes

of violence?

Here are some brief examples to illustrate:

A reformed alcoholic has a history of seriously assaulting his wife. At the time of his violence, his marriage and job were important sources of stress. He coped poorly by excessive use of alcohol. At present, he has maintained sobriety for six months, has taken a job with lower demands well within his range of occupational capability, and he and his wife are proceeding toward divorce. The wife's father was an abusive alcoholic. In her marriage, she responded to her drinking husband with behavior patterns that seemed to provoke his drunken assaults.

The client's stress level is lower. He is coping better. It appears that he will remain sober. There will probably be other women in his future, but through AA counseling he has a clearer understanding of the type of woman his wife is and how she provoked him. The stress-victim combination likely in his future appears significantly less than the stress-victim combination at the time of his last violent episode.

A nineteen-year-year-old drug abuser has a history of assaulting elderly people and robbing them. At the time of his violence, he was unemployed and associated mainly with others in the drug culture. There was considerable stress from his family, occupational area, and from his peer group. The victims were elderly people who had little interaction with the client during the violent episodes. They usually offered minimal resistance to his robbery demands. The client entered prison to begin a five-year sentence.

The client has been drug-free for four months now. He will probably undergo vocational training while in prison. The future availability of drugs in prison is considered minimal. It is anticipated that he will have similar peer stresses in prison. The client is likely to be in prison for eighteen to twenty-four months. While his stress level will be only slightly lower or the same, he seems to be coping better while drug-free. The victim availability is much lower. A second examination at the time of parole hearing would be useful since victim availability would return to the status present at the time of past violence.

7. OFFER AN EXPLICIT OPINION. The ending of the report

should relate directly to your understanding of the question put to you as you enumerated it at the beginning of the report. Your opinion should specify what *potential victim* you considered, the *time period* you consider your opinion to cover, and *quantifying* adverbs. An example follows:

> I examined Mr. Robert Johnson to form opinions as to whether he is presently a danger to his *wife, Betty*, and whether it is likely that he will physically harm her in the future.
>
> After consideration of all the information described in the body of this report, it is my opinion that Mr. Johnson is *minimally* dangerous toward his wife and that it is *unlikely* that he will physically injure her. Since it appears highly likely that the Johnsons will not reunite, but will divorce, I express my opinions as holding true for the next year. My opinion time frame would be shortened to the *time spent apart* if they resume an intimate or cohabitational relationship.

Let me offer some general remarks about the examination process. Every available source of information should be used. Sources include the victim or potential victim, the client, relatives of both, employers, acquaintances, police reports, criminal record sheets, medical reports, school performance records, psychological test results, and any other source that can reasonably comment on the client. All of the sources used should be listed in the report. Be especially wary of submitting a report when the only source of information is the client. Give strong consideration to not submitting an opinion at all.

The assessment process is difficult enough. In the end, the decision of what to do about the assessed danger is heavier. Client, spouses, parents, and judges may be expected to perceive our opinion as disagreeable because it is they who must *do* something with it.

The anxiety and ill feeling is heightened further by the stakes. An obese person remaining obese is one thing. A person said to be dangerous and then set free only to kill or harm someone is another matter. Even the "false positive" situation—the client deprived of something of value—is highly distasteful. In short, the decision to invoke a specific action is a no-win bind. We are not likely to be thanked for our assessment. It is likely that we will be berated for our effort as failing on either side of the fence. Ironically, it is certain that we will be asked to assess other clients and render more opinions.

The assessment process does not include the specific actions generated by our assessment. Each assessment episode stands by itself. Today's evaluation episode does not mandate stability of opinion or sameness for the future or for other episodes of assessing the dangerousness of the same client. Above all, the actual future events are not part of today's assessment process.

EXPLAINING AND DEFENDING YOUR OPINION. If and when your opinion is challenged, begin by emphasizing the *differences* between dangerousness and violence. Dangerousness does no injury and sheds not one drop of blood. If a person is actually injured, we are no longer talking about danger. We are talking about violence.

Dangerousness can be assessed only as of the present moment. Conversely, violence is either past or in the future, but it is not in the present. Therefore, assign the past and the future to violence and the present to dangerousness. Express predictions of violence in terms of probability, not certainty.

In dealing with the prediction of a violent event, you have weighed predictor variables (age, sex, client/victim relationship, etc.) and you make a descriptive statement of probability, not a prediction, when you say it is likely, probable, highly probable, etc. that the client will injure someone. You *are* making a prediction if you state, "The client will (or will not) injure someone."

REFERENCES

Breiner, S.: The violent person in the community. *Psychiatric Forum, 2*:33-49, 1970.

Cocozza, J., and Steadman, H.: Some refinements in the measurement and prediction of dangerous behavior. *American Journal of Psychiatry, 131*:1012-1014, 1974.

Justice, B., and Birkman, R.: An effort to distinguish the violent from the nonviolent. *Southern Medical Journal, 65*: 703-706, 1972.

Justice, B., Justice, R., and Kraft, I.: Early warning signs of violence. *American Journal of Psychiatry, 131*: 457-459, 1974.

Kozol, H.: The diagnosis and treatment of dangerousness. *Crime and Delinquency, 18*: 371-392, 1972.

Marcus, A., and Conway, C.: Dangerous sexual offender project; *Canadian Journal of Corrections, 11*: 198, 1969.

Monahan, J.: The clinical prediction of violent behavior. *NIMH Monograph: Crime and Delinquency Issues*, DHHS Pub. No. (ADM) 81-92, 1981.

Monahan, J.: *The Preventing of Violence.* Paper presented at the meeting of the Western Psychological Association, San Francisco, April 1974.

Rubin, B.: Prediction of dangerousness in mentally ill criminals. *Archives of General Psychiatry, 27*: 397-407, 1972.

Satten, J.: *Murder without Apparent Motive: A Study in Personality Disorganization.* Paper presented at the meeting of the American Psychiatric Association, Philadelphia, April, 1959.

Shah, S.: Dangerousness: A paradigm for exploring some issues in law and psychology. *American Psychologist*, March 1978, pp. 224-238.

Smith, S.: The adolescent murderer. *Archives of General Psychiatary, 13*: 310-319, 1965.

Tanay, E.: Dangerousness and psychiatry. *Current Concepts in Psychiatry*, October 1975, pp. 17-26.

Wenk, E.: Can violence be predicted? *Crime and Delinquency, 18*: 393-402, 1972.

Chapter 3

THE PRACTITIONER'S INITIAL RESPONSE TO VICTIMS OF VIOLENCE

CAROLE A. ANDERSON

INTRODUCTION

ACCOUNTS of violence in daily newspapers, official crime statistics, a long history of involvement in wars, recurrent civil disorders, and cries of support for the death penalty support the thesis that violence is a fact of everyday life in American culture. Furthermore, violence is often justified by values and ideology. For example the supporters of the death penalty think it is necessary for the "good" of society, in spite of the fact that the death penalty does not deter capital crime, and involvement in wars is justified by the argument that the country needs to protect itself and its allies against a creeping, divergent political ideology.

Violence and violent acts or crimes are generally thought to be social problems and, thus, only within the purvue of the criminal justice system. However, in recent years it has become known that violence transcends the deviant subculture and is a pervasive influence in all facets of American life. The American home, for example, may well be the most dangerous place for women and children since violence between family members occurs more often than it does between any other individuals (excluding wars and riots).

Abuse of women by their husbands has come to be known as a major problem in recent years. Although no definite causes have been identified, such things as cultural norms legitimizing spouse abuse, the level of societal violence, socialization within families into violent modes of interacting, sex roles and sexism, economic frustrations, substance abuse, and power resources are all factors that have been associated with abuse (Gelles, 1974; Strauss, 1977; Steinmetz and Strauss, 1974; Roy, 1977; Carlson, 1977; Bard and Zacker, 1971; Gayford, 1975; Gelles and Strauss, 1975; Nichols, 1976; Parker and Schumacher, 1977; Pizzey, 1974; Strauss, Gelles, and Steinmetz, 1977).

The 1980 Surgeon General's report estimates that 2,000 children die each year as a result of being abused by their parents. Valid and reliable child abuse statistics are difficult to obtain, but what is known points to such abuse as a widespread and serious phenomenon that involves hundreds of thousands of children each year (Gelles, 1977; Nagi, 1975; Kempe, 1971).

Rape and incest are other examples of violent acts, and the incidence seems to be increasing. Reported rates are thought to be less than the actual rate due to underreporting, denial, social stigma, humiliation, and the like (Sarles, 1975; Summit and Kryso, 1978; *National Symposium*, 1972). Both of these acts have serious physical and psychosocial implications for the victims.

Victims of violence apear in newspaper headlines, statistical reports, and friendship circles. These victims also appear in significant numbers as clients in health and human service agencies. Workers with such agencies must respond daily to victims who are attempting to cope with the physical and psychological impact of the violent acts. These workers cannot defend against the powerful reality of violence by viewing it simply as a subcultural phenomenon.

RESPONSIBILITIES OF HEALTH CARE PROVIDERS

Victims are found in every health care setting: emergency rooms, clinics, private offices, and inpatient facilities. Sometimes they are seeking treatment for their primary injuries and at other times help for the secondary effects of violence, for example, depression. Health care providers, through an understanding of the network of associated causal factors, can be of assistance to victims of violence. Adequate and responsive treatment to victims consists of identifying victims, adhering to legal requirements, and providing emergency medical treatment, psychosocial crisis intervention, and referral.

Identification of Victims

Each health care profession has its own ethical standards to guide the care it provides. In spite of some of the differences that might exist among the various professions, all of them set the standard that care be given to individuals only after a complete data base has been obtained, that is a complete assessment of the individual must be done in order to decide upon appropriate care. Professionals are ethically and morally bound to acquire as much information as they can from individuals seeking their care. Accordingly, when victims present themselves with, for example, signs and symptoms that are suspicious, that is, cause the provider to suspect their origin, the provider is obligated to pursue a line of inquiry into the possibility of abuse, whether that be child, sexual, or spouse abuse.

Individuals must be directly questioned to discover the true nature of the injuries. Many times, however, victims are ashamed of what has happened to them and devise false stories about the nature of the injury. For example, battered women talk about an "accident," and parents, in an attempt to hide or deny abuse or incest, will fabricate a story. If we do not go beyond the story that is offered, we are not only being remiss, but also delivering substandard care, because it will be only partial care. That is to say, if we do not know the circumstances of the injury, we cannot provide the care, such as counseling, information giving, referral, etc., that is required for the care to be complete. To not pursue our suspicions is to essentially collude with individuals in perpetrating their own victimization. Health care providers must accept responsibility for trying to assist individuals to extricate themselves, if they can, from their violent situations or advocate for individuals unable to do so for themselves.

Determining Wife Abuse. A woman who presents herself for services with physical symptoms such as bruises, lacerations, and broken bones signals the possibility that this may be a battered woman. In addition, if the woman appears to be embarrassed or evasive about the details of the "accident," further suspicions should be aroused. Battered women frequently report that when they sought medical assistance they lied to the care giver, *and those lies were never questioned* (Flitcraft, 1978). A heightened awareness of the problem causes health care professionals to be suspicious of a woman's story and thus to take the first step in responding to the needs of the victim.

Sometimes a woman will provide other clues that might cause suspicions such as referring to her husband as someone who "gets very, very angry" or "has a quick temper." Careful attention paid to the woman and her accounts of her relationship with her husband can generate clues toward concluding that this is a woman who is being physically abused.

When enough data has been gathered to indicate that the woman is being beaten, the perception should be shared with her. There is no need to be afraid of making that judgment prematurely. In other words, if the assessment of the situation is incorrect, then the woman will simply correct it. However, on the other hand, if the assessment is correct, sharing that perception with the woman will help her to feel that someone is genuinely interested in her and her family and is willing to assist her to find ways of coping with her problem.

Often, it is the case that health care providers are very much aware of women who are being physically beaten but feel inadequate to provide them with any concrete form of assistance or are uncomfortable with the topic of family violence and, thus, do not talk about that possibility. However, once an assessment of intrafamily violence has been made, the woman can be helped to identify her alternatives. Without proper identification of the problem, complete care cannot be provided.

Determining Child Abuse and Incest. Child abuse is a widespread and common phenomenon involving thousands of children per year and causing the death of approximately 2,000 of them (Schmitt, 1978). Eighty-five percent of abuse is physical, 10 percent sexual, 10 percent nutrition deprivation, and 5 percent failure to thrive secondary to nutritional deprivation. The ages of abused children vary but the majority (two-thirds) are under three years. In 90 percent of the cases the abuser is a related caretaker; the others are boyfriend 5 percent, babysitter 4 percent, and sibling 1 percent. Identification of the abused child is extremely important since early detection and intervention can reduce the death rate by two-thirds (Schmitt, 1978*A*).

As mentioned above, physical abuse is the most common type of child abuse and can be suspected on the basis of history and a physical examination. The combination of an implausible, phony, or suspicious history and certain physical findings can lead to the identification of a child victim. It is not the intent of this chapter to provide a detailed discussion of intervention and treatment in child abuse cases since other comprehensive sources exist (Schmitt, 1978*A* and 1978*B*). Rather, what follows is a brief outline of certain findings that when present should raise suspicion and prompt health care providers to be diligent in pursuing and confirming the diagnosis of child abuse so as to provide the appropriate intervention, treatment, and referral. The following is a list of findings associated with confirmed cases of physical child abuse derived from the work of health care professionals associated with the National Center on Child Abuse and Neglect (Schmitt, 1978*A*, pp. 39-45*):

Unexplained injuries:
Injuries that are unable to be explained by parents or explanations that are vague and evasive.

Discrepant history:
Discrepancies in the history obtained in regard to the injury. The discrepancy can be related to differences between: the stories of the two parents, dates, times and causes of the injury, the physical findings and the history, the parents' dating of the injury and the physical findings, and the injury and the child's developmental level.

Alleged self-inflicted injury:
A history alleging that a very young child injured himself or that a child deliberately hurt himself, since children rarely inflict injuries on themselves.

Alleged third-party injury:
When the parents blame the child's injuries on someone other than themselves, e.g., babysitter, sibling, neighbor, etc.

Delay in seeking medical care:
Abused children are often not brought in promptly for care whereas children injured under other circumstances are brought in immediately.

History of repeated suspicious injury:
When a child has suspicious injuries on more than one occasion or when a parent identifies the child as "accident prone."

Diagnostic bruises, welts, lacerations and scars:
Bruises of the buttocks and lower back are almost always related to punishment as are bruises on the genital area or inner thigh usually inflicted for toileting mishaps. Bruises on the cheek from being

*Quoted by permission of the publisher, Garland Publishing Co., Inc.

slapped, tears of the floor of the mouth and bruises inside the lips and mouth, human hand marks and encircling bruises, strap marks, bizarre shaped bruises, e.g., from a shoe or a toy, choke marks and bruises found at multiple stages of healing and on multiple body places.

Diagnostic burns:

The most common inflicted burn is from a cigarette with characteristic shape found most often on the palms, soles or abdomen. Dry contact burns can occur from forcibly holding a child against a heating device and the shape is obvious and diagnostic. The most common type of hot water burn results from dunking the child into scalding water resulting in a circular burn usually of the buttocks or a burn showing a clear cut water level on the thighs and abdomen. In the latter, hands and feet are usually not burned, thus ruling out falling into a tub of hot water.

Brain injuries:

Usually resulting from a subdural hemorrhage caused by rapid shaking or from being hit up against a wall or door. Usually other bruises are also present on the body.

Eye injuries:

Bruises and bleeding into the internal structure.

Abdominal injuries:

These are the most common cause of death and result from the whipping force of a punch or a blow leading to internal hemorrhage and are different from injuries sustained in, for example, a car accident or a fall which usually results in the rupture of internal organs.

Bone injuries:

The most classic finding is a chip or corner fracture. Evidence of multiple healed fractures are also diagnostic of repeated abuse.

Incest is a variant form of child abuse; if it is suspected, reporting to the appropriate child protection agency is mandated. Providers in all settings, for example, schools, pediatric clinics, community health, and emergency departments, are ideally situated to assess the child and identify incest and to assist the child and parents to deal with their rage and guilt.

Incest should be suspected in instances of generalized signs of abuse (i.e. bruises, burns, vaginal or penile discharge, lesions around the mouth or perineum, painful urination or defecation, perineal itching, unexplained history of choking on mucous-like secretions, the presence of Trichomonas or gonorrheal organisms, or a positive test for syphilis) (Herjanic and Wilbois, 1978).

Incest often is not a physically violent act. However, since incest usually involves a young child and a parent (most often a girl and her father), it does involve undue emotional force related to the power position of the parent and the intrinsic vulnerability of the child. Furthermore, there is considerable evidence to suggest that child victims, as a group, are more vulnerable to pathological development in later life and that considerable numbers of them suffer lasting harm (Herman, 1981, p. 29).

Confirmed cases of incest are usually derived from the history obtained from the victim (Schmitt, 1978, p. 48). The confirmation and documentation is accomplished by a thorough evaluation of the following (Schmitt, 1978, pp. 48-49):

- Complaint of incest by the victim
- Unexplained pregnancy
- Venereal disease or vaginal bleeding in a prepubertal child
- History of running away from home
- Injury of the mouth, anus, or external genitalia
- Vaginal discharge

The child and parents need to be helped to understand that the reporting is designed to help them resolve their family difficulties. It is important to maintain a nonjudgmental attitude and to try to help the parents see that the services that will be provided will be of assistance to them in improving their parenting.

The incestuous family's needs are complex and require specialized treatment from family therapists. Therefore, after the incest is identified and reported, assistance can be given to obtain appropriate referrals for specialized care.

Adherence to Legal Requirements

When a person has been the victim of violence that may be a crime and if the state has a mandatory reporting law that requires health care providers to report the incident to the appropriate authorities, they must do so. For example, most states now do have such laws pertaining to child abuse victims (including sexual abuse) and victims with gunshot wounds.

Police officials should be informed, if they haven't been already, when rape victims come to the emergency room and request to file a report. In addition, the health care professional is obligated to perform a full medicolegal examination, regardless of whether the woman intends to prosecute, so as to ensure that prosecution is possible if the victim changes her mind.

Currently, it is not required of health care providers to report spouse abuse, regardless of its severity. If the victim does not want to call the police, she is not obliged, nor is anyone else, to inform the police of the violence that has occurred. Advocacy groups dedicated to delivering services to battered women do encourage health care providers to ask women directly if the injuries are the result of a beating and, if they are, to give information to her about available resources as well as her legal rights related to prosecution of her assailant.

Obviously, this necessitates that providers be aware of the legal rights of victims and community resources available to them. One of the most important legal considerations of providing emergency services to victims is the maintenance of an accurate, written record since that document is always subpoenaed in subsequent court actions. The record should contain an accurate and detailed description of all events and findings associated with the services provided. In addition, the general rules for obtaining patient consent must be followed and recorded (D'Amico and Sherman, 1978).

On behalf of the client and society, health care providers act as a liaison between the victim and the appropriate institution by reporting the act of violence. By providing care with adequate knowledge, the client's rights will be protected and justice will be hastened.

Emergency Medical Assistance

A significant responsibility of health care providers is to provide emergency medical assistance for physical trauma, beginning with a thorough physical examination. Therefore, it is especially important that victims be thoroughly examined for internal trauma, such as ruptured spleens, head injuries, and fractures. Health care providers must not underestimate the physical force that is used on these victims. Ideally, victims should be allowed some time prior to the examination to talk about their experience and express whatever emotions they are feeling. In other words, let them cry, yell, express anger and rage, etc., prior to any physical treatment. This is an important first step in beginning to resolve a crisis. However, at times, the nature of the injury is such that care must be provided immediately. When this is the case, then the provider must be understanding of the victim's emotional needs and not insist on silent compliance. In this situation, it is helpful to have at least one other provider, free from any responsibilities for physical care, to tend to the victim's emotional needs.

Physical examinations should be carried out in a calm, gentle, caring, and sensitive manner that communicates to victims an understanding of the depth of their distress and humiliation. If victim advocacy and support services are available in the community through other agencies, such as rape crisis centers, they should be employed to augment the services provided by health care professionals.

Most importantly, services should be provided in ways that will maintain the victim's dignity. Such things as being sensitive to individual beliefs and customs and involving the patient in and providing descriptions of the care that is being provided help to maintain dignity and communicate respect.

Since individuals who seek emergency services are in both physical and emotional crisis, particular attention needs to be paid to the emotional needs before or concomitant with providing physical care. Some common emotional responses of victims are anger, fear, confusion, and distrust and disbelief that call for interventions aimed at alleviating the associated distress before or accompanying any physical care.

ASSAULT VICTIMS. In most emergency rooms, there is a person, usually a nurse, assigned the responsibility for triaging all patients. General guidelines and standards exist and are used by most hospitals to guide this assessment. Responsibilities of the triage person include the following (Nelson, 1978):

Notification of law enforcement agencies for reportable injuries, e.g., gunshot wounds, child abuse, etc.

Gathering a history of the injury:

- Quality and location of the injury
- Effect of the injury on other body systems
- Details of the trauma, e.g., weapon used
- Any existing illnesses or past injuries

Conducting an initial assessment aimed at establishing the status of various body systems, e.g., respiratory status, motor function, emotional status, pain assessment including quality, location and intensity, level of consciousness, physical activity, etc.

Recording findings in an accurate and detailed fashion

Ordering appropriate laboratory and radiographic tests

BATTERED WOMEN. Often, battered women present to medical

facilities with vague complaints of traumatic injuries or complaints of trouble with their children. However, when suspicion of battering is aroused and the woman is asked a direct question as to whether or not she has been beaten by her husband, most will admit the abuse and discuss it with an interested professional.

Suspicion of wife battering should be entertained when the following are present in a woman seeking emergency care:

- Victim disclosure of abuse
- Evidence of beating, kicking, and punching especially about the head, face, chest, breasts and abdomen
- Multiple bruises and/or lacerations with an improbable, evasive, or insufficient cause identified
- Discernible bruises fitting the outline of a hand
- Evidence of injury inflicted with a weapon

The specific care that is provided would be dictated by the injuries identified and should follow the protocol for general assault victims outlined above. As mentioned earlier, it is important to not underestimate the amount of violence that is used in these situations. Therefore, a thorough physical examination, including appropriate radiographic studies, is indicated.

Another aspect of care is to respond to the victim's emotional status and following treatment, utilize all other available sources of referral, and follow-up so as to assist the woman to entertain all alternatives available to her.

RAPE AND INCEST VICTIMS. Treatment of rape victims involves an interface between medical and legal issues, and therefore, programs designed by medical facilities should be part of a cooperative effort between hospitals, citizen groups, law enforcement, and prosecuting agencies (Hilberman, 1976, p. 23).

Adequate treatment of the rape victim is facilitated by a team treatment model involving physicians, nurses, social workers, mental health workers, and victim services. Specific medical treatment consists of the following (Hilberman, 1976, pp. 17-21):

- Treatment of physical injury such as lacerations, fractures, vaginal tears, etc.
- Prevention of venereal disease
- Prevention of pregnancy
- A medico-legal examination to collect evidence for possible future use in a court trial and consisting of—

Assessment of physical and emotional status of victim
Details of the rape incident
Information of menstrual status
Behavior between time of rape and examination
Description of wearing apparel
Physical examination
  General appearance
  Evidence of trauma to external genitalia
  Vaginal examination and collection of specimens
Laboratory examination
  Pubic hair combings for possible typing
  Foreign material
  Smear for presence and typing of sperm
  Smears and cultures for venereal disease diagnosis
Photographs to document this trauma
Tagging of identifying evidence with the name of victim and person having custody of the evidence
Prevention of permanent psychological harm

The treatment of incest victims includes all of the same services provided to rape victims, depending on the nature of the incest, that is, whether forced or not. In addition, incest victims and their families need referral to appropriate agencies for family therapy.

CHILD ABUSE. Once the suspicion or confirmation of child abuse is made, appropriate treatment plans should ensue and include the following (Schmitt, 1978, p. 3):

- Appropriate treatment of the specific injury
- Reporting to appropriate agency
- Referral to a variety of services such as Parents Anonymous, therapeutic preschools, psychiatric services, crisis nursery, child rearing counseling, etc.
- A plan for a minimum of a 6 months follow-up

Psychosocial Crisis Intervention

The most appropriate model for psychosocial care for victims and their families is crisis intervention since, at the time of identification, the individual and family are in a crisis. That is, the "normal" state is disrupted and they are, at the time, in a state of disequilibrium. The health care professionals can be of significant assistance at this time. At the time of discovery or disclosure, the health care provider should—

1. *Establish a meaningful relationship* that includes listening and communicating concern, care, and understanding. It is also important to communicate confidence in the fact that the crisis can be resolved.
2. *Counteract feelings of helplessness/hopelessness* by assisting individuals and families to perceive their strengths and also to see that there are "solutions" for them.
3. *Avoid false reassurance.* It is important for individuals and families to begin to understand the full impact of the situation without becoming overwhelmed or frightened. Things can improve, but only if definitive steps are taken.
4. *Fact-find.* An attempt must be made to discover all of the relevant facts in the situation in order to assist the victim in setting priorities for action. For example, in a case of wife abuse, it is important to find out where the children are, if the husband owns any weapons, whether there are friends and relatives with whom she can stay, etc. At the time of the crisis, victims are not always able to think through even the most elementary facts of the situation, and they, therefore, need assistance.
5. *Avoid blame.* Victims sometimes blame themselves for what has happened, e.g. "If I hadn't left my daughter alone with my husband," "If I had only screamed and run for help I wouldn't have been raped," or "I knew my husband had been drinking, I shouldn't have told him about the car trouble." Providers need to communicate that no matter what has transpired prior to the violence, no one deserves to be beaten, abused, or raped and that the perpetrator should be the focus. In other words, it is the perpetrator of the act that should be judged and not the victim.
6. *Allow victims to cry.* Victims are frequently humiliated and have lost their self-respect. They are also angry and frustrated. They should be allowed to cry, which will help them discharge feelings and move on to problem solve.
7. *Offer assistance.* Victims need some direct assistance, for example, calling friends or family, making a referral to an agency for homemaker service, finding someone to stay with them, etc. This is particularly important to counteract a low self-esteem, which interferes with an individual's asking for "help" (*see* below).

8. *Escort*. Because victims are distraught, they often need someone to accompany them. In many communities, agencies that serve and advocate for victims such as rape crisis centers and battered womens' shelters offer these services and will accompany victims home, to the court, etc.
9. *Follow-up*. It is very important that a mechanism exists to obtain follow-up information from victims especially in regard to utilization of referral services. In many communities, a referral is made to a public health or visiting nurse for follow-up. This procedure should ideally contain a feedback mechanism to the crisis service.

Crisis intervention is integral to a health care provider's role and is an important first step in helping victims gain the strength needed to acknowledge their situation and begin to problem-solve for the future. However, since all of us are socialized in a culture that teaches various stereotypes of victims, we must first confront our own attitudes related to such things as violence, marriage, roles of husbands and wives, and attitudes toward someone who remains in an abusive situation. Unless we can be honest with ourselves about how we feel about these things, any attempt to engage in a helping relationship will fail since victims are acutely sensitive to the attitudes of others.

Referral

A careful assessment of the individual and family needs to be made in order to provide the needed data base upon which appropriate referrals can be made. For example, it is sometimes appropriate to refer a battered woman to a mental health center. This is not because the woman is mentally ill but because assessment reveals this person to be at high risk or already clinically depressed. Referral to specialized care is then appropriate if it is accompanied by careful explanation of the rationale.

Rape victims experience both an acute and long-term reaction (Burgess and Holstrum, 1974), necessitating crisis intervention and possibly continued counseling at a mental health facility. Furthermore, husbands and boyfriends often respond in a dysfunctional manner and, for example, view the rape as a sexual act rather than a violent crime, hold the woman responsible, feel personally wronged, and see the victim as devalued and unclean (Silverman, 1978). In this instance, to avoid long-term complications, the victim and her boyfriend or husband must be referred to a mental health specialist for counseling.

As previously stated, incestuous families need treatment from individuals specially trained in family therapy. The referring professional should make it clear to the family that the referral is appropriate treatment and the means toward ending their family difficulties.

Frequently there is a need for other social services, such as financial assistance, child care, homemaker services, legal services, and special interest groups (that specialize in self-help for victims). Professionals need to be aware of the services available in the community so as to make appropriate referrals and to help people put their lives back in order.

One of the results of the emergence of a variety of agencies, each devoted to specific victim services, is that those services are frequently uncoordinated and are therefore dissipated and random. It is not unusual, for example, that one family can be in care with several different agencies for a variety of problems related to violence and abuse. It could be the case that the family is known to, for example, child protective services, the department of social services (welfare), a mental health center, and a primary health care provider. Unfortunately, it is usually the case that there is no centralizing or coordinating body within the community to rorganize the family's care. Given this reality, providers should strive to obtain information from the individual and family as to what other agencies are providing care or services. Aggressive and direct contact with other providers needs to be established if the care is to be truly comprehensive and not redundant or contradictory. Coordinating care in this way maximizes benefits and is a way of preventing issues or problems from "falling through the cracks" in the complex service delivery system.

In addition, health care agencies need to strive to develop formal and informal linkages with other agencies in the community that provide services. Providers would be well served if they made a point to acquire as much information as possible about other agencies and then to develop both formal and informal contacts within them. In this way, referral and coordination can be better accomplished.

Knowledge of Community Services

Professionals need to be aware of the services in their community that are targeted for victims of violence and abuse. If they are not, then they will find it difficult to carry out their role successfully, Recently, groups that serve victims have been established in many communities, for example, rape crisis centers, battered women's shelters, and Parents Anonymous. The groups frequently have a strong self-help component in their services and are designed to provide direct care such as counseling, referral, and advocacy. Often few or no "professionals" are on the staffs of such agencies. Because of a strong commitment to self-help there is a concomitant reliance on victim volunteers. This way of organizing is often at odds with a professional's orientation. However, a willingness to work cooperatively with these groups should be fostered. Special interest groups provide those needed services that have been identified as lacking in the existing network of services in a community. Thus, they are not only willing but also able to provide care that is not otherwise available or that has been historically viewed as the prerogative of the more traditional agencies. A good example of this is advocacy for the victim through the criminal justice system. Most health care providers do not see that as within the scope of their role. However, it is an important service for victims because of the potential it holds for a permanent resolution to the victim's dilemma.

PRINCIPLES RELATED TO PRACTICE

Victim-Centeredness

In order for health care providers to assist victims of violence, they must transcend the constraints that keep them from responding appropriately to violence. They must forego easy explanations and come to understand the complex factors associated with the origin and perpetuation of violence. They must stop blaming victims for their plight, understand their own violent impulses, and lastly, since much of the everyday violence involves women as victims, confront their sex role ideology and stereotyping.

Violence that victimizes women and children is a very serious problem that does not lend itself to easy conclusions or stereotyping, such as thinking that if women would leave their abusive husbands, they could end the violence; if they do not leave, they "enjoy"/"need" the abuse; if children are removed from their families, the abuse will stop and the child will develop into a whole, intact person; or finally, if women would not go out alone, they would not be raped. The problems and situations of victims are complex and involve many different factors that allow for or perpetuate violence and abuse, such as the value placed on intact families and the stigma associated with disrupted families, economic forces that keep women victims in violent relationships, the victims' childhood experiences, which might predispose them to victimization as adults, the "trade-offs" that victims make, and the external constraints, such as an unresponsive legal system, that hinder victims from pursuing certain options. A common response to victims of violence is to blame them for what has happened. Blaming the victim is a cultural process described by Ryan (1976) that refers to focusing on the victim rather than on the social structure that allows the violence to occur. Accordingly, rape victims are often queried as to *their* behavior and how they might or might not have "provoked" the rape, rather than attempting to identify the social structure and processes that provoke men to assault women and, for the most part, remain relatively immune from punishment. Or, women who have been beaten by their husbands are asked what they did to provoke the attack. Likewise, the social situation (no money, nowhere to go, fear of retaliation, etc.) of women is ignored as a factor that keeps them in the situation while the focus is on the women's personal traits, such as provocative behavior or a pathological need to stay with an abusive spouse.

In order to help victims of violent acts, providers must confront and understand their own aggressive impulses. If that is not done, they will be inhibited from dealing directly with victims out of fear of hearing the frightening, violent details that remind them of their own aggressive impulses and how they deal with anger in situations that provoke rage. Perhaps they might have been exposed as children to abuse. If so, what impact has that left on them? Does it prevent them from dealing directly with victims? Also, they must ask themselves how they resolve conflicts in their daily lives, within their families and social groups. Do they avoid conflict and allow pressures to build or do they engage in constructive conflict resolution? Providers must ask themselves all of these questions and be honest with the answers. If they are not, then an unconscious need to *not hear* about the violence will prevent them from pursuing their suspicions and helping the victim to understand the situation and the available options and alternatives.

As mentioned above, many of the victims of violent acts are women, and numerous social scientists believe that sexism in the culture encourages this form of violence and also precludes appropriate punishment for the perpetrator (Straus, 1977). This is especially clear in the case of domestic violence insofar as the sexist structure of the family in our society contains the most fundamental set of factors associated with the physical abuse of wives (Straus, 1977). In other words, the norms and values that permit and sometimes encourage husband-to-wife violence are reflective of a hierarchical and male-dominated society, characteristic of the Western world, and are most clearly illustrated by our traditional marriage contract (Straus, 1977). Health care providers must recognize their own sex role biases and understand their sex role expectations; that is, what are appropriate male and female behaviors and how do they influence the analysis of the victim's situation? Furthermore, it is also important to think about how, as individuals, they function on a day-to-day basis relative to their own gender expectations. For example, if a provider possesses a traditional orientation, which emphasizes male dominance and female passivity, then it might be difficult to assist a woman beaten because she was "too assertive." The provider might agree with the abuser and believe that the woman needed to be put in her place.

In summary, it is imperative that health care providers engage in some "soul searching" in regard to the aforementioned factors in order to make sure that they approach the victim with a nonjudgmental attitude that will allow them to provide care, including understanding the situation, the act itself, and the alternatives available for changing the situation. They must

- Understand the complexity of violence
- Stop blaming victims
- Avoid oversimplification and stereotyping
- Understand the social context in which violence occurs
- Confront and understand their own aggressive impulses
- Recognize sex role biases
- Examine own behavior vis-à-vis sex role expectations

Provider-Centeredness

Health care providers who come into frequent contact with victims of violence and abuse need to be aware of the possible implications for themselves by virtue of the services they provide. A common response is to become insensitive to the needs of the victims. Initially, the response to victims of violence may be outrage and deep concern. Over time, however, it is possible for concern and outrage to be replaced by apathy or a casual cavalier attitude. Since what was once an unusual event becomes to the provider usual, the naive response is lost. This can be accompanied by a seeming disinterest in the predicament of the victim since the situation has become routine.

Fear is another response to violence. If direct experience with violence is not something that has been an integral part of life, hearing accounts of violence can be very frightening. Fright can be expressed in different ways, such as withdrawal from the victim, anger, anxious lightheartedness, blaming the victim, and so on.

Burnout is a term that, in the health professions literature, refers to a stress syndrome characterized by such things as physical and emotional exhaustion, involving the development of a negative self-concept, negative public attitudes, and loss of concern and feelings for clients (Storlie, 1979; Pines and Maslach, 1978). Factors that lead to burnout are such things as the intensity of the work, high expectations, and intimate and prolonged client contact (Pines and Maslach, 1978).

Working with victims of violence is very intense. When they present, they are in a severe crisis having both physical and psychosocial aspects. Their needs are great, and they are usually quite expressive in making them known. The provider must respond. In many ways responding means that the provider must relive the violence with the victim. This reliving can be very stressful and anxiety provoking.

Health care providers are, by nature of their education and training, dedicated to alleviating suffering. That is why they entered their profession. Their education and training have taught them how to provide ideal care and, unfortunately, all too often without regard for the realities that they will experience. Because they want to provide ideal care, they hold themselves (and others) to very high expectations. When they encounter situations in which they are unable to do anything directly to stop the violence, such as in the case of battered woman, they may become disillusioned and feel impotent and helpless.

Some victims of violence have a long history of violence and victimization. For example, many battered women are beaten, leave their husbands, and then return to them to be beaten again. Health care providers who initially understand her plight and the many factors keeping her in the situation may, over time, come to hold the victim responsible for not changing her own situation.

Many victims of violence are unable to garner the emotional resources necessary to follow through with suggestions, referrals, legal options, etc. For many different reasons they may use their resources to cope with the situation at hand and are unable to extend beyond that. This is very frustrating for providers who have worked to provide necessary information, etc., for the follow-through. It is not that victims do not want to follow through at the time, but many are unable to follow through when the immediate crisis is over. Over time, the realities and demands of working with victims of violence may exceed the provider's resources.

All of these—insensitivity, fright, and burnout—are, in essence, barriers to providing therapeutic care to victims. Professionals need to have outlets for themselves to express the feelings that are experienced in working with this group so as to diminish the chance of destructive interaction. Group sessions can be organized with the goal of providing a forum for the direct expression of feelings that are aroused in the course of providing services to victims. By having the opportunity to express directly the effect that is generated from their work, health care providers experience diminishing risk of dysfunction and destructive adaptation. Each individual, department, or agency needs to determine the strategy that best fits with them and their organization.

SUMMARY

The preceding chapter has provided the reader with an overview of the factors associated with violent acts and the potential impact on the victims. Victimization should be of particular importance to health care providers since the pervasiveness of physical and sexual abuse renders the problem of epidemic proportions and continued and repeated abuse does not provide a level of health consonant with contemporary societal resources.

Little is known of the long-range effects of repeated violence. However, common sense would lead to the conclusion that there are long-range negative consequences *if* appropriate care is not given at the time of the incident or disclosure. Furthermore, little evidence exists to indicate that victims are treated in the health care system with sensitivity and understanding. Indeed, some victims report that their requests for help, albeit at times vague, have been ignored. In some instances, health care workers have also reinforced negative stereotypes of the victim. Surely, we do not wish to compound an already existing crisis with insensitivity. We must strive to deliver care in a sensitive, caring, and responsive manner so as to maximize the victim's coping and ultimate adaptation.

REFERENCES

Bard, M., and Zacker, J.: The prevention of family violence: Dilemmas of community intervention. *Journal of Marriage and the Family, 33*: 667-676, 1974.

Burgess, A., and Holstrum, L.: *Rape: Victims of Crisis.* Bowie, Md., Robert J. Brady Co., 1974.

Carlson, B.E.: Battered women and their assailants. *Social Work, 58*: 455-460, November, 1977.

D'Amico, S., and Sherman, S.: Legal considerations. In Warner, C.G. (Ed.): *Emergency Medical Care.* New York, C.V. Mosby, 1978, pp. 13-18.

Flitcraft, A.: *Battered Women: An Emergency Room Epidemiology with a Description of a Clinical Syndrome and Critique of Present Therapeutics.* Unpublished paper given to the Subcommittee on Domestic and International Scientific Planning, Analyses and Cooperation, February 15, 1978.

Gayford, J.J.: Battered wives. *Medicine, Science and the Law, 15(4)* 237-245, 1975.

Gelles, R. *The Violent Home: A Study of Physical Aggression Between Husbands and Wives.* Beverly Hills, Calif., Sage Publications, 1974.

Gelles, R.J.: *Violence Towards Children.* Paper read at American Association for the Advancement of Science, Denver, Colo., 1977.

Gelles, R.J., and Straus, M.: Family experience and public support of the death penalty. *American Journal of Orthopsychiatry, 45(4)*: 596-613, July, 1975.

Herjanic, B., and Wilbois, R.P.: Sexual abuse of children: Detection and management. *Journal of the American Medical Association, 239(4)*: 331-333, January 23, 1978.

Herman, J.L.: *Father*-Daughter Incest. Cambridge, Mass., Harvard University Press, 1981.

Hilberman, E.: *The Rape Victim.* Washington, D.C., American Psychiatric Association, 1976.

Huggins, M.A., and Straus, M.A.: *Violence and the Social Structure as Reflected in Children's Books from 1850–1970.* Paper presented at the Eastern Sociological Society Meeting, 1975.

Kempe, C.H.: Pediatric implications of the battered baby syndrome. *Archives of Disease in Children, 46*: 28-37, 1971.

Lustig, N., et al.: Incest: A family group survival pattern. *Archives of General Psychiatry, 14*:31-40, January 1966.

National Symposium on Child Abuse. Denver, Colo., American Humane Association, Children's Division, 1972.

Nelson, D.: Triage and assessment. In Warner, C.G. (Ed.): *Emergency Medical Care.* New York, C.V. Mosby, 1978, pp. 45-57.

Nichols, B.B.: The abused wife problem. *Social Casework, 57*: 27-32, January 1976.

Parker, B., and Schumacher, D.N.: The battered wife syndrome and violence in the nuclear family of origin: A controlled pilot study. *American Journal of Public Health, 67(8)*: 760-761, August 1977.

Pines, A., and Maslach, C.: Characteristics of staff burnout in mental health settings. *Hospital Community Psychiatry, 29*:233-237, New York, April 1978.

Pizzey, E.: *Scream Quietly or the Neighbors Will Hear.* New York, Penguin Books, Ltd., 1974.

Rounsaville, B.J.: Battered wives: Barriers to identification and treatment. *American Journal of Orthopsychiatry, 48(3)*:487-43, July 1978.

Roy, M.: A current survey of 150 cases. In Maria, Roy (Ed.): *Battered Women: A Psychosociological Study of Domestic Violence.* New York, Van Nostrand-Reinhold Co., 1977, 25-44.

Ryan, W.: *Blaming the Victim.* New York, Vintage Books, 1976.

Sarles, R.M.: Incest. *The Pediatric Clinics of North America, 22(3):633-641, August, 1975.*

Schmitt, B. (Ed.): The Child Protection Team Handbook. New York, Garland STPM Press, 1978*A*.

Schmitt, B., et al.: *Guidelines for the Hospital and Clinic: Management of Child Abuse and Neglect.* U.S. Dept. of Health, Education, and Welfare, 1978*B*. DHEW Publication No. (OHDS) 79-30167.

Steinmetz, S., and Straus, M.: *Violence and the Family.* New York, Harper and Row, 1974.

Storlie, F.J.: Burnout: The elaboration of a concept. *American Journal of Nursing, 79(12)*: 2108-2112, December 1979.

Straus, M.A.: A sociological perspective on the prevention and treatment of wife beating. In Maria, Roy (Ed.): *Battered Women: A Psychosociological Study of Domestic Violence*, New York, Van Nostrand-Reinhold Co., 1977.

Straus, M.: Wife beating: How common and why? *Victimology, 2(3-4)*:443-458, 1978.

Straus, M., Gelles, R., and Steinmetz, S.: *Normative and Behavioral Aspects of Violence Between Spouses: Preliminary Data on a National Representative U.S.A. Sam-*

ple. Paper read at symposium on Violence, Simon Fraser University, March 12, 1977.

Summit, R., and Kryso, J.: Sexual abuse of children: A clinical spectrum. *American Journal of Orthopsychiatry, 48(2)*, April 1978.

Surgeon General's Report on Health Promotion and Disease Prevention. *Healthy People*, PHS .79-55071. U.S. Department of Health, Education, and Welfare, Washington, D.C., 1979.

Chapter 4

STRATEGIES FOR CRISIS INTERVENTION WITH VICTIMS OF VIOLENCE*

BARRIE LEVY AND VIVIAN BROWN

VICTIMIZATION is a traumatic life event, which, like other events such as divorce or death of a family member, can precipitate a crisis. Crisis is a period of disequilibrium for an individual that cannot be resolved with usual problem-solving mechanisms. Accumulating evidence supports the idea that victimization is a generic issue, with similar consequences for many diverse groups of victims, including victims of rape, mugging, terrorism, and disaster. Sudden unpredictable violence is experienced as intensely stressful, and for many victims this precipitates a severe crisis reaction. The severity of the crisis appears to vary with preexisting factors and aspects of the violent experience, as shown in Table 4-I.

Lazarus (1978) stated that a stressful episode is not just a "momentary static stimulus" to which the individual gives a single response, but the entire process may extend over a long period of time and encompass many encounters and psychological changes. Using the grief work of bereavement as a model, he described the process of recovery that begins with the discovery of the loss through the full realization of the loss, then its acceptance, and finally a

*We wish to thank Doctor Susan Vivell for her contributions to this chapter. We also wish to acknowledge, in memoriam, Valerie Nordstrum, whose caring for victims was an inspiration.

Table 4-I

Factors Affecting Severity of Crisis

Pretrauma	The Assault	Posttrauma
1. Developmental and/or life cycle issues 2. Previous coping skills 3. Availability of support systems	1. Victim's relationship to assailant 2. Degree and kind of coercion or force 3. Severity of violation of self	1. Reaction of others 2. Number and kind of stressful events that occur as a consequence of the assault

reinvestment in living. Each of these coping tasks is accomplished as related events occur. This process is quite similar to the crisis matrix concept of Jacobson (1981). In his research on separation and divorce, he discussed the time period of six weeks between the event and the restoration of a level of equilibrium and the longer time periods of a year to two years during which the impact of the major life change lasts. The process of resolution bridges these time periods.

A similar process takes place following a violent assault, beginning with the occurrence of the event through full realization of physical and psychological damage, then the reactions of all others, including care givers, its acceptance, and finally reinvestment in living. This extended process allows for a number of time periods during which crisis intervention can assist in the recovery.

The intensity of the usual emotional reactions to a violent experience indicates that crucial life issues are involved and that these emotional reactions may be further intensified by unresolved conflicts from earlier life events. Individual psychodynamics are extremely important in understanding and planning intervention and have been described by Horowitz (1976) and Jacobson et al. (1968). In addition, intervention can be guided by expectations of the generic *victim response syndrome*, a posttraumatic stress reaction that "intensifies feelings of personal helplessness and vulnerability leading to a revision in self-concept and loss of self-esteem (Bard and Sangrey, 1979). Humiliation and shame, reinforced by family and societal withdrawal, bring into focus a view of the self as weak and helpless" (Salasin, 1981; Bard and Sangrey, 1979).

This chapter focuses on strategies for generic crisis intervention with victims of violence, particularly victims of sexual assault. Recovery is seen as a process by which the *victim* becomes a *survivor* of victimization.

The generic crisis intervention approach, described by Jacobson et al. (1968) consists of techniques designed to be effective to a target group as a whole. Intervention activities include general support, environmental manipulation, direct encouragement of adaptive behavior, and anticipatory guidance.

General support involves listening, accompanying a client in an unpleasant (or stressful) situation, and allowing ventilation (without interpretation). Environmental manipulation involves direct assistance in contacts with community systems, such as welfare agencies, police, or hospital staff. Direct encouragement of adaptive behavior involves exploration of old and new adaptive coping behavior. Anticipatory guidance prepares the client for feelings and events that may be expected to take place, based on the experiences of others in similar circumstances. Anticipatory guidance helps the client to prepare for these changes and to feel less traumatized or overwhelmed when they take place. It also enables the client to plan coping strategies, for example, to seek treatment or to stay with a relative.

EMOTIONAL REACTIONS TO VICTIMIZATION

The generic approach can be effective with victims of violence because of the universal nature of emotional reactions to victimization. Generic reactions most frequently described in the literature on assault and most frequently observed in the authors' practice are symptoms of anxiety and depression, feelings of guilt, fear, powerlessness, anger, and embarrassment or shame. In addition, long periods of general disruption of usual routines and life-styles have been observed. Effective intervention combines (1) generic crisis intervention activities (support, environmental manipulation, encouragement of adaptive behavior, and anticipatory guidance), (2) understanding of the individual victim's unresolved conflicts triggered by the victimization, and (3) sensitivity regarding the impact of social attitudes towards victims.

The specific objectives of the crisis intervention are to (1) assist victim in retaining or regaining a sense of competence; (2) assist victim in accepting any unalterable consequences of the victimization; (3) assist in adaptive actions, including the maintenance of support systems; and (4) assist in the reestablishment of a sense of continuity and meaning for life. These are integrated in the practitioner's approach to dealing with feelings of fear, powerlessness, guilt, anger, and shame or embarrassment.

FEAR. The usual reaction to a threat of survival is fear; fear mobilizes a person's capacity for "fight or flight." When neither fight nor flight is possible, fear increases. The assault victim may appear to be or report being shaky or jumpy following the assault and may overreact to people and noises. He or she may talk about being afraid to go out alone or to be in a crowd, may be uneasy being at home alone and concerned about locks or open windows, and may worry constantly about whether or not the assailant will return. If the assailant is a family member or friend, fear may be repeatedly stimulated by continued contact. The victim may express fears of specific situations that are similar to when, where, and/or how the assault took place, such as going to work at night or getting into an elevator. Frequently, the worst fear is of "going crazy" or of always being intensely afraid.

In general, the client describes a fear for his or her life. He or she may describe the terror felt during the assault and the fear that he or she would be killed. Victims generally reexperience the terror in flashbacks or nightmares that are extremely intense, but these gradually diminish with time. In an episode of victimization in which the individual faces "near death" (assailant threatens to kill victim), death imagery (Lifton, 1980) is often evidenced. The victim suddenly is confronted with his or her mortality and vulnerability, and there may be a break in the victim's sense of the continuity and meaning of life. This reaction increases the fear.

Various life cycle issues also may compound the fear reaction. For example an adolscent in the process of emancipation and increasing independence may be frightened by the sudden experience of vulnerability; parents may become overprotective. The result may be a serious interruption of this developmental process.

Burgess and Holmstrom (1974) recommend that the counselor use ventilation as a technique to reduce the intensity of the client's fear. Sutherland and Scherl (1972) suggest discussing with the victim that others feel similar fear and that these feelings are to be expected. He or she may always be more cautious than before, but the fear can be manageable. The client needs to identify what he or she is specifically afraid of and needs to develop a plan to feel and be more safe and secure. For example, a survivor may consider moving, staying with a friend, or getting a dog. The reality of making oneself safe and regaining control makes one less fearful. Clients may not follow through on these plans of action, but may still report a reduction in level of fear as a result of discussing plans. The survivor should be taught "dosing" (Horowitz, 1976), which is remembering the event for a time, putting it out of mind for a time, and continuing that cycle.

POWERLESSNESS. Feeling helpless and easily overwhelmed is a common sign of stress; however, the victim feels that control over his or her life, environment, safety, and ability to take care of oneself has been seriously threatened. A life-threatening, violent experience confronts a person's denial of mortality and the illusion that he or she is in control of his or her life. Powerlessness affects family members and friends, as well as the survivor.

Counselors often observe victims behaving in an overwhelmed and scattered manner. Victims report not feeling able to handle even routine tasks, inability to focus on any one thing, and a sudden need to rely on others, including the counselor, to do things and to make decisions. It is important to note that this behavior did not exist before the assault; the victim might have felt fairly self-confident and independent. The sudden feeling of vulnerability and powerlessness results in a new feeling of dependence.

Feelings of vulnerability are present regardless of the degree of violence (whether coerced or physically endangered). However, a greater degree of violence and perceived threat of death seems to result in a more intense sense of mortality. The extent to which the victim felt able to influence the outcome of the assault has an effect on the resolution of feelings of powerlessness.

Feelings of powerlessness and loss of control also are affected by developmental issues related to dependence. For example, an older victim who may be struggling to take care of himself or herself and live independently in spite of physical limitations may feel immobilized and/or may find overprotective family members deciding to change living arrangements.

An important task of the helping person is to encourage active participation of the victim in treatment. This enhances the regaining of feelings of control and mastery. It is important to help clients identify feelings of powerlessness and to understand the connection between feeling overwhelmed and the loss of control involved in victimization. They may express anger towards the assailant and others who have made them feel so helpless. The client can be encouraged to formulate a plan for making life tasks manageable at a pace that is individually appropriate.

The objective of the crisis intervention to deal with powerlessness is for the client to feel that what he or she has to deal with is manageable and that he or she is able to regain feelings of control over the environment. A counselor should be careful, therefore, of "rescuing" or responding to the client's helplessness by doing things for him or her. If the victim's powerlessness is real, for example, in the case of a child or an institutionalized elderly person, the counselor may need to change roles and become a change agent (advocate) in the client's environment. In this instance, it is important to validate these feelings by acknowledging that vulnerability is real.

GUILT. Prolonged guilt reactions seem to be a universal response of survivors. Survivors of personal violence are affected both by internalized victim blame and by the reactions of friends, family members, colleagues, and helping people. Victim blame can be seen as an attempt to maintain the illusion of control in a world in which traumatic events take place in an unpredictable and arbitrary manner (Ryan, 1976; Symonds, 1980). If the event can be explained by faulting the victim or by seeing the victim as different, then the illusion continues that anyone not behaving as the victim did would not be vulnerable to victimization. The victim may sustain feelings of guilt and responsibility for his or her own victimization as a means of defending against overwhelming feelings of vulnerability and powerlessness.

Feelings of guilt may be manifested directly; for example, victims may report feeling guilty or say the assault was their fault. The feelings also may be manifested indirectly; for example, victims may exhibit somatic symptoms or self-destructive behaviors. Victims who feel guilty feel responsible for the victimization because of something they did or did not do to avoid or stop the assault because they feel that something characteristic of them brought on the assault or because they feel for some reason they deserved it. Notman and Nadelson (1976) and others have observed that victims often say they feel they should have handled the assault situation differently, regardless of the reality of the situation. The inner sense of guilt is often revealed by the manner in which the victim reports or tells someone about the assault.

In situations in which the assailant is known or very familiar to the victim, the victim is likely to feel more intensely responsible and upset with his or her participation in the assault. Subtle threat or coercion, for example, the threat of the loss of a job or a threat of violence without visible means to follow through, more often results in the victim's self-doubt and self-blame than clearly violent threats or injury.

People close to the victim may experience intense guilt for not protecting the victim or preventing the assault, regardless of the reality.

The age of the victim sems to be a variable in the pervasiveness and prolongation of guilty feelings. Young people seem more quickly than adults to assume their own responsibility when things "go wrong."

Notman and Nadelson (1976) and Symonds (1980) suggest that the practitioner offer nurturance, support, and reassurance about the way the victim handled the assault to deal with guilt feelings. Sutherland and Scherl (1972) emphasize the importance of relieving guilt feelings to restore self-esteem. This is accomplished by a realistic appraisal of the victim's own responsibility for the assault. They caution against challenging guilt prematurely, as this can be perceived by the victim as false reassurance. Burgess and Holmstrom (1974) suggest that the counselor alleviate guilt by identifying the victim's coping during the threat of attack, the attack, and immediately afterwards. The counselor defines for the victim the coping behavior as a "positive adaptive mechanism used to survive a life-threatening situation."

It is recommended that the counselor review each step of the assault with the victim until it is clear that although there may have been some decision or action he or she wishes to have taken differently, he or she was not responsible for the assault.

The victim needs to be helped to (1) understand that he or she is feeling guilt; (2) understand that guilt is an almost universal reaction to misfortune; (3) look at each step in the assault as a series of hazards, be helped to see if he or she did do something to feel guilty about, and be helped to forgive himself or herself; (4) understand that the guilt had reactivated early childhood feelings of "having caused it" and, therefore, deserving parents' punishment; (5) understand that most, if not all, of the events were out of his or her control; and (6) understand that the assailant was responsible for the act.

ANGER. Anger may be felt towards the assailant, towards people close to the victim, or towards himself or herself. Anger expressed towards family members and friends may be displaced from the assailant or may stem from the belief that they did not help to protect him or her or have not been supportive enough. Anger towards the assailant can be very direct and open, accompanied by feelings of wanting revenge and threats, such as, "I'm going to kill him." Sometimes the anger is diffuse, and this may take the form of hostility towards the practitioner. Ochberg and Spates (1981) refer to the rage that "can come from being suddenly shifted downward on the dominance hierarchy."

Anger often appears in recurrent nightmares, explosive outbursts, and displacement of anger onto others. The behaviors represent attempts by the victim to "master" the assault. Symonds (1975) describes the acute reaction to attack as disbelief, followed by fright or anger. Fright is more typical of women; anger more typical of men. Several authors (Hilberman, 1976; Notman and Nadelson, 1976) are in agreement that overt anger is usually absent from the reaction of the sexual assault victim. According to Hilberman, the "universality of guilt and shame stand in striking contrast to the absence of anger." Sutherland and Scherl (1972) describe subdued anger in the "pseudo-adjustment" phase of reaction to the assault, when the victim attempts to return to his or her ordinary life. In this phase, he or she may rationalize his or her anger, for example by attributing the assault to chance or the assailant's "sickness."

Ventilation of anger should be encouraged and should be seen as a natural response to victimization. It is important to direct or focus anger, if it continues to be diffuse or generalized. After the survivor has expressed anger, energies can be redirected to whatever constructive or positive things can be done, for example, reporting to the police and organizing a crime watch for neighbors.

SENSITIVITY OF MENTAL HEALTH PRACTITIONERS

It is difficult for practitioners to maintain personal objectivity in relation to victimization. To effectively implement diagnosis and counseling strategies, any counselor must be additionally aware of the counselor-centered factors involved in the intervention.

Caplan (1964), in a discussion of consultee-centered case consultation, described four categories of difficulty that interfere with a counselor's ability to deal with client problems. These are (1) lack of objectivity, (2) lack of skill, (3) lack of understanding, and (4) lack of confidence. The practitioner experiencing lack of objectivity finds that his or her feelings interfere with his or her response. The counselor may feel unable to deal with violence or may become frightened when hearing about the assault. Counselors frequently reported feeling vulnerable themselves when talking to victims like themselves or their family members. Counselor needs, such as "rescue fantasies" or the need to see clients "cured" and client problems resolved, may result in intervention that is unrealistic for the client.

Due to societal myths and the misconceptions about victimization, especially sexual assault, it often happens that counselors' values interfere with effective intervention, the counselor may react judgmentally to the client's situation; for example, the counselor may feel that the client should not have been hitchhiking or out at a bar and then finds it difficult to be supportive.

In addition to the Caplan categories, a fifth factor was noted in the authors' experiences. Obstacles often exist in the agency or in the counseling environment. Lack of agency or staff support can make the counselor's job difficult. Counselors need opportunities to ventilate, especially because of the emotional intensity of many victims' reactions and the complexity of their problems. Counselors can experience too much stress from seeing too many victims in too short a time. This has been observed in emergency room settings, as well as rape crisis centers.

CASE EXAMPLE

L, 23, an office worker and student, was awakened one night by unusual noises. When she got up to check, she startled two men as they ransacked her living room. She screamed. They grabbed her, held a knife to her throat, and threatened to rape her. They held her and harrassed her for an hour until her neighbors, hearing her screams, banged on the door, and the assailants fled.

Following the assault, *L* was too frightened to stay alone in her apartment. A friend stayed with her, and within a week, she moved to a new apartment. After moving, she seemed to feel unaffected by the assault, except for her difficulty sleeping. She had nightmares and was restless all night, frequently jumping out of bed to check "noises." She coped with this with the support of two close friends, who talked with her on the phone or stayed with her, if she became terrified or extremely anxious during the night.

Three months following the assault, she had an especially difficult night and was unable to reach either of her friends. She felt they must be "sick and tired" of her. The next morning she could not get up for work. She had a migraine headache, cried easily, and did not feel able to do anything without feeling overwhelmed. She stayed home for two days and returned to work because she was afraid of losing her job. She could not concentrate and felt overwhelmed by every task and demand. She decided to take a leave from her job and called her parents, who lived 100 miles away, to pick her up and take her home with them. She contacted the mental health clinic at her parents' suggestion.

L described herself as very capable, confident, and self-sufficient, living independently since her graduation from high school. With the therapist's help she understood how the assault had confronted her sense of security and her confidence in her ability to take care of herself. Even though the assailants had fled, she felt that was just luck and that she had no real control over whether she lived or died. She felt overwhelmed by her vulnerability and powerless to control anything that happened to her. She felt angry with herself for demanding so much help from friends, and, when she realized that they would not always be available, she felt isolated and alienated because of her constant fear and anxiety. She was afraid that she would never recover.

L was very relieved when reassured that her fear and anxiety were "normal" reactions to an assault and that her intense fear would gradually diminish. She talked about her fears, her nightmares, and getting up at night to check noises. She realized that she was feeling compulsively vigilant, as if the moment she stopped watching for danger, something life-threatening would occur. In her nightmares, she was trapped and helpless. She became most fearful at night and when she was at home alone. She planned measures to maximize her actual safety and to manage her anxiety and gradually increased the amount of time she could stay alone in her parents' house. New coping was encouraged, and her intense fear began to subside.

L's story of the assault contained numerous comments, such as, "I knew better than to leave the front window open," and "I just sat there, when I should have run." As she reviewed the sequence of events with the therapist, she remembered her perceptions of her options at the time of the assault and realized that she had actually done the best she could to survive under the circumstances. She became furious with the intruders for robbing her of her sense of security. She also remembered that her screams brought help and that she had not been so passive and helpless. When *L* began to perceive herself as having made sensible choices during the assault, she began to regain her sense of control in other areas of her life.

L was appalled that she had become so completely dependent on her friends and her parents. With the therapist's help, she began to understand how unresolved dependency needs had been stimulated by her vulnerability during the assault, distorting her perception of her ability to take care of herself. The identification of this developmental issue was central to the resolution of the crisis.

CONCLUSION

In the case example above, generic crisis intervention consisted of anticipation of reactions to be expected, encouragement of adaptive behaviors, recognition of unresolved conflicts triggered by the assault, and the resolution of feelings of intense fear, powerlessness, guilt, and anger. As *L* moved from the powerless and fearful victim position, she regained a sense of competence and control and identified herself as having survived a trauma, instead of continuing to feel victimized.

REFERENCES

Bard, M., and Sangrey, D.: *The Crime Victim's Book*. New York, Basic Books, 1979.
Bard, M., and Sangrey, D.: Things fall apart: Victims in crisis. *Evaluation and*

Change, Spring 1980.

Burgess, A., and Holmstrom, L.: The rape trauma syndrome. *American Journal of Psychiatry, 131*, 1974.

Burgess, A., and Holmstrom, L.: Coping behavior of rape victims. *American Journal of Psychiatry, 133(4)*, 1976.

Caplan, G.: *Principles of Preventive Psychiatry*. New York, Basic Books, 1964.

Hilberman, E.: *The Rape Victim*. Washington, D.C., American Psychiatric Association, 1976.

Horowitz, M.J.: *Stress Response Syndromes*. New York, J. Aronson, Inc., 1976.

Jacobson, G., Strickler, M., and Morley, W.: Generic and individual approaches to crisis intervention. *American Journal of Public Health, 58(2)*, February 1968.

Jacobson, G.F. (Ed.): *New Directions for Mental Health Services: Crisis Intervention in the 1980s*. San Francisco, Jossey-Bass, 1980.

Katz, S., and Mazur, M.: *Understanding the Rape Victim: A Synthesis of Research Findings*., New York, John Wiley and Sons, 1979.

Krupnick, J., and Horowitz, M.J.: Victims of violence: Psychological responses, treatment implications. *Evaluation and Change*, Spring 1980.

Lazarus, A.: *Stress and Coping Paradigm*. Paper presented at American Psychological Association, 1978.

Lifton, R.J.: *The Broken Connection*. New York, Simon and Schuster, 1980.

Notman, M., and Nadelson, C.: The rape victim: Psychodynamic considerations. *American Journal of Psychiatry, 133(4)*, April 1976.

Ochberg, F., and Spates, R.: Services integration for victims of personal violence. In Salasin (Ed.): *Evaluating Victim Services*. Beverly Hills, Sage, 1981.

Ryan, W.: *Blaming the Victim*. New York, Vintage Books, 1976.

Salasin, S.: Services to victims: Needs assessment. In Salasin (Ed.): *Evaluating Victim Services*. Beverly Hills, Sage, 1981.

Sutherland, S., and Scherl, D.: Crisis intervention with victims of rape. *Social Work*, January 1972.

Symonds, M.: The second injury to victims of violent crimes. *Evaluation and Change*, Spring 1980.

Viano, E.: *Victims and Society*. Washington, D.C., Visage Press, 1976.

Chapter 5

THE VIOLENT PATIENT: ASSESSMENT AND INTERVENTION

DENNIS J. KUTZER AND JOHN R. LION

DEFINITION OF A VIOLENT DISORDER

THE American Psychiatric Task Force on Clinical Aspects of the Violent Individual has defined the violent patient as one who "acts or has acted in such a way as to produce physical harm or destruction" (*Clinical Aspects*, 1974). That task force acknowledges that there are individuals who fantasize harm but are not properly defined as violent because the harm had not been committed. Yet, clinicians may often see individuals who are contemplating violence or who are afraid of running "amuck" or losing control over their impulses. Heuristically speaking, it would be clinically prudent to identify patients with severe violent urges as *violent* in order to render treatment. Yet, the labeling of anyone who has violent thoughts as *violent* has serious social, political, or legal repercussions and should be done cautiously. The complexities inherent in such labeling are illustrated by the recent *Tarasoff* decision in California, where the Supreme Court found that a psychiatrist has a duty to warn when he or she encounters a patient who threatens violence to someone in society (Gurewitz, 1977; Roth and Meisel, 1977). In such an instance, the psychiatrist must decide whether the patient is simply fantasizing harm or is actually dangerous to the point of requiring reporting. In no other field of inquiry is there as much anguish in the decision-making process as in this area. Confidentiality, also, is severely disrupted by such a ruling. In any event, it is difficult to identify potentially aggressive patients based upon ideation alone. However, there is evidence that individuals who commit homicide often "cry for help" prior to the act just as persons who are suicidal (Lion, 1972).

The clearest definition of violence occurs in a patient who has been unequivocally violent and who has, for example, been incarcerated with a history of aggressive acts.

DESCRIPTION OF THE VIOLENT PERSON

The violent patient may present to the clinician in several ways. When the person has already lost control and has acted in a violent manner, he or she is brought by law enforcement officers to an emergency setting with that history. Another way a person may present is in the emergency room, where he or she verbalizes fears of becoming violent and acting on impulses.

Patients with these chief complaints may be agitated or disconcertingly quiet. The latter is more likely in individuals who have well thought out plans for violence. Patients may well simply state that they are afraid that "something terrible is going to happen," or they may specify a particular target or vector. When the complaint is vague or diffuse, it often cloaks a true victim whom the patient has ambivalent feelings about, and some probing may be necessary. The relevance for such probing to the clinician is that a victim may be identified and brought into the picture in order to resolve some ongoing conflict between the two.

Patients with various diagnoses can be identified in the emergency room. Perhaps the most common type of individual seen in an emergency setting is a psychotic individual with paranoid delusions who threatens harm. Manic patients may be aggresive also. Other types of patients are the belligerent alcoholic, the rebellious adolescent, or the agitated, depressed patient who is explosive. Personality disorders of the antisocial, paranoid, or passive-aggressive type may exhibit violence. Other individuals less commonly seen but who are no strangers to emergency rooms are child-abusing parents (Green, 1975), husbands who "batter" wives (Hanks, 1977), or senile individuals who are agitated and combative. The point to be made is that violence cuts across a wide spectrum of diagnoses and is in itself a symptom of an illness, not an illness itself. Further, social factors play a role. Some violence is subcultural; examples are certain adolescents demonstrating a "macho" attitude.

COURSE OF VIOLENT BEHAVIOR

It is difficult to define a course of violence as an illness because of its complex etiology. Generally speaking, violence begets violence so that a history of violence in a family leads a patient to react to frustration with violence. Hence the clinician is usually likely to find that violent patients have been violent before and have engaged in previous violent actions, such as wife abuse or child abuse on several other occasions than the presenting one. Patients with temper outbursts also commonly give a history of many years of such outbursts. Exceptions to a long duration of violent behavior are toxic conditions, such as amphetamine or PCP (phencyclidine) psychosis, where the violence is a relatively new occurrence, or other organic factors, such as head injury, where violence may appear in a nonviolent person for the first time. Violence is more or less a life-style, and the appearance of it as something unordinary in a patient should make the clinician consider underlying organic etiologies.

ASSESSMENT

The biggest obstacle to assessment is the clinician's denial. Many clinicians become frightened by violent or incipiently violent individuals and would rather deal with them dispositionally by sending them to state hospitals or placing them in the hands of the law enforcement agencies. Nevertheless, there is room for clinical assessment.

First, the clinician must establish mental status and determine whether the patient's reality testing is intact. Thus, a patient who hears delusions telling him or her to kill is at risk.

Severely depressed patients should not be considered safe from the standpoint of being suicidal rather than homicidal since they may well commit homicide first and suicide second; such occurrences are not uncommon in published series of violent patients.

Thus, the clinician needs to ask a seriously depressed patient whether he or she has ever thought of doing harm to anyone else besides himself or herself.

A history of exposure to drugs, such as alcohol, or other agents that heighten impulsivity or lability are important. Paranoid psychoses resulting from amphetamines have already been mentioned, and homicide has been associated with abuse of such drugs and with barbiturate abuse (Tinklenberg and Woodrow, 1973). Violence has also been reported in association with hallucinogen drug intoxication and glue sniffing (Peterson and Stillman, 1978). These patients should be considered risks and hospitalized.

Overt homicidal ideation and the availability of a victim always signal the need for limits and temporary confinement until the situation can be resolved. The clinician should inquire about the availability of weapons. He or she should also query the use of an automobile, which should also be considered a weapon; the patient may drive recklessly and misuse his car as a part of violence (Selzer, Rogers, and Kern, 1968). Finally and most obviously, the clinician should ask the patient outright how violent he or she has ever been and what the most violent thing he or she has ever done is. A history of previous incarcerations or difficulties with the law should signal the patient's capacity to repeat such acts. Again, the clinican needs to ask questions that are more forensic than those ordinarily asked.

As is the case with most medical conditions, intuition plays a strong role. Before deciding upon hospitalization or commitment, the clinician must depend upon his or her own urges and inclinations toward the patient and assess the establishment of a rapport. Many patients are aloof and distant and generate within the clinician a feeling of alienation or coldness that is ominous (Kozol, 1975). Generally speaking, patients who have the capacity for warmth can strike bargains and alliances with medical staff, and they work in treatment, thus precluding commitment. Other patients in an interview or therapy reveal little capacity for the reverence of life when seen and are more distinct threats to society. Some patients blame all their problems on the environment while others are more introspective and willing to look inside themselves as a way of gaining relief from angry urges. As a rule, violence is a dysphoric state and something that a patient does not enjoy. Thus, the clinician should recall that violent individuals and those who think about becoming violent want controls established and do not enjoy the rage that they show. Hence, controls are welcomed more than one might think, and hospitalization is not to be feared and will not lead to retributive or retaliatory threats by the clinican any more than a suicidal patient would threaten the doctor who incarcerates him or her.

Much work has been devoted toward the discovery of childhood events that are predictive of violence. Little has been found of substance, though many parallels can be drawn between violence in childhood and violence in adult life. Some ominous findings are the existence of childhood brutal traits, which include pyromania and cruelty to animals (Hellman and Blackman, 1966). If such traits are noted, referral for psychiatric treatment is warranted. Some adult patients mention that they showed these traits in childhood; such a discovery might make the clinician more seriously evaluate the patient's propensity toward violence. Other findings in childhood may be enuresis, frequent fights, school problems with truancy, and interpersonal difficulties culminating in fights and rebelliousness. These behaviors are often associated with antisocial personalities seen in later life. Severe parental deprivation or abandonment together with brutalization by one or both parents has been associated with violence in later life.

Common psychological themes evoking violence are helplessness and insults to masculinity. Men are susceptible to outbursts of rage when their identities are threatened. This is particularly likely to occur when self-esteem is tenuous, although the determination of the patient's level of self-esteem is difficult to make in an emergency room setting and usually requires several interviews. At the time, the clinician may discover that the patient is more fragile than he or she looks and that there are severe identity problems. Violence often occurs among those who feel the most fragile about themselves and cannot tolerate ridicule (Lion, 1972).

Object loss is a most vital etiologic consideration for all mental illness including suicide and homicide. Questions must be asked regarding the alienation of affection between the patient and a lover or a spouse, recent separation or divorce, or even death. Such losses are often handled by rage rather than by sadness and the patient who has sustained major loss is at risk for depression and possibly violence or both.

Also difficult to evaluate in a single interview is the patient's sexual identity. Rage towards women together with sadistic pleasure associated with violence at the opposite sex may herald tendencies toward aggressive deviant behavior, such as rape. The discovery that the patient has pedophiliac tendencies often is noteworthy, and psychiatric referral is important. These patients, under the provocation of frustration by a child they approach, may become violent. Other sexual habits, such as voyeurism and exhibitionism, are less commonly linked with violent behavior and occur among more passive people (Cohen, Grofalo, Boucher, and Seghorn, 1975; Groth, Burgess, and Holstrom, 1977).

From the standpoint of etiology, one of the most important things a clinician can do is to establish the identity of a victim. The discipline of victimology is now well established as a social phenomenon. Since violence most often is dyadic and occurs between two people, it is mandatory that inquiry be made about the possibility of confronting the victim and informing the latter about his or her potential danger. At the same time, the victim's provocativeness can be assessed. Many times, seeing both parties together sheds light on a pathological interaction (Ervin and Lion, 1969).

In addition, neurologic dysfunction is important to assess. Certain brain anatomical structures have been implicated in the expression of aggression in man. These areas include limbic system structures, such as the amygdalae and hippocampus. Surgical manipulation of these structures has been shown to lead to violent behavior while diseases in these areas, such as epilepsy or neoplasms, can also result in temper outbursts (Mark and Ervin, 1970; Sheard, 1975). Hence, the clinician should complement his psychiatric assessments with neurological questions. Generally speaking, brain dysfunction can manifest itself in mood lability, temper outbursts, and a tendency to become violent under condition of frustration. This can be seen in a diverse number of diseases ranging from mental retardation (Haberland, 1969; Jervis, 1948) in children to the senile dementias (Roth, 1968). The clinicians should carefully inquire about head injury and conditions that might have predisposed the patient to such injury. Examples are anoxia in childhood, convulsion, and trauma. Some patients with paroxysmal outbursts of violence may have such neurologic dysfunction. This is particularly likely when the outbursts are of sudden onset and remission and are of precipitous appearance. Sometimes, patients' histories contain symptoms with strong flavorings of epilepsy, states of consciousness, or other prodromal events, such as micropsia, or gustatory or olfactory sensations may precede the violent outbursts. The patients may complain of anger building up and complain of sleepiness or drowsiness following the angry outbursts or discharge. This may make the clinician think of temporal lobe epilepsy. Current thinking regarding the association of this form of epilepsy with violence is that the aggression may well be associated with such brain dysfunction but may be more prevalent during the interictal or postictal phase rather than the epileptic discharge (Brown, Wienckowik, and Bevins, 1973; Rodin, 1973). That is, patients may become violent when restrained after an epileptic outburst or may show heightened irritability in between the epileptic discharges, which themselves are manifested merely by changes in the consciousness. Some clinicians have categorized patients with "epileptoid" outbursts of temper as having an episodic behavior disorder (Benson and Blumer, 1975; Monroe, 1970). This concept has been formalized in the *Diagnostic and Statistical Manual of Mental Disorders III*, 1980) and described as intermittent explosive disorder.

As noted above, such a disorder is viewed as paroxysmal violence associated with "soft" neurologic signs and symptoms, EEG evidence of central nervous instability, and a history indicative of head trauma. If the clinician finds such a syndrome, referral to a neurologist is warranted. However, the neurologist should be an individual interested in the delineation of cortical dysfunction and be one who is interested in determining the existence of possible temporal lobe disorder, which may underlie the aggressiveness and poor impulse control the patient shows.

Trauma to the orbital regions of the frontal lobes and temporal lobes have been associated with changes in personality and violent outbursts (Blumer, 1974).

It is noteworthy that alcohol has been described as a possible activator of temporal lobe epilepsy (Marinacci, 1963), though a more carefully controlled study has not supported such a finding (Bach-Y-Rita, Lion, and Ervin, 1971). Nevertheless, the term *pathological intoxication* has been used to describe bizarre changes in mood and behavior following minimal alcohol intake. Thus, discovery of a patient with such a constellation of symptoms should alert the clinician to possible underlying brain dysfunction.

ADDITIONAL DIAGNOSTIC CONSIDERATIONS

Further clarification of the patient's propensity for harm and the diagnosis can be obtained from psychological testing and neurological assessment.

If a thought disorder is being considered and the patient is seen as psychotic and paranoid, psychological testing may ascertain the existence of such a disorder and may give some information regarding how distorted the patient's reality testing is. Projective tests such as the TAT or Rorschach Ink Blot Tests are useful here. Even if the patient is not psychotic but simply depressed, these kinds of clinical tests may give some idea of the level of rage and anger.

Neurological tests include a sleep EEG in order to determine the existence of temporal lobe dysfunction. The sleep study is desirable because the incidence of interictal abnormalities is very low with a wake tracing (Ervin, 1967). The EEG may show spike discharges indicative of temporal lobe dysfunction or it may show more equivocal findings, such as the common 14 and 6 per second spike and wave form. In an event, the appearance of an abnormality or even borderline abnormality may help the clinician decide on a rational psychopharmacologic treatment program.

Evidence of organicity associated with temper outbursts may also be determined by specialized psychological testing such as the Reitan-Halstead Battery. This test can pick up minor neurologic dysfunction that is not detectable by gross clinical examination (Reitan and Davidson, 1974).

DIFFERENTIAL DIAGNOSIS

The various diagnoses associated with violence have already been mentioned; a recapitulation is in order and is diagrammed in Table 5-I. It always must be kept in mind that aggression is symptomatic of weakness and reflects the patient's need to be strong, rather than weak. Thus violence will be seen in a variety of illnesses and is in itelf not a circumscribed disease process. The risks of it occurring are influenced by the factors that follow:

1. History of previous violence
2. Availability of weapon
3. Availability of victim

4. Pathological relationship with victim
5. Toxic substance (alcohol)

Table 5-I

Mental Disorders Associated with Violent Behaviors

Disorder	Examples
Thought disorder	Functional psychosis schizophrenia Toxic psychosis amphetamine barbiturate hallucinogenic drug solvent inhalation
Affective disorder	Agitated depression Manic stage of manic-depressive illness
Behavior disorder	Personality disorder Alcoholism
Organic dysfunction	Minimal brain dysfunction Temporal lobe dysfunction
Situational reaction	Adolescent adjustment

TREATMENT

Emergency room treatment faces the clinician with simple control in order to quiet the patient. Often, patients are brought in by many people such as the police, and a one-to-one relationship eliminates the need of the patient to be belligerent. This is not a hard and fast rule, however; the clinician should feel comfortable. If the patient is not quieting down, an aide should be summoned. The patient should be told that he or she is scaring staff and frightening personnel. Open acknowledgement of feelings is mandatory during the initial stages of emergency control. Offering the patient some medication orally lends dignity to the situation. The patient can be told exactly what drug is being given; it is important that the patient realize that he or she will not be drugged or rendered lethargic since this often exacerbates the violence if the patient feels that he or she is going out of control. Small amounts of medication are the rule. Thus 5 or 10 mg. of diazepam (Valium®) could be given orally, and the oral route is preferable from the standpoint of absorption since parenteral absorption is so poor.

More agitated patients will require antipsychotic drugs. In the past, chlorpromazine (Thorazine®) was the drug of choice for emergency room use. It has been replaced by the high potency drug such as haloperidol (Haldol®), which has fewer hypotensive effects. This drug of choice for emergency rooms can be given parenterally in 5 or 10 mg. dosages. These dosages can be given every thirty minutes sequentially until the patient is calm. This is referred to as the rapid titration technique (Donlon, Hopkin, and Tupin, 1979). The usual tactic is for the nurse to give the injection, but the physician should be present and explain to the patient what is going on. In some cases, it is preferable that the physician give the injection for the patient who is quite frightened, and his or her belligerence is directly proportional to his or her fears. It is often hard for a physician to calm a violent patient by talking, but it should be recalled that anxiety and agitation go hand in hand. Thus, simply saying to a violent patient that you are going to help him or her stay in control may be highly reassuring.

The process of giving the injection requires that the patient be relatively calm. The patient's extremities should be immobile, and the site of injection should be the gluteal region since the deltoid quadrants involve the arms that the patient may swing. Physical restraints have a place in emergency room management, but the emergency room team should be knowledgeable in their use. Whether a belt or a sheet arrangement is used, it should be practiced ahead of time. Security personnel are also crucial in the management of the violent patient, but the intervention should not be haphazard. Security personnel should strip themselves of weapons and other devices that can be used against them and have a practice technique for restraining the patient (Guirguis, 1978; Rosen and Di-

Giacomo, 1978). Once the patient is restrained, the clinican can then begin the talking process or call in the family. The point to be remembered is that sedating the patient does not end the intervention. If a patient requires parenteral tranquilization, he or she almost invariably requires hospitalization, and oral medication should be continued during the acute phase. Generally speaking, oral requirements are two to three times that required during the parenteral phase. Thus, a patient requiring 10 mg. IM of haloperidol in the emergency room will require 30 mg. a day of the same drug to achieve antipsychotic effects.

Acute brain syndromes caused by drug toxicities are often best treated without medication if possible. Thus, a belligerent alcoholic should be observed carefully unless he or she has brain injury, such as a subdural hematoma. It would complicate the picture to give the patient large and sedating doses of an antipsychotic drug that would impair consciousness to some extent, and physical restraints are preferable. However, some patients are so agitated and belligerent that some tranquilization is necessary and small amounts of an antipsychotic drug can be given. If it can be clearly established that the intoxicant is a hallucinatory drug, an antipsychotic drug is in order. Phencyclidine (PCP) psychoses have been reported to worsen with the use of antipsychotic drugs, and the matter is still controversial as to which drug to use. An alternate to antipsychotic drugs is an antianxiety agent such as diazepam (Valium®) (Peterson and Stillman, 1978).

The nonemergency use of medications to control aggressive patients is more problematic. There is no drug that is specific for aggression. Rather, aggression abates as a symptom of any illness that is responsive to medication (Lion, 1975). To this extent, any medication that controls the specific illness is useful.

With respect to psychotic patients, any antipsychotic drug may be useful for the control of violence. This is true for manic patients as well, and lithium may well be the drug of choice for the violence seen in manic-depressive illness not because it possesses specific antiaggressive properties but because it is of utility in this affective disease state (Lion and Hill, 1975; Sheard, 1975; Tupin et al., 1973). Antidepressants may also be useful to control depression that has associated violence. In both these cases, psychiatric consultation should be sought to determine optimal drug and dosage. Some violence associated with excited catatonic schizophrenia may be best treated with electroconvulsive therapy.

With personality disorders, the matter is more complex. Some of these individuals show target symptoms of anxiety that may be responsive to pharmacologic control. Thus, drugs of the benzodiazepine class, such as diazepam or chlordiazepoxide, may be useful though they may also be abused by the patient. Again, consultation should always be sought for these individuals. Some borderline patients may warrant small amounts of an antipsychotic drug (Lion, 1974; 1978).

Patients with epileptoid forms of violence who are diagnosed as having intermittent explosive disorders or true seizure disorders may benefit from anticonvulsants. The drug of choice for these related group of illnesses is probably carbamazepine (Tegretol®) (International Drug Therapy Newsletter, October 1979). Dosages should be adjusted according to patient response, and a blood level will determine both compliance and the adequacy of the drug regimen. Other drugs useful for this condition are diphenylhydantoin (Dilantin®) or primidone (Mysoline®) (Monroe, 1975). These drugs should also be used in conjunction with blood levels to determine adequacy or compliance.

The cardinal point to be remembered by the clinician is that a patient is not refractory to a drug unless the drug has been used in adequate amounts for adequate lengths of time. One of the main reasons for "drug failures" is the inadequate use of a drug for too short a time. One drug should be used after another in an orderly and systematic fashion, titrating the drug slowly upwards to the point of incipient toxicity or to the point where it can be demonstrated that the patient does not respond. Many patients respond idiosyncratically to one class of drug when another class has failed.

Central nervous system stimulants such as dextroamphetamines (Dexedrine®) or methylphenidate (Ritalin®) have been used to control hyperactivity and aggressiveness associated with minimal brain dysfunction. Traditionally, these drugs have been used in children only, though recent literature indicates that they may be of utility in adolescents and young adults (Allen, Safer, and Covi, 1975; Bellak, 1979). However, they are still considered experimental in this age group, which is prone to abuse drugs. Hence, the clinician can only use them in an experimental fashion.

The same is true with the use of hormones or hormone analogues, such as medroxyprogesterone acetates (Provera®) (Blumer and Migeon, 1975; Money, 1970). This drug is useful for sexually aggressive men and lowers serum testosterone. Its use is still experimental, and FDA approval would be required by the clinician who elects to try it on an individual basis.

Surgical treatment such as amygdalotomy has been used for some intractably violent temporal lobe epileptics (Mark and Ervin, 1970; Sweet, Ervin, and Mark, 1969). This method is also innovative and to be considered in patients in whom all avenues have been exhausted. Certainly, psychiatric consultation and neurological evaluation should preclude any consideration of such a treatment modality.

Patients with violent tendencies should be referred for psychotherapy. Not all patients wish to change, but some are amenable to insight. Psychotherapy of aggressive individuals is difficult since violence is a behavior that occurs before the patient has a chance to think about it; hence, the first goal of therapy is to get the patient to realize when he or she is angry and to appreciate rage within. This is done by acquainting the patient with the somatic accompaniments of anger. A patient must be able to tell, by paying attention to his body, his tight chest, his clenched fists, etc., that he is indeed angry. This is a first step toward verbal expression rather than translation of discomfort into action. A second agenda is fantasy. These patients often have impoverished fantasy lives and respond to stimuli with an immediate physical reply, rather than meditating on the consequences of their actions. They must be trained to contemplate the outcome of violence in detail, ranging from how it would feel if they hit someone to how it would feel if they were in jail. These mundane tasks are requisite in therapy. With time, depression ensues as the patient comes to grips with his or her helplessness and can no longer strike out (Lion, 1972).

Group therapy has proven in our experience to be a valuable and readily available tool of treatment. Many violent patients think they are alone in their impulsivity; a group experience corrects such distortions (Lion et al., 1977).

Violent patients evoke many sentiments in those who care for them. Actual fear or overreactions that are manifestations of the clinician's own attitudes toward violence can arise. These are referred to as countertransference responses, or strong feelings stirred up within the therapist by the patient (Lion and Pasternack, 1973). Therapists often are repulsed by the violence they see in a patient. Anger at the patient can lead to punitive sanctions, heavier medication, or even repudiation. On wards, chemical and physical restraints and seclusion may be outcomes of unexpressed attitudes in which staff dislike patients and come to fear them. Frequent discussion should be held between the treating clinician and staff about such emotions.

The clinician electing to treat violent patients must be open and verbal, someone with whom they can identify. Availability by phone is crucial in states of stress, and patients can be educated to call first rather than hit.

Family therapy has recently made contributions to the treatment of violence. Symonds (1978) has looked at violence-prone marriages and found two types: one in which violence is brought into the marriage as early as courtship and is due to the preexisting character structure of the husband and the other in which violence is produced within the marriage over conflicts from the marital relationship. He finds that the latter group are amenable to conjoint therapy while the fomer seems refractory. Other researchers have found that violence is more than twice as likely to occur in families with alcohol problems than in those without. Harbin (1977) found in treating adolescents with episodic dyscontrol that families showed two types of pathological adaptive functions. One was an overly close alliance with one parent with the other parent being ineffectively involved. This seemed to heighten the normal conflict the adolescent was experiencing over becoming independent and resulted in intense rage. Another pattern noted was the parents' inconsistency in values and setting limits concerning aggression. The adolescent may be punished one minute and ignored the next. Sometimes, fear by the parent was involved with the inconsistency. The type of therapy used in this study was a problem-oriented practical approach with well-structured plans and tasks set for the family. This type of family therapy has been described in work by Haley (1976).

SUMMARY

A violent patient is one who acts, or has acted, in such a way as to produce physical harm or destruction (*Clinical Aspects*, 1974). Violence cuts across a wide spectrum of diagnoses and is in itself a symptom of an illness, not an illness itself. Violence is more or less a life-style, and the appearance of it as something unusual in a patient should make the clinician consider underlying toxic or organic conditions.

The clinican must overcome denial of the violence potential. In assessing a violent individual, the clinician must obtain as much clinical history as is possible, perform a mental status examination, and rely on clinical judgment and intuitiveness. If at all possible, identify the potential victim. The neurologic status should eventually be assessed in all violent individuals. The clinician must always question the accessibility of dangerous weapons.

Treatment of the violent patient varies with the situation and etiology of the violent behavior. When possible, a one-on-one approach is best in an emergency setting. Various medications can be useful, but keep in mind that no medication is specific for aggression. For longer-term treatment, patients should be referred for psychotherapy. Both individual and group psychotherapy is useful and should focus on the patient recognizing anger before acting upon it. Clinicians working with violent patients must be open, verbal, and willing to be available by phone. Family therapy of a well-structured, problem-oriented approach seems most promising in cases of violence within the family.

It always must be kept in mind that aggression is symptomatic of weakness and reflects the patient's need to be strong, rather than weak. Thus, violence will be seen in a variety of illnesses and is in itself not a circumscribed disease process. The risks of it occurring are influenced by factors listed previously in this chapter.

REFERENCES

Allen, R.P., Safer, D., and Covi, L.: Effects of psychostimulants on aggression. *Journal of Nervous and Mental Disease, 160*:138-145, 1975.

Bach-Y-Rita, G., Lion, J.R., and Ervin, F.R.: Pathological intoxication: Clinical and electroencephalographic studies. *American Journal of Psychiatry, 127*:698-703, 1971.

Bellak, L. (Ed.): *Psychiatric Aspects of Minimal Brain Dysfunction in Adults*. New York, Grune and Stratton, 1979.

Benson, F.D., and Blumer, D.: *Psychiatric Aspects of Neurologic Diseases*. New York,

Grune and Stratton, 1975.

Blumer, D.: Organic personality disorders. In Lion, J.R. (Ed.): *Personality Disorders: Diagnosis and Treatment*. Baltimore, Williams and Wilkins, 1974.

Blumer, D., and Migeon, C.: Hormone and hormonal agents in the treatment of aggression. *Journal of Nervous and Mental Disease, 160*:127-137, 1975.

Brown, B.S., Wienchowski, L.A., and Bevins, L.W.: *Psychosurgery: Perspective on a Current Issue*, DHEW Publ. 73-9119, Washington, D.C., U.S. Government Printing Office, 1973.

Clinical Aspects of the Violent Individual, Task Force Report 8. Washington, D.C., American Psychiatric Association, July 1974.

Cohen, M.L., Grofalo, R., Boucher, R., and Seghorn, T.: The psychology of rapists. In Pasternak, S.A. (Ed.): *Violence and Victims*. New York, Spectrum Publications, 1975.

Cutler, N., and Heiser, J.F.: Retrospective diagnosis of hypomania following successful treatment of episodic violence with lithium: Case report. *American Journal of Psychiatry, 135*:753-754, 1978.

Diagnostic and Statistical Manual of Mental Disorders. Washington, D.C., American Psychiatric Association, 1980.

Donlon, P.T., Hopkin, J., and Tupin, J.P.: Efficacy and safety of rapid neuroleptization with injectable haloperidol. *American Journal of Psychiatry, 136*:273-278, 1979.

Ervin, F.R.: Brain disorders. IV: Associated with convulsions (epilepsy), In Freedman, A., and Kaplan, M. (Eds.): *Comprehensive Textbook of Psychiatry*. Baltimore, Williams and Wilkins, 1967.

Ervin, F.R., and Lion, J.R.: Clinical evaluation of the violent patient. In *Crimes of Violence*, Staff Report 13. Washington, D.C., National Commission on the Causes and Prevention of Violence, U.S. Government Printing Office, 1969.

Green, A.H.: The child abuse syndrome and the treatment of abusing parents. In Pasternack, S.A. (Ed.): *Violence and Victims*. New York, Spectrum Publications, 1975.

Groth, N., Burgess, A.W., and Holstrom, L.L.: Rape: Power, anger and sexuality. *American Journal of Psychiatry, 134*:1239-1243, 1977.

Guirguis, F.F.: Management of disturbed patients on alternatives to the use of mechanical restraints. *Journal of Clinical Psychiatry, 34(4)*:295-299, 1978,

Gurewitz, H.: Tarasoff: Protective privilege vs. public peril. *American Journal of Psychiatry, 134*:289-292, 1977.

Gutheil, T.C.: Observations on the theoretical bases for seclusion of the psychiatric inpatient. *American Journal of Psychiatry, 135*:325-328, 1978.

Haberland, C.: Alzheimer's disease in Down's syndrome: Clinical-neuropathological observations. *Confinia Neurol., 29*:153-158, 1969.

Haley, J.: *Problem Solving Therapy*. Washington, D.C., Jossey-Bass Publishers, 1976.

Hanks, S.E.: Battered woman: A study of women who live with violent alcohol-abusing men. *American Journal of Orthopsychiatry. 47*:291-306, 1977.

Harbin, H.T.: Episodic dyscontrol and family dynamics. *American Journal of*

Psychiatry, 134:1113-1116, 1977.

Hellman, D.S., and Blackman, N.: Enuresis, firesetting and cruelty to animals: A triad predictive of adult crime. *American Journal of Psychiatry, 122*:1431-1435, 1966.

International Drug Therapy Newsletter, 14:29-31, October 1979.

Jervis, G.S.: Early senile dementia in mongoloid idiocy. *American Journal of Psychiatry, 105*:102-106, 1948.

Kozol, H.: The diagnosis of dangerousness. In Pasternack, S.A. (Ed.): *Violence and victims*. New York, Spectrum Publications, Inc., 1975.

Lion, J.R.: Conceptual issues in the use of drugs for the treatment of aggression in man. *Journal of Nervous and Mental Disease, 160*:76-82, 1975.

Lion, J.R.: *Evaluation and Management of the Violent Patient*. Springfield, Illinois, Charles C Thomas, Publisher, 1972.

Lion, J.R.: *Personality Disorders: Diagnosis and Management*. Baltimore, Wiliams and Wilkins, 1974.

Lion, J.R.: *The Art of Medicating Psychiatric Patients*. Baltimore, Williams and Wilkins, 1978.

Lion, J.R.: The role of depression in the treatment of aggressive personality disorders. *American Journal of Psychiatry, 129*:347-349, 1972.

Lion, J.R., and Hill, J.: Lithium carbonate and aggression: A case report. *Diseases of the Nervous System, 36*:97-98, 1975.

Lion, J.R., and Pasternack, S.A.: Countertransference reactions to violent patients. *American Journal of Psychiatry, 130*:207-210, 1973.

Lion, J.R., et al.: A group approach with violent outpatients. *International Journal of Group Psychotherapy, 27*:67-74, 1977.

Mark, V.H., and Ervin, F.R.: *Violence and the Brain*. New York, Harper and Row, 1970.

Malamud, N.: Psychiatric disorder with intracranial tumors of the limbic system. *Archives of Neurology, 17*:113-123, 1967.

Marinacci, A.A.: Special type of temporal lobe (psychomotor) seizures following ingestion of alcohol. *Bulletin of the Los Angeles Neurological Societies, 28*:241-250, 1963.

Menkes, M.M., Rowe, J.S., and Menkes, J.H.: A twenty-five year follow-up study on the hyperkinetic child with minimal brain dysfunction. *Pediatrics, 39*:393-399, 1967.

Money, J.: Use of an androgen depleting hormone in the treatment of male sex offenders. *J Sex Res, 6*:165-172, 1970.

Monroe, R.R.: Anticonvulsants in the treatment of aggression. *Journal of Nervous and Mental Disease, 160*:119-126, 1975.

Monroe, R.R. *Episodic Behavior Disorders: A Psychodynamic and Neurophysiologic Analysis*. Cambridge, Harvard University Pres, 1970.

Peterson, R.C., and Stillman, R.C.: *Phencyclidine (PCP Abuse: An Appraisal)*, NIDA Research Monograph 21. Washington, D.C., DHEW, Government Printing Office, 1978.

Reitan, R.M., and Davidson, L.A. (Eds.): *Clinical Neuropsychology: Current Status and Applications*. Washington, D.C., V.H. Winston and Sons, Inc., 1974.

Rosen, H., and DiGiacomo, J.N.: The role of physical restraint in the treatment of psychiatric illness. *Journal of Clinical Psychiatry, 39*:228-232, 1978.

Rodin, E.A.: Psychomotor epilepsy and aggressive behavior. *Archives of General Psychiatry, 28*:210-213, 1973.

Roth, L.H., and Meisel, A.: Dangerousness, confidentiality and the duty to warn. *American Journal of Psychiatry, 134*:508-511, 1977.

Roth, M.: Cerebral disease and mental disorders of old age as causes of antisocial behavior. In de Reuck, A.V.S., and Porter, R.A. (Eds.): *The Mentally Abnormal Offender*. Ciba Foundation Symposium, Boston, Little, Brown, 1968.

Selzer, M.L., Rogers, J.E., and Kern, S.: Fatal accidents: The role of psychopathology, social stress and acute disturbances. *American Journal of Psychiatry, 124*:1028-1036, 1968.

Sheard, M.: Lithium in the treatment of aggression. *Journal of Nervous and Mental Disease, 160*:108-118, 1975.

Sweet, W.H., Ervin, F.R., and Mark, V.H.: The relationship of violent behavior to focal cerebral disease. In Garattini, S., and Siggs, E.B. (Eds.): *Aggressive Behavior*. New York, Wiley, 1969.

Symonds, M.: The psychodynamics of violence prone marriages. *American Journal of Psychoanalysis, 38*:213-222, 1978.

Tinklenberg, J.R., and Woodrow, K.M.: Drug use among assaultive and sexual offenders. In Frazier, S.H. (Ed.): *Human Aggression: Proceedings of the 1972 Annual Meeting of the Association for Research in Nervous and Mental Disease*. Baltimore, Williams and Wilkins, 1973.

Tupin, J.P., Smith, D.B., Clangn, T.L., et al.: The long term use of lithium in aggressive prisoners. *Comprehensive Psychiatry, 14*:311-317, 1973.

Chapter 6

A COGNITIVE-BEHAVIORAL APPROACH TO CHILD ABUSE: IMPLICATIONS FOR TREATMENT

Craig T. Twentyman, Cynthia A. Rohrbeck, and Patricia L. Amish

A COGNITIVE-BEHAVIORAL approach describes the abusive process as consisting of the four stages which involve behavioral deficits and cognitive dysfunctions, identified below:

Stage 1: Inappropriate parental expectation for the child

Example: Upon having a difficult day at work, a father returns home expecting his newborn infant to give him love and nurturance.

Stage 2: Child disconfirms parental expectations.

Example: The newborn infant cries due to hunger.

Stage 3: Parent makes idiosyncratic interpretations of child's behavior.

Example: The father believes that the infant hates him and wants to annoy him.

Stage 4: Parent responds aggressively toward child.

Example: The father repeatedly hits the infant to produce obedience and compliance.

Each of the four stages presented in the cognitive-behavioral reformulation can be assessed at the time of an abusive incident. A brief statement describing each of the stages follows:

Stage 1. Maltreating parents have deficits leading them to have unrealistic expectations about the appropriateness of their child's behavior. Such unrealistic expectations may lead the parent to discipline the child for behaviors that the child is incapable of modifying and in a manner that the child is incapable of understanding.

Abusing parents often disregard their child's needs, limited abilities, and general helplessness. Instead, they frequently perceive the essence of the child's role as providing for their own emotional needs.

Stage 2. The child acts in a way to disconfirm parental expectations. Obviously, a child cannot meet expectations that are inappropriate to his or her age and behavioral capacity. Furthermore, many abused children have a history of risk factors, such as prematurity, which further limit their ability to even minimally meet their parent's expectations.

Stage 3. The parent interprets the child's inability to meet expectations as willful acts of disobedience and parental disrespect by the child.

Data by Shorkey (1980) suggests that abusing parents may interpret their child's disobedience as negative feedback, for example, "He didn't obey me, therefore he thinks I'm a bad mother." Such parents may also negatively misperceive their child's innocuous behaviors. Thus, when an infant wets his diaper, a parent may suspect that "he wet his diaper because he's mad at me."

Stage 4. The parent aggresses against the child. Bousha and Twentyman (1981) have presented evidence that abusing mothers aggress more frequently against their children than do either neglectful or comparison mothers. It is not clear at this time whether this parental aggression is reinforced because it stops the child's negative behaviors (instrumental aggression) or because it serves as a release of frustration. To date, several investigators have suggested that maltreating parents have a difficult time controlling angry impulses (Wasserman, 1967; Spinetta and Rigler, 1972). When the aforementioned cognitive and behavioral distortions are combined with a lack of impulse control, an aggressive parental response is not surprising.

CURRENT EVIDENCE SUPPORTING THE COGNITIVE BEHAVIORAL MODEL

At this point, it has been suggested that abusing parents have unrealistic parental expectations, their children act to disconfirm these expectations, and these parents systematically misinterpret their child's actions. In working with a large number of abusing parents, at the Mt. Hope Family Center in Rochester, New York, it has become clear that the preceding stages do occur frequently.

In this section, anecdotal and research evidence generated at the Family Center will be presented in support of the cognitive behavioral model. Anecdotal evidence and case studies at the Mount Hope Family Center provide limited evidence for the four stage cognitive – behavioral model.

CASE 1. One mother, upon coming to the Family Center for an assessment, had recently delivered a premature infant with birth complications. After one week, the mother was able to bring her daughter home. The mother reported that the infant had been crying and would not stop despite the mother's admonitions to stop crying. Finally, she spanked her daughter since the daughter was "obviously not listening" to her. This incident indicates that not only did this woman have little knowledge of the cognitive capabilities of a seven-day-old infant, but that she also interpreted the continued crying as "not listening" which eventually made her frustrated enough to spank the infant.

CASE 2. A young mother abused her four-year-old son, who, after the birth of a sibling, proceeded to repeatedly wet his bed. The mother told her son not to wet the bed; however, he continued to do so, and she interpreted this as his "getting even" with her. She raged that he was doing this so "she would have to slave around the house" and punished the child with a severe whipping, which left extensive welts.

CASE 3. A pattern of unrealistic expectations and idiosyncratic interpretations eventually led to court action for child maltreatment and treatment. In this case, a young father related what had become almost a nightly occurrence to his therapist. He would read his two sons, ages two and three, bedtime stories and play in bed with them. Then he would leave them to fall asleep by themselves. His sons, however, stimulated by the play and stories, would not fall asleep immediately and would often talk. This angered the father who believed that they did not "care for the kindness" he gave them and showed him "no respect" by their failure to obey his instructions. This father regularly beat his children when he believed that this was the case. It should be noted that such aggressive responses are fundamentally related to the father's misreading of his sons' actions and that, ironically, in this case, the father was exciting his sons with the play and stories and then punishing them for their reaction.

Such case studies are suggestive that for many of these parents, the proposed four-stage model is in operation. In these examples, the parents expected too much of their child, their child did not meet their expectations, the parent angrily misinterpreted this failure and aggressively punished the child.

Despite the clinical evidence for the cognitive-behavioral model of child abuse, it has been only recently that controlled studies capable of providing evidence supporting this position have been conducted. Plotkin, Azar, Twentyman, and Perri (1981) reviewed the literature on causative factors of child maltreatment and found it characterized by explanatory models based on clinical impressions, rather than rigorous methodological experimentation. In the past two years, several controlled studies at the Family Center have been completed and provide and suggest emperical cognitive-behavioral evidence in support of the model.

One study (Twentyman and Plotkin, in press), using the Developmental Expectations Questionnaire derived from the Vineland Social Maturity Scale, gives evidential support for the first stage of the model. This study tested the hypothesis that child-abusing parents are less knowledgeable about child development than matched, nonmaltreating parents. This questionnaire consisted of twenty developmental milestones, and the parents were asked, first, at what age their child would achieve each milestone; second, at what age the "average child" would achieve each milestone. Results supported the hypothesis that parents who maltreat their children are less knowledgeable about child development than matched, nonmaltreating parents. The study also pursued the hypothesis that parents who maltreated their children have more unrealistic expectations than matched, nonabusing parents. In the research to support this there was a greater variability of response on the part of the abusing aprents. In some cases, abusing parents had *lower* expectations for their children than for the "average child." In other cases they had unrealistically higher expectations. Twentyman and Plotkin suggest that low expectations may promote cognitive or emotional delays in children, whereas unrealistically high expectations may increase the parent's frustration eventually leading to child maltreatment.

The second stage of the model, the assumption that the child acts in a way that disconfirms parental expectations, is also supported by research. Bousha and Twentyman (1981) completed an observational study of abusing, neglectful, and control families. In this study, family interactions were observed during three sessions in the home. Observation was directed to the following behavioral categories: verbal and nonverbal instruction and affection; active physical affection; verbal aggression; passive nonverbal aggression; and initiations, social interactions, noncompliance, and play behaviors.

Initial results illustrate that children in maltreating families demonstrated more active physical aggression and more noncompliance with parental requests. This was especially the case of children in abusing families. Children of abusers also showed significantly more passive, nonverbal aggression than either neglected or comparison children. The findings that the child in an abusing family was actively aggressive, cried more, and was more noncompliant suggest that abused children may play a significant role in abusive incidents.

Thus far, we have seen that research data support elements of the first two stages of the proposed cognitive-behavioral model. The third stage posits that abusing parents idiosyncratically interpret their child's behavior. Although numerous case studies support this view, until recently empirical demonstration was lacking. Larrance and Twentyman (1981) devised an assessment technique in which parents were asked to generate explanations for their child's behavior. In this study, abusing, neglectful, and comparison mothers told stories designed to elicit their feelings, attributions, and interpretations about their child's behaviors. These stories were about their own children and unknown children of the same age and race who were engaged in a variety of behaviors. Mothers told the stories in response to a set of photographs that depicted a sequence of activities in which toys were broken, walls were crayoned, and skill and chance games were completed. Blind raters assessed each story for its positive and negative content. Abusing mothers judged their children significantly more negatively. Abusive mothers made external attributions when their child succeeded at a task; for example, "He was just lucky." When the child failed or showed inappropriate behavior, the mothers attributed the misbehavior to sources in the child; for example, "He always misbehaves." This was in direct contrast to comparison mothers, who made internal attributions when their child succeeded and external ones when their child failed. Neglecting mothers made attributions between these extremes.

Data from a recent study (Plotkin and Twentyman, 1981) provide further support for the third stage of the model that abusing parents have idiosyncratic interpretations of their children's behavior. In the study, mothers were read stories of various problem situations, which included aversive child behavior, and were asked what they would do in each situation. Stories varied according to cues for causal explanations of the child's behavior. For instance, in one case, a child soiled his pants after a long drive in the car. In another case, a child soiled his pants soon after being taken to the toilet while expressing anger to the parent. Mothers were asked to rate each story for the degree of aversivenes of child behavior, how threatening the child behavior was, and how much the child intended the behavior. Parents were then given several ways to react to or punish the child, including taking away prizes from the child and squeezing a hand dynamometer to indicate the degree that they would punish the child. Abusing mothers judged the child's behavior to be significantly more aversive and punished the child more according to all the punishment measures. Importantly, abusing and neglecting mothers also rated that the child was being aversive "to annoy" them more than did the comparison mothers.

In the fourth stage of the model, the abusing parent aggresses against the child. Data from our laboratory clearly shows that abusing mothers respond more aggressively to their children than do neglectful and comparison mothers. In the home observation study discussed earlier (Bousha and Twentyman, 1981), abusing mothers showed both the most active physical aggression and verbal aggression of all the groups studied. Abusing and neglecting mothers showed fewer positive responses, were less affectionate (both verbally and nonverbally), initiated less play behavior, gave their child less nonverbal instruction, and were more verbally aggressive than comparison mothers.

In summary, data exist to support elements of each stage of the cognitive-behavioral model. Still open to question is the interdependence between stages and the presence of a causal sequence linking the stages together. The relative importance of each stage also needs to be determined in order to develop assessment, treatment, and prevention procedures.

IMPLICATION OF A COGNITIVE-BEHAVIORAL APPROACH FOR PSYCHOLOGICAL ASSESSMENT

When a clinician working with child abuse cases adopts the cognitive-behavioral model of child abuse, two major implications for assessment become clear. First, family members must be assessed to determine whether cognitive defects are present. Secondly, an assessment of the family's social interactional system must occur to determine the extent to which parenting skill deficits and dysfunctional child behaviors are involved in the production and maintenance of child abuse.

Assessment of Parental Cognitive Structures (Stages 1 and 3)

A person's cognitions can interfere with his or her production of effective and appropriate behavior sequences (Meichanbaum, 1972). In assessing the potential for child abuse, it is essential to determine (a) the parent's cognitions about child development and behavior and (b) the appropriateness of the expectations they hold for their child's behavior as a result of their cognitions. A clinician can employ several mechanisms to assess a parent's cognitions and expectations.

Despite the limitations that interview techniques have in terms of reliability and social desirability, important antidotal information may be uncoverd by this method. Information about the frequency and severity of physical punishment and use of alternative methods of discipline are important to obtain. Moreover, as one's own childhood affects future child care practices, a thorough history of a parent's own child-rearing experiences ought to be collected. This may include interviewing the parent about his or her childhood, as well as interviewing the client's parents, if that is possible (Wolfe, Kaufman, Aragona, and Sandler, 1981). Parents' individual experiences with parenting behaviors (e.g. babysitting siblings) prior to the birth of their own children should be collected to document previous interactions and practice as well (Wolfe et al., 1981).

The clinical interview is useful also in revealing additional information about a client's cognitive structures and specific distortions concerning a child's intentions or abilities. It has been our experience, for example, that child abusers attribute highly specific negative characteristics to their children that are related to negative characteristics in individuals such as old boyfriends, ex-spouses, or disliked parents. Because of the highly specific nature of these attributions and expectations, it is often difficult to assess them outside a structured interview.

Many of the measures discussed in the previous section on research have been used in clinical assessments and provide information about parental cognitive distortion. The Parental Opinion Questionnaire, for example, is useful in determining whether the parent has unrealistic expectations across a number of different areas of child behavior (e.g. the child's ability to provide love and nurturance). A modification of the Vineland Social Maturity Scale (Twentyman and Plotkin, in press) focuses upon the existence of a deficit in knowledge of when children typically are able to perform various tasks.

Information that specifically focuses on parents' idiosyncratic interpretations of their child's behavior may be obtained through the use of a measure similar to the one used in the attributional study discussed previously. It is believed that presenting semistructured information in a format where the parent tells a story about their child will elicit more useful information than standard projective instruments, because the latter typically does not pull for information about the child. The storytelling format also has the advantage of not requesting specific information concerning what a parent dislikes about their child; this might possibly lead to a defensiveness in responding.

A number of other measures might be employed to assess additional relevant areas. For example, the cognitive capabilities of the parents to solve problems have been investigated, and assessment devices have been standardized that are now used for clinical assessments (Spivak, Platt, and Shure, 1976; D'Zurilla and Goldfried, 1971). Moreover, measures of a client's overall cognitive abilities, such as the WAIS or Shipley, are useful to administer in cases where questions arise about whether the client would be able to benefit from training or additional information about child developmental sequences. Thus, if a parent is mildly or moderately retarded, the educational training sequences would be considerably different from those offered to parents with a higher intelligence.

Assessment of the Social Interactional System and Parenting Behaviors (Stages 2 and 4)

While information obtained from testing frequently provides useful data, it is our contention that the assessment of sociointeractional system provides the most useful information about current deficits and dysfunctional familial patterns. Assessment of the interactional system specifically focuses upon how the family interacts and whether the mother and father can demonstrate effective parenting behavior. This assessment provides a sample of the family's *current* behavioral repertoire.

As with any behavioral observation, it is important that a representative sample of typical interactive sequences of the family be obtained. Of course, the mere presence of observers in a setting is likely to change a family's behaviors to some degree. However, it has been our experience that families in which maltreatment occurs typically do not inhibit aggressive responses after the first part of the initial session. The data from Bousha and Twentyman (1981) also have shown that abusing mothers exhibited approximately twenty high-intensity aggressions during observation as opposed to virtually none in the neglect and comparison groups. This clearly suggests that even if the rate of aggression is reduced during observation, it is still of such a high frequency that useful clinical information can be obtained by sending trained observers into the home.

A positive aspect of observing within the home setting is that it allows greater insight into the family's natural interactions. In this regard, it is beneficial to choose a time period to observe when all the members of the family are present with a need to interact. We have found that the dinner hour and the surrounding time fulfills this requirement. Others (Burgess and Conger, 1978) have also found this time appropriate for observation.

Behavioral observation in a structured laboratory setting may not have all the richness that observing in the home has but may be useful when assessment of parenting skills related to specific child management needs to be continued. In observations, Wolfe and his colleagues (1981) utilized the Parent–Child Interaction Form (PCIF), which was developed from the Parent Performance Checklist by Sweitzer and Boyd (1979). Essentially the PCIF is a compilation of behaviors that a parent should be able to demonstrate in order to effectively teach and control his or her child. It yields information on whether or not parents perform behaviors at an appropriate level under various circumstances. This information can tell the observer what skills the parent has in his or her behavioral repertoire. A typical session includes observing the natural interactions of parent and child, followed by the parent teaching the child a new task, which is purposely set to be slightly above the age level of the child, concluding with requesting the parents to have the child put away the teaching materials.

Behavioral observations of children in both home and classroom settings are useful in several aspects. If the children are aggressive, disruptive, or withdrawn across both settings, this suggests that generalized behavioral dysfunctions may be occurring in the child and that the child may need to be treated independently of the family. If dysfunctional behaviors occur only in the home setting, however, this suggests that the child may be responding to parental contingencies and treatment should be focused within the family setting alone. Although we recommend that behavioral observations occur in both home and school settings, observation in the home setting is particularly important in determining what the child does prior to parental aggressive episodes and in determining if there is potential risk of the child being further abused.

Finally, in addition to direct behavioral observation, samples obtained through role playing may prove useful to examine situations that clients suggest occur at low frequency but result in high-intensity aggression. The role-playing format is particularly useful in assessing the client's range of alternative responses to such "trigger" situations. This assessment is not possible in observation unless the clinician wishes to intervene in the family's interaction.

IMPLICATIONS OF THE MODEL FOR TREATMENT

Although the treatment is not directly relevant to the proposed model of child abuse, the model does suggest that a number of specific factors are related to child maltreatment. Thus, there is the implication that if these factors were changed, the incidence of child maltreatment would be less likely to occur.

Treatment of the particular factors emphasized in the model is focused on both the parents and children. Treating child-abusing parents should focus on (1) decreasing cognitive distortions about the child, self, and others; (2)correcting parental expectations; (3) improving knowledge of child development patterns; (4) challenging idiosyncratic misperceptions of the child; (5) increasing child management skills; (6) treating/altering aggressive response tendencies; (7) supplying positive interaction models; (8) increasing social skills with other individuals in order to decrease dependence on the child; (9) improving stress coping and impulse control; and (10) increasing total social interaction of the parent and child. Treatment targets for children include (1) addressing and ameliorating aggressive tendencies, (2) identifying and decreasing cognitive deficiencies, and (3) improving social interaction skills with peers and adult care givers.

As has been discussed throughout this chapter, family dynamics involved in child abuse are complex. They are not unilateral with respect to the parents or the children. Rather, the sequence of actions is best viewed as an interaction that occurs among all family members. Therefore, it is not sufficient to isolate and treat only one or two family members or to treat only problem areas that affect particular members of the family. Thus, one implication of the model is to suggest that a multimodal treatment program be utilized, addressing major areas of concern for all the family members.

Admittedly, when working with families in which child abuse has occurred, there are pragmatic difficulties one encounters that are not present in other populations. In particular, parents are often mandated by the courts to attend treatment. Though the importance of adjudication for successful completion of treatment has been noted (Wolfe, Aragona, Kaufman, and Sandler, 1980), the voluntary nature of the interaction makes noncompliance to treatment likely, and dealing with this issue is inevitable. The abusing population is likely to include individuals from lower-class backgrounds who typically have had a limited amount of formal education. Both these characteristics have been associated with poor attendance rates and the need for concrete structured forms of treatment. Furthermore, these families are less likely to have telephones and a readily accessible means of transportation, which is likely to inhibit therapeutic contact. Such factors as these force the therapist to place greater emphasis on outreach programs rather than programs typically utilized with other populations.

The difficulties mentioned above are addressed by various treatment modalities that differ in their underlying premises. We will consider two major types of treatment in particular: cognitive and behavior modification approaches.

THERAPEUTIC PROGRAMS DIRECTED AT THE PARENT

Cognitively oriented therapies are directed at the modification of maladaptive beliefs and attitudes, which are believed to be the basis of dysfunctional behaviors (Beck, 1976). Thus, cognitively oriented therapy with abusive populations is directed at modifying misinterpretive styles and unrealistic expectations. This is done by teaching realistic developmental milestones and promoting more realistic interpretations about children's behavior. Information is frequently presented within the context of teaching problem-solving skills and encouraging clients to produce socially acceptable alternatives to problem situations (Beck, 1970), as well as increasing self-control through positive self-statements (Meichanbaum, 1972).

Behavioral approaches to therapy, in contrast to cognitive therapy, place greater emphasis on the client's actions rather than on his or her cognitions. A basic premise is that the observable changes should occur in the client's behaviors in precisely those areas where the client previously demonstrated deficiencies or excesses. Specific child management techniques are taught that can be put into direct use by the parents. For example, teaching appropriate disciplining techniques, such as placing the child in time-out, and learning to give positive reinforcement for appropriate behavior in acceptable situations are foci of behaviorally oriented treatments.

There are many treatment programs for abusive parents in the literature, ranging from those working mainly within a behavioral framework to multimodel programs combining behavioral and cognitive therapy techniques. Helfer (1980) reported a skill-relearning program for adults who have had poor parental histories. A basic premise in this therapy is that clients have learned maladaptive child-rearing techniques by observing and participating in their own parents' maltreatment of them. The program relies essentially on systematic desensitization, allowing parents to relearn the behaviors that have been associated with negative affective experiences. Positive reinforcement is freely provided by lay therapists who serve as new role models for the parents. The therapist-parent interaction facilitates friendship, encourages positive interaction, and provides the parent with a more effective source of information of child management problems. Although this program has many commendable features, currently no data is available on its effectiveness.

Justice and Justice (1976) advocate a treatment program integrating several treatment modes. Cognitively, they utilize structural analysis in working with abusive parents. Based heavily on transactional analysis (Gordon, 1970), the emphasis is upon making members recognize which part of their personality structure (i.e. parent, adult, or child) is involved in particular transactions. Once aware of maladaptive interactional styles, parents are taught to alter maladaptive roles. Behavioral components of this process include parents' carrying out assigned "prescriptions" and using goal attainment scaling techniques. In addition to the above, hypnosis and relaxation training is advocated. While empirical research has not been given for this program, the author claims that the program is successful based on clinical observations.

Gilbert (1976) demonstrated the efficacy of developing and implementing a set of individual target behavioral goals to increase both positive mother-child interactions and maternal physical affection through therapist modeling and self-monitoring in a case study with an abusive mother. Sandler, VanDercas, and Milhoun (1978) also altered negative interactions between parents and child in two families through a parent-training program designed to improve child management skills and reduce aversive interaction. With the addition of contingency contracting to the above parent-training component, it was purported that parents learned more rapidly, as illustrated by decreased use of punitive forms of control and improvements in the child's behavior (Wolfe and Sandler, 1981). Furthermore, with the expansion of a third component, cognitive-behavioral training parents were found to cope more effectively with problem situations in specific reference to the control of explosive anger (Denicola and Sandler, 1980).

Based on the success of their treatment studies, Wolfe, Sandler, and Kaufman (in press) expanded their program into a group design in order to include more parents and to evaluate the treatment's effectiveness with greater control variables. They combined the advantages of group support and interaction with a home-based training component aimed at reviewing and generalizing skills presented at group sessions. The program involved an eight-week intensive parenting course with the two major components, covering child management, knowledge of child development, and methods of anger control. Within the classroom instruction period, modeling and rehearsal of behaviors were utilized. The emphasis was placed upon acquisition of appropriate child management and anger control skills as applied to a wide variety of child behavior problems. Secondly, the competency-based parent training within the home allowed parents to progress at their own pace in order to establish successful improvements in child rearing in the natural setting. Established learning principles were heavily relied upon through verbal and written instructions of new material, modeling of new behavior via videotaped parent and child actors, behavioral rehearsal in the group and home settings, and reliance upon feedback. Evaluation measures consisted of home observations of parenting skills, parental reports of child behavior problems, and casework reports of family problems.

The authors reported that those receiving services designed to train parents in handling difficult child management situations and controlling their aggression exhibited fewer child-related problems in the home, demonstrated a continued reliance upon appropriate management skills within the home, and were noted to be functioning more effectively in general by their caseworker. Parallel improvements were not demonstrated by the control group who simply received biweekly supervision in accordance with standard services mandated by the state. Follow-up data after a one-year period illustrated maintenance of these original findings.

MODIFICATION OF THE CHILD'S BEHAVIOR

To treat the parents without treating the child in an abusing family either assumes that the child is not a significant part of the family system or that the child does not play any part in eliciting the abuse. Although one need not ascribe any responsibility or blame to the child for abusive incidents, it is clear that certain factors that may be present in a given child may place that child at a greater risk for abuse. In this regard, it has even been suggested that some children may invite abuse (de Lissovoy, 1979). Based on the proposed model, the second step recognizes that children can elicit negative treatment when they act in a manner that disconfirms parental expectations. From a number of studies completed to date, it has been found that abused children are more aggressive and are frequently developmentally delayed (Hoffman-Plotkin and Twentyman, 1981), interact less with their parents (Bousha and Twentyman, 1981), demonstrate avoidance of friendly overtures in a classroom setting (George and Main, 1979; Hoffman-Plotkin and Twentyman, 1981), and in essence are viewed as being more aversive by their parents than control children.

It is believed that early intervention with behavioral techniques may alleviate many of these risk factors, but conclusive evidence for such a position has not been presented to date. If this were the case, however, special facilities, such as therapeutic schools or day service programs, would permit the systematic reinforcement of socially acceptable behavior across a variety of contexts.

Two behavior techniques are particularly applicable to the difficulties demonstrated by maltreated children. As illustrated in the home observational study (Bousha and Twentyman, 1981), abusive parents are less likely to reward their children with positive reinforcement. Teachers, however, have an excellent opportunity to encourage and reward children for attempts at socially acceptable behavior for many hours a day. Through the use of shaping techniques (i.e. gradually working toward a goal with children through a step-by-step process), children may be encouraged to interact more frequently with their peers and adult caretakers. Also, as a result of being members of a classroom, children are able to learn proper behavior through the observation of others.

Secondly, abused and neglected children demonstrate high rates of disruptive behavior in the classroom, with abused children in particular demonstrating a high frequency of aggressive responses/ interactions (Hoffman-Plotkin and Twentyman, 1981). Thus, treatment must be directed at reducing negative behavior without also reducing the likelihood that the child will engage in more positive social activities. Initiallly, redirecting the child engaged in minor disruptive incidents toward more socially acceptable behaviors while repeating the message that their original behavior was unacceptable may be sufficient to change the child's behaviors. More severe incidents require stronger responses and may involve removing the child from the group and placing him or her in a time-out area. After a brief period, when the child is in a calmer state, the care giver should repeat his or her displeasure and speak with the child about alternative solutions to the problem situations. The child can then be returned to the classroom or setting from which he or she was removed. It should be noted that time-out procedures are only likely to be effective if the setting from which the child was removed is more reinforcing than the time-out area in which he or she is required to sit. Thus, placing the chair in a spot where the child is not likely to get a lot of positive attention is essential for the effectiveness of this procedure.

THE MT. HOPE FAMILY CENTER TREATMENT MODEL

The Mt. Hope Family Center is a facility dedicated exclusively to the treatment of abused and neglected children and their families. Its comprehensive program serves approximately forty families at any one time. The services provided by the Family Center are uniquely tailored to the goals of preventing the occurrence of further episodes of child abuse and neglect, providing an alternative to long-term foster care, and reuniting families who have had the child removed from the home.

Prior to entering Mt. Hope Family Center the entire family undergoes a thorough psychological assessment. Preschool children entering the Family Center undergo psychological and educational assessment to determine their cognitive, social-emotional, and physical development. This assessment enables the staff to design a treatment and educational program specific to each child's needs.

The parents are assessed to determine their knowledge of child development and expectations of children, feelings toward individual family members, and personality structures. As with the children, parental assessment allows a therapy plan that is tailored to the parent's needs.

The center provides a year round, five-day-a-week program for preschool children aged three to five that are referred through child protective services. An enriched environment consisting of materials for play and peers exists. The classrooms are staffed by certified teachers as well as classroom aides. The ratio of adult to child is approximately a one to four ratio, allowing for considerable individual attention. In addition to the normal classroom activities, special education services are available for children with emotional, behavioral, and/or speech problems. A staff of special education teachers work with the children to promote cognitive/learning skills in attempting to ameliorate the children's developmental deficiencies. The teachers also work in conjunction with the child psychologist to implement behavioral programs for children who are aggressive, withdrawn, or hyperactive. Professional speech therapy is utilized with children exhibiting language deficits, and play therapy is utilized with children exhibiting behavioral disturbances. An important feature of the day service program is the fact that the trained staff exercises consistency in a positive manner, promoting a predictable and stable environment for the children.

Treatment effects have been found among the children after a year's period of time in the classroom setting. Scores on intelligence tests have increased over time, as well as the progressive development of positive social interaction skills. Through the use of time-out periods, redirection, and consistency in responding to the child, the incidence of aggression has been shown to decrease sharply within the first month of the child's participation in the program. For example, in one case, a family was referred in which the child was previously dismissed from a local day-care center because he was viewed as being overly aggressive and out of control. An initial two-week baseline revealed that the boy displayed approximately fifty high-intensity aggressions per day. Following the baseline, the child was placed on a time-out program in which he was not allowed access to toys or classroom activities for two minutes following each incident of aggression. Within a month, the rate of aggression was approximately two per day.

The therapy for parents who participate in the Mt. Hope program is designed to meet the needs of individual families and may take the form of individual, group, couple, or family sessions. Typically, treatment consists of a combination of a number of these treatment modalities. Evening and weekend psychotherapy is available for working parents. The focus of the psychotherapy sessions includes child management information about developmental sequences, anger and stress management, and problem-solving skills (i.e. generation of alternative solutions to difficult situations). Methods for enhancing effective communications and increasing social contacts are also areas covered in therapy.

Visits to the homes are extremely valuable in both the assessment and treatment of families, as family dynamics can be most accurately evaluated by direct observation by staff in the home setting. The home visits also provide information about the child's behaviors and may result in a change in the child's treatment program and/or the parents' psychotherapy focus. In some instances, the home visits result in positive reinforcement of the parents' child management skills and parent-child interaction patterns.

The parent-training groups conducted by the staff at Mt. Hope allow the program to intensify its efforts of educating the parents in proper child management techniques. The parents meet once a week to discuss problems they encounter and to receive support from one another. The group emphasis has been found to decrease social isolatuion and further reinforce the parents' changes. A variety of skills are taught, including child management and problem solving. Discussions pertaining to child development, health, and nutrition are also considered.

PREVENTION

The cognitive-behavioral model of child abuse and its implications for assessment and treatment have been examined. Various methods for assessment and treatment based on this model have been proposed. One of the most difficult, although presumably most rewarding, approaches to the problem of child abuse is that of prevention. While improving services to identified neglectful and abusing families is an effective means of preventing abuse and neglect from reoccurring, the ultimate goal would be to prevent child maltreatment from ever occurring. Prevention efforts should focus on three areas: the parents, the child, and the culture or environment. Prevention would also focus on child-rearing strategies and sociological characteristics, such as unemployment and isolation, that might escalate the risk of abuse.

Three aspects of prevention include: (1) interventions provided through educational systems, (2) interventions that aim to provide or extend support systems, and (3) media interventions. Suggested interventions in these three realms will be discussed in the order they are listed below:

Educational Interventions

1. School programs throughout the life cycle
2. Parenting groups
3. "How-to" tapes

Support System Interventions

4. Emergency "drop-in" child care
5. Parent-support groups
6. Buddy programs
7. Child-support groups
8. Hot lines

Media Interventions

9. Radio and television advertisements
10. Notices on products: cereal boxes, milk cartons, etc.
11. "How-to" cartoons for children

EDUCATIONAL INTERVENTIONS

An educational strategy for prevention must provide parents (and future parents) with educational experiences throughout their educational career. The goal of the educational approach would be to emphasize that parenting is not just a biological act; instead it requires a repertoire of behavioral skills, experience, and maturity. The educational curriculum could stress normal child developmental sequences, parental skills, ways to strengthen family bonding, and disciplinary techniques.

Often such broad-based programs may be too costly or impractical to operate. In this case, identified "at-risk" populations could be the target of such training programs. Predictive questionnaires or other assessment devices might be administered to new parents and parents-to-be. Such groups as adolescent parents (a high-risk group for child maltreatment) could be specifically targeted for intervention efforts. Some clinicians have suggested a mandatory parent-training course, similar in setup to driver education courses often required for licensing. Such training courses could also include practical experience, for example, working with children in a day-care center. When young adults see that all children have behavior problems and disobedient or disagreeable periods, they are less likely to react with anger in the future when their own child misbehaves. In essence, they will have more realistic expectations concerning their own children.

Schools could provide the site for parental skill-training programs; however, early childhood programs such as day-care centers may be a more effective site for specific targeted groups of parents. Such programs could offer parenting groups and provide excellent information and advice concerning common problems in child raising to interested parents. Since teachers and day-care directors are already known to the parent, they can be approached as nonthreatening, accepted authority figures in child rearing.

Parental skill-training programs can educate parents about normal childhood developmental patterns and processes. They can advise parents on common problems such as toilet training and temper tantrums. Inexperienced parents who do not realize that nearly all young children have temper tantrums at some time may become extremely frustrated and think of themselves as failures. Uninformed neighbors or family members may add to the frustration, and ineffective or harmful discipline can result.

One way to stretch the tightly limited budgets of many parent groups and educational programs would be to utilize all forms of media available, for instance brochures, movies, and "how-to" tapes. Tapes or movies that a parent could watch, or even phone in and listen to, would be economically practical and enable the parent to seek advice in a nonthreatening, independent manner. Such tapes and films could focus on normal growth and developmental patterns and suggest alternative disciplinary techniques.

SUPPORTIVE INTERVENTION

Educational interventions are not always enough, or perhaps not what the isolated and unsupported child-abusing parent wants. Supportive interventions, those that provide additional help to the parent, may be beneficial. For instance, one service that day-care programs could provide is "drop-in" child care. Parents who are having particularly difficult times with their children would be encouraged to participate in these programs and reduce their child-caring responsibilities during a stressful period. It is believed that this would help the parent cope with stress and help him or her to maintain self-control, thus preventing a potentially abusive incident.

Yet another approach would be to provide opportunities for parents to meet each other and share child-rearing difficulties and experiences. Such groups could be self-run support groups focusing on other life problems, for instance looking for a part-time job, sibling rivalry, and communication problems. Families that become abusive or neglectful are often socially isolated, and these programs allow parents to experience social involvement and broaden support systems.

It is helpful to ask such parents which persons in their environment are the most helpful to them (Wolfe, Kaufman, Aragona, and Sandler, 1981). Such individuals may include clergy, family members, or neighbors. The parents' permission can often be elicited to include these one or two persons on home visits. Such resource persons can provide a "buddy system," prompting parents to improve and praising them for their performance. Buddies can serve as modeling agents for the parents to learn better child management techniques and ways to control impulsive feelings. Such "buddies" can also provide parents with a "sounding board" when they are faced with a problem they cannot solve on their own.

Such a program would be relatively simple and cost-efficient to develop. Similar companion programs have been initiated with psychiatric patients, for example the Compeer Program in Rochester, New York, and have proven helpful to both the patient and the companion. Both college students and community people could provide pools from which volunteers could be elicited. Such a program could be specific, focusing on identified at-risk parents, or it could be nonspecific. An example of a nonspecific program is a program developed in the United Kingdom (*c.f.* Justice and Justice, 1976), in which health visitors make home visits to all families with newborns to check for possible educational deficits or risk factors for child abuse.

Support groups can be as useful for appropriately aged children of abusers as they are for the abusing parents. Such groups could be easily administered through the educational system. Their aim would be twofold. They would allow children to express their feelings about being the target of abuse and also show them their possible role or "elicitation" of the abuse.

Yet another intervention to provide support would be the use of hot lines. Such hot lines could provide educational information in addition to providing supportive listeners. Parents could call the hot line when distressed or worried about their potential for an abusive act. Hot lines could be managed by trained nonprofessionals, thus lessening the cost of professionals' involvement.

MEDIA INTERVENTIONS

Although educational or supportive interventions come to mind most often, one potential method for interventions is virtually untapped: that of media. Media interventions can reach a large audience at low cost and can be less intimidating to both parents and children.

Television or radio advertisements could be utilized to inform both abusers and abused children of their rights and of services available to help them. Advertisements like these, when made in a supportive, nonthreatening way, may reach parents who may not be initially willing to seek help from human service providers. Such advertisements might also encourage children to report abusive incidents despite the fear of retaliation abused children often have.

Another type of media intervention would be to provide information on products that children often see and read like cereal boxes. When Sweden instituted its law banning corporal punishment, notification was printed on all the milk cartons in an attempt to reach children who may not have been aware of the new law. Similar information on packaged products would reassure an abused child that he or she is not an isolated case and that help is available.

Media interventions need not only be educational or informative; indeed they could provide a therapy of types. "How-to" cartoons for children could teach them alternative behaviors in potentially abusive situations. Children or characters who are faced with the problem of an angry parent could model alternative responses. Those children participating in a cycle of abusive patterns with their parents might see alternative ways to act and thus avoid or modify an abusive incident.

SUMMARY

In the preceding sections, clinical and empirical evidence has been presented supporting our belief that child abuse is best conceptualized as a complex cognitive-behavioral phenomenon. We suggest that a cognitive-behavioral model is more useful, both in research and clinical enterprises, than is the traditional psychodynamic model. This view may in part be justified by the fact that we have been able to present tentative *evidence* supporting our position. Future research will, however, determine whether the present model is adequate for explaining abusive acts or whether modification or elaboration is necessary.

The implications of our model for treatment have been previously stated. It is our belief that the present model will prove useful for the human service provider, as it allows a multitude of therapeutic approaches, focusing on one or several stages and on the parent, child, or family system. This is in contrast to the traditional psychodynamic approach, which focuses on the parent alone. The cognitive-behavioral model allows the provider to approach the problem from more than one front. Moreover, with its emphasis on behavioral and educational deficits, this model is complementary with recent trends in psychotherapy, which emphasize short-term, behaviorally oriented programs and prevention through the use of mass media approaches.

REFERENCES

Beck, A.T.: *Cognitive Therapy and the Emotional Disorders*. New York, International Universities Press, 1976.

Beck, A.T.: Cognitive therapy: nature and relation to behavior therapy. *Behavior Therapy, 1*:184-200, 1970.

Bousha, D.M., and Twentyman, C.T.: *Mother-child Interactions in Abuse and Neglect Families*. Unpublished manuscript, 1981.

Burgess, R.L., and Conger, R.D.: Family interactions in abusive, neglectful and normal families. *Child Development, 49*:1163-1173, 1978.

Caplan, G.: *Principles of Preventive Psychiatry*. New York, Basic Books, 1964.

de Lissovoy, U.: Toward the definition of "abuse provoking child." *Child Abuse and Neglect: The International Journal, 3*:341-350, 1979.

Denicola, J., and Sandler, J.: Training abusive parents in cognitive-behavioral techniques. *Behavior Therapy, 2*:263-270, 1980.

D'Zurilla, T.J., and Goldfried, M.R.: Problem solving and behavior modification. *Journal of Abnormal Psychology, 78*:107-126, 1971.

Elmer, E.: A follow-up study of traumatized children. *Pediatrics, 59(2)*:273-279, 1977.

Galston, R.: Observations on children who have been physically abused and their parents. *American Journal of Psychiatry, 122*:440-443, 1965.

George, C., and Main, M.: Social interactions of young abused children: Approach, avoidance, and aggression. *Child Development, 50*:306-318, 1979.

Gilbert, M.T.: Behavioral approach to the treatment of child abuse. *Nursing Times*, 1976, pp. 140-142.

Gordon, T.: *Parent Effectiveness Training*. New York, Wyden, 1970.

Helfer, R.E.: *A Self-Instructional Program on Child Abuse and Neglect*. Committee on Infant and Preschool Children, American Academy of Pediatrics, Chicago, Ill., and the National Center for Prevention and Treatment of Child Abuse and Neglect, Denver, Colo., 1974.

Helfer, R.E.: *Childhood Comes First: A Crash Course in Childhood for Adults*. First evaluation edition published by author, 1978.

Helfer, R.E.: Retraining and relearning. In Kempe, C.H., and Helfer, R.E. (Eds.): *The Battered Child*. Chicago, University of Chicago Press, 1980.

Hoffman-Plotkin, D., and Twentyman, C.T.: *Cognitive and Behavioral Characteristics of Abused and Neglected Children*. Paper presented at the Third International Congress on Child Abuse and Neglect, Amsterdam, April 1981.

Justice, B., and Duncan, D.: Physical abuse of children as a public health program. *Public Health Review, 4*:183-200, 1975.

Justice, B., and Justice, R.: *The Abusing Family*. New York, Human Services Press, 1976.

Larrance, D.L., and Twentyman, C.T.: *The Role of Abusive and Normal Mothers' Causal Attributions of Their Children's Behaviors in Understanding Child Abuse Patterns*. Workshop paper presented at the National Conference for Family Violence Researchers, Durham, N.H., July 1981.

Kempe, C.H., and Hopkins, J.: The public health nurse's role in the prevention of child abuse and neglect. *Public Health Currents, 15*:1, 1975.

Kempe, G.H., and Kempe, R.S.; *Child Abuse*. Cambridge, Mass., Harvard University Press, 1978.

Kihlstrom, J.F., and Nasby, W.: Cognitive tasks in clinical assessment: an exercise in applied psychology. In Kendall, P.L., and Hollon, S.D. (Eds.): *Assessment Strategies for Cognitive – Behavioral Interventions*. New York, Academic Press, Inc., 1981.

Meichenbaum, D.H.: Ways of modifying what clients say to themselves: A marriage of behavior therapies and rational – emotive therapy. *Rational Living, 7*:23-27, 1972.

Morris, M.G., and Gould, R.W.: Role reversal: A necessary concept in dealing with the battered child syndrome. In *The Neglected – Battered Child Syndrome*. New York, Child Welfare League of America, 1963.

Plotkin, R., Azar, S.T., Twentyman, C.T., and Perri, M.P.: A critical evaluation of the research methodology employed in the investigation of causative factors in child abuse and neglect. In *Child Abuse and Neglect*. In press.

Sandler, J., VanDercas, L., and Milhoun, M.: Training child abusers in the use of positive reinforcement practices. *Behavior Research and Therapy, 16*:169-175, 1978.

Shorkey, C.T.: Sense of personal wealth, self-esteem and anomia of child abusing mothers and controls. *Journal of Clinical Psychology, 36(3)*:817-820, 1980.

Spinetta, J.J., and Rigler, D.: The child-abusing parent: A psychological review. *Psychological Bulletin, 77*:296-304, 1972.

Spivack, G., Platt, J.J., and Shure, M.B.: *The Problem-Solving Approach to Adjustment*. San Francisco, Jossey-Bass, 1976.

Steele, B.F., and Pollock, C.B.: A psychiatric study of parents who abuse infants and small children. In Helfer, R., and Kempe, L. (Eds.): *The Battered Child.* Chicago, University of Chicago Press, 1968.

Steele, B.F., and Pollock, C.B.: A psychiatric study of parents who abuse infants and small children. In Helfer, R., and Kempe, C. (Eds.): *The Battered Child*, 2nd Ed. Chicago, University of Chicago Press, 1974.

Sweitzer, M., and Boyd, A.: *Parent Performance Checklist: A Behavioral Assessment of Parent Skills.* Unpublished manuscript, Florida Mental Health Institute, 1979.

Twentyman, C.T., and Plotkin, R.: Unrealistic expectations of parents who maltreat their children: An educational deficit pertaining to child development. *Journal of Clinical Psychology*, in press.

Twentyman, C.T., Plotkin, R., Dodge, D., and Rohrbeck, C.A.: *Development and Cross-validation of an Unrealistic Expectations Questionnaire for Parents Who Maltreat Their Children.* Presented at the annual meeting for the Association for the Advancement of Behavior Therapy, Toronto, Canada, November 1951.

Wasserman, S.: The abused parent of the abused child. *Children, 4*:175-179, 1967.

Wolfe, D.A., and Sandler, J.: Training abusive parents in effective child management. *Behavior Modification, 5*:135-148, 1981.

Wolfe, D.A., Aragona, J., Kaufman, K., and Sandler, J.: The importance of education in the treatment of child abusers: Some preliminary findings. *Child Abuse and Neglect, 4*:127-135, 1980.

Wolfe, D.A., Kaufman, K., Aragona, J., and Sandler, J.: *The Child Management Program for Abusive Parents: Procedures for Developing a Child Abuse Intervention Program.* Winter Park, Fla., Anna Publishing Co., Inc., 1981.

Wolfe, D.A., Sandler, J., and Kaufman, K., *A Competency-based Parent Training Program for Abusive Parents*. In press.

Chapter 7

THERAPY WITH VIOLENT FAMILIES

RODNEY J. SHAPIRO

VIOLENCE in contemporary society is a growing concern of Americans, and more recently, the public is recognizing that violence between family members is far more common than between nonrelated persons. A number of investigations have disclosed an alarming degree of marital violence and child abuse in American family life (Saunders, 1977; Straus et al., 1980; Rosenbaum and O'Leary, 1981). Despite the widespread occurrence and seriousness of family violence, few assessment and treatment strategies have been developed by clinicians (Barnhill, 1980). Family therapists have only recently begun to attend to problems of family violence. This chapter presents family therapy as a process for better understanding and treating problems of violence between family members.

Family therapy strategies for the assessment and treatment of family violence were developed by the author over a period of several years of work with violent families at the Family and Marriage Clinic in Rochester, New York, that offers treatment for families and couples seeking help for a wide array of disorders. Most cases at the clinic presented with marital difficulties or problems with children, particularly adolescents. Referrals come from a variety of sources including inpatient and outpatient services, community mental health agencies, schools, physicians, and self-referrals. Some form of violence was evident in approximately

20 percent of families seen. Wife beating was involved in almost all of these cases, with child abuse as the next most frequent problem. Violence against parents was infrequent, though this may have been partly a function of the type of population, which mostly included marital partners or parents with younger children. Serious violence between siblings was rarely cited as a problem, although physical attacks between siblings were quite common in families experiencing spouse or child abuse.

The Family and Marriage Clinic provides training in family therapy for staff and trainees at different levels of experience. The educational format facilitated the gathering of detailed data and clinical impressions. Colleagues and trainees collaborated in sharing information on all cases involving violence.* Like most family therapy programs, this program emphasizes the use of live observation and videotape, which allowed monitoring of the family treatment process in vivo. As experience was gained, an overall treatment approach evolved, and specific strategies were developed that seemed best suited to particular types of problems in work with violent families.

DIMENSIONS OF THE PROBLEM

Definition of Family Violence

For purposes of this chapter, the following sociological definition of family violence will be used: Family violence comprises those acts that result in, or are likely to result in, physical injury (Straus, 1980). In their research, Straus and his colleagues define a family as violent if at least one such act occurred within the year. They also identify *acts of minor violence* as those with the least potential for causing serious injury, for example, pushing, shoving, slapping, and throwing things. Minor violence is distinguished from *acts of severe violence*, which are those with a high likelihood of causing serious injury, such as kicking, biting, punching, hitting with an object, "beating up," and attacking with a knife or gun.

Families seen in the Family and Marriage Clinic were rarely pre-

*Particular thanks go to Doreen Smethurst, M.S.W., Elta Green, M.S.W., and Ralph Gallope, Ph.D.

cise in reporting frequency of violence, and it was not always possible to ascertain the exact incidence of *minor* versus *severe* episodes of violence. These families were understandably defensive and vague or uncertain about such details. Nevertheless, sufficient information was forthcoming to conclude that all of the families designated as violent had experienced at least one act of severe violence within the past year.

The definition of violence as a physical act is operationally sound, but it belies the fact that family violence is an extremely complex phenomenon. Any therapist who works with families becomes privy to numerous acts of nonphysical violence. Expressions of hatred, ridicule, or contempt, particularly if inflicted on children from an early age, can have as much destructive potential as most acts of physical abuse. Hostility does not necessarily require the medium of physical force to find its mark and take its toll. A comprehensive exploration of violence must take account of these nonphysical interpersonal behaviors. For this chapter, it seems prudent to confine the definition to the narrow but unambiguous definition of violence as a physical action. Once providers of human services achieve some fundamental understanding of physical violence, they may be able to investigate other more complex and intangible modes of destructive human interaction.

CONTRIBUTING FACTORS

Sociological Factors

The primary causes of violence are uncertain. Controversy rages as to the relative significance of genetic and environmental determinants, and these are matters best left to academic debate and future research. However, some variables are known to be associated with the incidence and expression of violence, and these have relevance to clinical understanding. The therapist must take these factors into account to ensure adequate understanding and to determine appropriate methods of intervention. Cultural norms play a complicated role in permitting or discouraging the expression of violence. Economic and occupational factors are also implicated (Lystad, 1975; Straus, 1977). Familiarity with sociological studies of family violence can be helpful to the clinician (Steinmetz et al., 1974; Straus, 1974; Straus et al., 1980). Exploring traditional norms, values, and socioeconomic circumstances can shed light on how and why violence may occur in a particular family.

The Perpetrator and Victim as Factors

Evaluation of the antecedent variables of violence must include a diagnostic assessment of each individual member of the family, particularly the perpetrator and victim of violence. A propensity for violence of the perpetrator may be associated with individual psychopathology and personality characteristics (Spinetta and Rigler, 1972; Pinderhughes, 1972). Neurological abnormalities may diminish judgment and impulse control (Elliott, 1976), and there is a strong link between substance abuse and violent behavior (Roy, 1977). Substance abuse and alcoholism may require additional interventions, but family therapy is particularly appropriate for these problems, too (Shapiro, 1977). Most violent individuals and victims have learned to rely on physical force as an effective means for stress reduction and problem solving. Invariably, their own family of origin provided "a training ground for violence" (Straus, 1977). Children who survive violent families often equate love with violence and are at risk for both perpetrating violence or assuming a victim role. For example, Gelles (1976) reports that women who experience violence as children from their parents stay in abusive situations as adults.

The role of the victim is frequently significant in determining whether or not violence occurs. Walker (1978) emphasizes that the victim role is a result of socially learned behavior characterized by a conviction of helplessness. Individuals who tend to assume a victim role have learned from experience that they cannot control events in their lives. They are more prone to passively submit to violence because they perceive the event as uncontrollable (Seligman, 1975).

The role of the victim has been documented as a critical factor both in wife and child abuse (Walker, 1978). In the case of child abuse, infants with physical and temperamental characteristics are at risk for becoming victims. Unattractiveness, excessive crying, and irritability can prove intolerable to parents, etc., already prone to violence. The abused infant may consequently develop behavioral patterns that actually increase the likelihood of continued abuse

(Bakan, 1971). The individual characteristics of either the violent person or the victim may be missed by the clinician who works with only one patient, or by the family therapist who is exclusively concerned with the relationship dynamics.

Interactional Factors

An assessment of each individual is important but not sufficient. Whatever his or her particular characteristics may be, each family member behaves in ways that are influenced by and exert influence on every other family member. Violence between family members is an expression of interactional behavior. The key to understanding family violence is in understanding the family as an interacting system of relationships (Minuchin, 1981).

AREAS AND TARGETS OF VIOLENCE

At the onset, the clinician can differentiate families according to the areas in which violence is expressed. Three broad categories of family violence can be distinguished: (1) families in which violence is expressed only within the boundaries of the family; (2) families in which violence is expressed outside the family; and (3) families who express violence both inside and outside the family. By far the most common category in the Family and Marriage Clinic were those families that inflicted violence on family members, that is spouse and children, rather than directing violence toward outsiders. The violent individual in these families either did not experience violent impulses toward outsiders or was able to inhibit such impulses. Frequently there was a need to hide the abuse from public view. Secretiveness was strengthened by concern with public opinion and fears of damage to social standing and occupational status. If violence was restricted to persons within the family, the treatment focus of attention was mainly confined to the dynamics operating within the boundary of the family system.

The second category comprised those families in which violence was expressed outside the home, but not between family members. Most of these situations also involved a child or adolescent acting out against peers or authority figures. Although treatment is offered to these families, they are not included in the present study since they do not involve violence between family members.

The third group was families characterized by the expression of violence both within and outside of the family. These families were marked by both marital violence and/or child abuse at home, as well as assaultive behavior, usually by a child or teenager against others. For such cases, we explored the dynamics of violence between family members, but also attended to the broader social system of the family. The relationship of the child with his peers and school environment sometimes revealed stresses that helped account for the violent behavior outside the family boundaries. The attitudes of the parents toward school authorities and other social institutions were important determinants in reinforcing or impeding their children's behavior.

Targets of Violence

Families also differ according to which member is selected as the victim of violence. Specific targets of abuse may be a child, a spouse, a parent, or a combination of these. Each of these situations requires the clarification of some questions preliminary to assessment and intervention. In cases of child abuse, it is important to ascertain whether one child is victimized or whether violence is directed at more than one family member. It is equally important to determine whether one or both parents are involved in child abuse. Even if one parent is the sole aggressor, the role of the other parent is significant. The investigator must bear in mind that the definition of child abuse is broader than other forms of family violence and includes sexual abuse and emotional or physical neglect. The dynamics of child abuse will be considered further in later sections.

When spouse abuse is the dominant form of violence, it is also important to ascertain whether there is a clear and consistent delineation of aggressor and victim. When one spouse is the attacker, it is usually the husband. We rarely saw cases in which a wife was abusing a husband who did not respond. It was common in the Family and Marriage Clinic population, as it is in other studies (Straus, 1978), for wives to physically attack their husbands, but these attacks were usually retaliatory and much less damaging than those perpetrated by the men. Abuse against parents, though rarer than child or spouse abuse, is a serious problem. The aggressor is invariably an adolescent or adult, and often the parents are old and unable to defend themselves. In the cases seen at the clinic, it was noted that one parent in particular was selected as the primary target for attack.

Frequently this would be a parent who had been physically abusive towards the attacker when the latter was a child. In these families, the parent who is not attacked and the siblings play important roles in preventing or encouraging such violence. For most of the families seen, violence was confined to marital and child abuse, and these will be the areas of primary concern in this chapter.

THE THERAPIST ROLE WITH VIOLENT FAMILIES

Most therapists reflect a customary middle-class abhorrence of violence, and personal issues are unavoidable in working with violent patients. Treatment will be uncomfortable and probably unsuccessful if the therapist has not come to terms with his or her own fears and impulses towards violence. Self-awareness is critical in this regard. Consultation and supervision are potential resources for exploring and understanding the subjective reactions of the therapist.

Techniques are clearly important in working with violent families, and these will be elucidated when treatment is discussed, but perhaps even more important than techniques is the ability of the therapist to maintain a stance of impartiality and objectivity. Violence invariably translates into victim and aggressor, right and wrong, good and bad. This dichotomy is engrained in our historical and cultural knowledge of ourselves and our world. To transcend this viewpoint is a difficult task for the therapist, and yet to be fully effective, it is necessary to do so.

Violent families are often polarized into those for or against the aggressor or victim, and they exert pressure on outsiders to join ranks with one or the other faction. Therapy with members of these families inevitably elicits strong countertransference reactions. To see the family through the eyes of any one member is to have a limited perspective. For this reason, traditional individual psychotherapy is unlikely to affect much change because the therapist is impelled into a one-sided view of the situation.

Family therapy is particularly advantageous as an approach to understanding and treating family violence. The conceptualization of behavior as systems determined rather than intrapsychically motivated, and the practice of working with several family members rather than one individual, is more likely to ensure an objective and impartial perspective. Objectivity is no simple matter, however. Experience teaches the family therapist that constant self-monitoring is essential and consultation with colleagues is advisable in working with family violence. Marital violence and child abuse tax the ingenuity of the family therapist and buffer his or her tenuous hold on impartiality. Consideration of these issues can help the therapist anticipate the personal reactions that he or she may be experiencing in working with these couples and families

Therapist Reactions to Spouse Abuse

The common view of wife beating is that of brutality inflicted on a wife by her husband. Cultural norms actually condone wife beating (Straus, 1977; Pagelow, 1976). Clearly there are examples of men who are brutal and intimidate and physically injure their spouses with impunity. Also, it is known that women often are unable to escape from situations in which they are victimized by such men (Gelles, 1976; 1977). However, in the Family and Marriage Clinic cases, all of whom are urban couples but ranging from low socioeconomic to high socioeconomic status, not one couple matched this description. It was found that the wife beating could be best understood as a significant component of interactional behavior sequences between the partners. Translating violence into interactional behavior makes sense because of the staff's adherence to a system's theoretical viewpoint, but this cognitive understanding constantly collided with our deeply held attitudes and values.

The wife and husband each enter the treatment situation with expectations and anticipations that pose immediate problems for the therapist. The wife hopes that she will win some sympathy for her plight and consciously or otherwise seeks an alliance with the therapist against the husband, but reluctance is likely to develop at the first insinuation that she is a participant and not simply as innocent victim in the marital strife. The husband is invariably resistant from the outset. He is the clearly designated villain and fully expects to be blamed. Most of these men unwillingly enter treatment under the duress of legal pressure or fear of losing their wives. The immediate challenge for the therapist is to supportively involve the man without condoning his violent behavior. Issues of resistance are considered in greater detail in the section on clinical interventions.

In work with these couples, the family therapists learned to recognize countertransference reactions as valuble indicators of the marital dynamics. Therapists reported that they initially experienced negative feelings, such as fear, dislike, and disapproval toward the husbands, while feeling concern or pity for the wives. As the first session or two unfolded, a typical shift took place in therapists, irrespective of the therapist's gender, in that the man was perceived more sympathetically and the wife was seen more negatively. This shift coincided with an awareness of interactional behaviors in which the wife's behavior was seen to be as hostile and damaging as that of the husband. However, the bias against the wife also proved to be one-sided. Before the evaluation was completed (usually by the third session), the therapist was able to recognize both the husband and wife as equally culpable and victimized. That is, the husband was no longer seen as a gratuitous victimizer, nor was the wife seen simply as a provacateur. During the course of treatment, the therapist repeatedly experienced an inclination to side with one or the other partner. These shifts tended to coincide with an empathetic awareness of how each viewed the other. The process of identifying with one person provided an intimate glimpse into the "truth" as subjectively experienced by each spouse. As long as the therapist was aware of these identifications with one or the other partner, it remained possible to shift when necessary and maintain a balanced and flexible stance.

Case Example

A couple in their mid-forties was referred to the therapist by a colleague who knew them socially. They had contacted him following an altercation that ended with the husband severely beating the wife. They confided to him that attacks on the wife had occurred periodically over several years, but they had avoided treatment until now. The therapist was rather shocked at this news since he knew the husband as a well-known scholar whose writings reflected deeply felt humanitarian values and ideas. He felt indignant and somewhat critical of what seemed like a hypocritical posture by this man whose public image of sensitivity and thoughtfulness contrasted so dramatically with his private life of violence.

When the couple arrived for their first session, the therapist was surprised. He had expected the husband to be aggressive and imposing, even intimidating. Instead he was extremely anxious, soft spoken, and timid in relation to both his wife and the therapist. He seemed to be a man under great stress. He smoked incessantly and admitted to bouts of heavy drinking. In recent years, his writings had brought him great academic success and national prominence. The pressures of constant productivity and public demands put considerable strain on the coping skills of this normally reticent scholar.

The wife was a physically imposing woman, forceful and aggressive in her movements and verbalizations. She lauded her husband's accomplishments, but feared that he might no longer be interested in her. She was convinced that he was having affairs with other women. She commanded the beginning of the meeting by delightedly reeling off his defects of character. Whenever he talked, she would interrupt with critical statements or accusations. At the onset, she regarded the therapist with condescension, and she reminded him of her husband's brilliance, disclosed that she came from an illustrious family, and made it clear they they currently enjoyed privileges of wealth and fame. In contrast to this arrogant trumpeting, the husband modestly glossed over his accomplishments and seemed uncomfortable with public adulation. I began to see the wife as obnoxious and felt increasing warmth and sympathy for the husband. For much of the first session, their resistance was reflected by the wife's belittlement of therapists and therapy and by the husband's resistive silences and evasiveness. As the meeting progressed, however, I became aware of a change in my perception of this couple. The wife, while continuing to criticize and argue with both the therapist and her husband, relaxed somewhat and modulated her tone to good humor and even affection. The husband, on the other hand, showed a different side as his anxiety abated. He was quietly contemptuous of any ideas or feelings expressed by his wife, and he constantly questioned the therapist's interventions by treating them as mediocre scholarly assertions that could be analyzed and dismissed. By the time of the second session, the therapist had developed a warm regard for the wife but began to feel dislike for the husband.

The pendulum reactions were bewildering and discomforting until the therapist realized that they actually provided helpful clues about the couple. The therapist was experiencing what the husband and wife liked and disliked in each other. It became clear what it was in the wife that enraged the husband and what it was in the husband that enraged the wife. Beyond that, the therapist could also experience what it was that endeared each to the other. The negative behaviors were defensive reactions to each other, as well as to the therapy. They saw the therapist as a potential source of help, but also as an enemy whom they had to keep at bay. At one point during the third meeting, they both admitted to apprehensions that therapy might, to quote the wife, "make things worse." Inquiries brought to light a common fear (which they shared with their grown-up children) that therapy might somehow lead to a separation or divorce. It thus became clear that therapy indeed was perceived as a threat to this family, and once this was acknowledged, it helped the therapist to understand and take distance from their unpleasant defensive reactions. As the sessions progressed, the couple became reassured that the therapist would not take sides or issue judgmental opinions about the violence and other behaviors (such as the husband's drinking or the wife's excessive jealousy and verbal criticisms) and that it would not (as they feared) be suggested that they needed to separate or divorce.

Therapist Reactions to Child Abuse

If personal reactions are likely in treating violent couples, they are inevitable when it comes to working with cases of child abuse. Nothing arouses as much public outrage as news of an adult inflicting harm on a child. It is virtually impossible for a therapist to feel warm and receptive in anticipation of meeting a child abuser referred for treatment. Often that parent makes contact only because evidence of child abuse has surfaced. He or she may be facing legal action, and treatment may be regarded as part of the machinery of indictment. Defensive postures including denial, dishonesty, and withholding are unlikely to endear the patient to the therapist. Conversely it is almost impossible not to feel compassion for the child who is abused. The younger the child, the more graphic the scenario of a defenseless and innocent victim at the mercy of a cruel and sadistic bully appears.

Therefore, at first contact, it is to be expected that the therapist will feel negatively towards the assaultive adult and sympathetically towards the child. To pretend otherwise and effect friendliness and acceptance of the abuser would not even impress the family, since they would readily recognize it as feigned and inappropriate. A more reasonble and appropriate stance for the therapist is likely if the initially disparate feelings aroused in him or her are accepted and tempered by the knowledge that a fair and neutral understanding of the case may modify these initial reactions.

Experience in family therapy at the Family and Marriage Clinic has shown that familiarity with the family may result in increased acceptance of the abuser without diminishing the concern felt for the child. The abusing parent often experiences himself or herself as helplessly driven by violent impulses towards a child. Recognition of the violence as a problem for the adult can stir empathy in the therapist, particularly if the abuser manifests genuine distress and contrition.

Most clinicians would acknowledge that an adult who is abused may behave in ways that maintain the violent interactions. There is understandable reluctance, though, to consider the child as contributing in any way to the violence. To even suggest as much is akin to blaming the child, and that could make the therapist feel as if he or she is somehow joining in assaulting the child. The problem lies with the implication of blame. If the therapist can translate behavior into interpersonal reactions rather than intentional acts, then the imputation of blame disappears.

The abused child should be closely observed by the therapist for clues as to what may trigger hostility or rage reactions in the parent. The risk of violence towards infants or young children may be dramatically decreased by discovering and (where appropriate) modifying certain behaviors. For example, excessive crying or sleeplessness commonly tax the tolerance of parents and are often cited as triggering events for violent interventions. Some commonsense guidance can provide the parents with skills that ameliorate the child's difficulties and hence avert the consequence of violence.

The parental violence may have nothing to do with what the child does, but rather with what the child is. A parent will often concede that the child gets the brunt of displaced anger or is seen as a source of demands that the parent cannot cope with or even that some physical characteristics are distasteful to the parent. In such cases, the child is an object of the parent's wrath rather than a participant in the interactions leading to violence, and the therapist must contend with a situation in which the adult seems gratuitously violent. It is no easy matter, but it is still essential for the therapist to establish a positive therapeutic relationship that will help that adult understand and moderate the violent and irrational reactions.

In the case of the older child, it is imperative to understand ways in which the child participates in interactions with the family. As mentioned earlier, there is evidence that abused children may inadvertently develop behavioral patterns that continue to evoke violent reactions. The therapist must discover these behaviors so as to modify interactional sequences involving both the child and the adult. Information about the child's behavior can come from parental and sibling reports, school personnel and peers, and direct observation during sessions. While it is obvious that the abusive adult's behavior must be scrutinized, it is less obvious that the child's behavior is often an essential element in the interactions culminating in violence. Overemphasizing the role of the abusive adult and neglecting that of the child is a risk even in family therapy. There is an unfortunate tendency for many family therapists to work with couples rather than with whole families. Reasons for this have been documented elsewhere (Shapiro, 1980). Suffice it to say that the therapist's understanding of the family system is limited if the index child and siblings remain unobserved.

If one parent is not abusive, the relationship with the parents is even more complicated than if both are violent. The therapist may overlook the role of the nonabusive parent by regarding him or her as an innocent bystander, particularly when that parent voices criticisms of the violent spouse. This may engender a discrepant perception of the parents as "good" (nonabusive) and "bad" (abusive), an attitude that is sure to increase the defensiveness of the abusive adult. This trap can be avoided if the therapist realizes that the role of the nonabusive parent is a critical factor in the interactions between the other spouse and the child. Noninvolvement is an illusion. Parents who claim neutrality (whatever their rationalizations) are implicitly permitting the violence. The nonabusive partner may actually encourage the abuse or may incite strife between the spouse and the child.

The parents play the major role in child abuse, but the therapist should not overlook the participation of the siblings of the abused child. Their behaviors may contribute to a lessening or heightening of conflictual interactions. Once the therapist understands the ways in which all family members interact, he or she gains a comprehensive perspective that transcends the temptation to place blame or absolution on any one individual.

Case Example

A couple was referred for therapy because of problems with their eleven-year-old daughter. The couple had two girls, ages eleven and four, both of whom had been adopted two years before. The parents complained that the eleven-year-old was difficult to manage: "lies a lot" and did not get along well with other children. The mother's attitude towards the daughter was decidedly negative. She expressed no affection or warmth towards the child and at one point even admitted to disliking her. It became evident that this woman rarely experienced affection for others, including her husband and younger daughter. She seemed somewhat indifferent to most people, but for some reason intensely disliked the older girl. The husband was an awkward and extremely passive man. He admitted to an awareness of holding back a great deal of rage. He seemed fearful of his wife; this was not surprising since she seemed to treat him with contempt. The children were attractive, bright, quiet, and well behaved. The older girl had a stricken look about her. An initial reaction of the therapist was an inability to like or empathize with the parents and a feeling of warmth and concern for the children.

A dramatic event occurred soon after the sessions began. The parents informed him that they had been reported by the older daughter's schoolteacher for suspected child abuse. The girl had come to school with bruises on her face and that had led to the report. The social service agency had sent an investigator to the family's home, and the parents admitted having struck their daughter. In admitting this incident, both parents seemed shaken, as much by the exposure of their violence as by the act itself. The therapist's regard for them sank to a new low. The daughter did not seem frightened so much as angry, and the therapist identified strongly with her. He was tempted to collaborate with child protective services in seeking placement for this child outside of the home. Fortunately, he resisted making such recommendations and decided to devote some time to getting to know the family better.

At the onset, the therapist stated that further violence was unacceptable. He maintained a matter-of-fact and nonjudgmental tone, which seemed to reassure the couple, and they honored the limit setting. The family was treated over a long term, and the therapist came to know the family very well. The mother had been physically abused as a child and had herself not experienced physical or emotional affection. She felt empty and inadequate as a wife and mother. Intimacy with others was obstructed by deep distrust and hostility. During the course of therapy, the mother formed an extremely positive relationship with the male therapist and learned to relate to her husband and children in a more caring and effective manner. The husband had also been abused as a child, and he needed help in coping with tremendous unresolved rage at his own parents. He was a lonely man, with feelings of inadequacy as a father and husband and in his work. He made good use of therapy and developed a much healthier sense of self-esteem and self-regard.

The older daughter had experienced unusual trauma in her early life. Her natural parents were both alcoholics who physically abused her. She and her sister were generally neglected. At age seven (when her sister was nine months old), both of them had been left alone in the house for a period of four days while their parents went on a drinking binge. They were finally rescued by child protective services and removed from the home and placed into foster care. After a period of two years, they were adopted by the couple. The older girl had learned to survive by growing up fast. At age eleven she had the disposition of a street-wise seventeen-year-old. She was extremely intelligent and perceptive. In her relationship with the adoptive parents, she betrayed a blatantly defiant and contemptuous attitude.

For good reason she was distrusting of others, and she survived by rapidly discerning the weaknesses and harmful intentions of others. Her high intelligence and critical scrutiny were unnerving to this couple. They talked about feeling inadequate when in conflict with this daughter. She stultified any possible affection from them by maintaining a cold and indifferent stance, and she met their criticisms and anger with feigned indifference or devastatingly critical comments. It was a pathetic prospect to see two adults so intimidated by an eleven-year-old. Clearly it was impossible for the child to change the situation; the change had to be initiated by the parents. For this reason, the therapist concentrated on helping the parents feel less defensive and threatened by their daughter.

As they gained more confidence in developing parenting skills and as they learned to understand this child better, the situation improved. Long-term therapy was required to effect lasting changes in this family. However, such therapy may not have occurred had the therapist acted on his initial dislike of the parents. Conversely, he might have focused treatment on the daughter only, and this would have been inefficient and probably unsuccessful. Maintaining the whole family in therapy maximized objectivity and enhanced the efficacy of the intervention.

CLINICAL INTERVENTION

A cardinal issue in dealing with violent families is that of resistance, particularly in the early phase of treatment. The actions of the therapist will largely determine whether or not families become invested or drop out prematurely. This rule holds true for most cases seen in family therapy (Shapiro and Budman, 1973) but is particularly significant in work with the problems of domestic violence. The successful involvement of all the pertinent family members makes possible a thorough evaluation of the problems and the formulation of appropriate treatment strategies.

Violence as Presenting or Emergent Problem

Most studies of domestic violence are based on persons making contact either as a volunteer or under compulsion with agencies or treatment facilities because of problems of violence. An interesting aspect of the clinic population is that a number of families did not present with violence as one of their problems. These families came to the clinic for any number of reasons, and it was only in the course of treatment that violence emerged as one of the issues. Some of these families chose not to disclose the violence simply because it was experienced as syntonic and therefore not worthy of mention. Comments such as, "Of course I hit my son with a belt when he misbehaves," or, "Yes, he hits me, but it's only when he is jealous," were typical in these cases. The challenge for the therapist was to make this behavior take on a dystonic connotation in the family; otherwise, there was little incentive to change. This sometimes requires educational emphasis such as actually teaching people that they do not "deserve" abuse or that discipline is more effective without physical punishment.

Invariably there was some disagreement between family members concerning the violence, and the therapist could tap such conflict to encourage change from within. For other families where violence emerged later as a problem, it was clear that fear of retribution or feelings of disloyalty delayed such disclosures.

The actual status of violence at the point of contact with the therapist is a critical factor in deciding on an appropriate intervention. If a family presents because of a current violent episode, then crisis intervention may be necessary. Immediate steps must be taken to bring in the family or couple. The violence must be addressed as the primary difficulty requiring immediate resolution, and this might necessitate actual separation of a family member from the home or home visits and frequent contacts until the crisis passes. Therapists must even be alert to the possibility of violent eruptions in their waiting rooms or offices, and clearly some training in active intervention with violent individuals is imperative. The principles for such crisis intervention are relatively simple and clear-cut (Barnhill, 1980), but they do require practice and appropriate resources. When there is no immediate threat of violence, or after the crisis has passed, a more thorough evaluation and treatment procedures can be implemented.

Issues of Resistance

A good deal of the groundwork can be laid during telephone contact with the family prior to the first meeting. Families usually telephone for an initial appointment, and it facilitates the work of the therapist if he or she handles the contact from the first call. This was a policy followed for all cases at our clinic. A brief telephone interview can clarify the presenting problem, indicate which family members are involved, and furnish relevant information about the family. Given such information, it is easy for the therapist to determine who should attend the first session. The therapist should make a point of speaking with both parents, and when appropriate, with any children who are implicated. This gives the therapist an opportunity to convey concern and impartiality even before the family is seen, and this may significantly reduce the initial resistance.

As noted earlier, it is the offender who is likely to be the most resistant participant to begin with. He or she is already identified as the wrongdoer, and contacting a therapist may be construed as part of the process of labeling and blame. An immediate task for the therapist is to establish positive contact with that person. The violent individual is understandably resistant. What may not be appreciated, though, is that the victims are also resistant. The most obvious fear is that of retribution following meetings in which the violent individual felt threatened or offended. The therapist must bring such concerns into the open and establish credible rules permitting open discussion and prohibiting retaliation. More complicated forms of resistance stem from ties of loyalty.

Accusing a spouse or parent in front of the therapist is akin to an act of betrayal in families. If disclosure or discovery of violence results in legal intervention, the victim may be regarded as a fifth columnist. Family members are usually torn between discomfort with the violence in their midst and the need to preserve unity. This dilemma may not be apparent to representatives of legal and social agencies. To an outside observer, the situation may simply be that one person has done something reprehensible to another person—a simple matter of right and wrong. For the family, though, it is far more complicated. In the Family and Marriage Clinic experience, there has not been an instance when all members of a family concurred in a rejection of the violent individual. Some more than others are able to separate what the person does from what the person is; for example, a wife explained that "sometimes he loses his temper, but he's a good husband and father." Negative feelings may be modified by explanations of extenuating circumstances: "His drinking makes him violent," or "If she didn't nag him he wouldn't hit her." More often than not the family is divided into those who are somewhat sympathetic versus those who are rejecting of the violent member, but these differences may be concealed from outsiders.

For many victims of abuse, a sense of their own wrongdoing can be an obstacle in treatment. An assumption of guilt in the victim may erode his or her motivation for change. These assumptions may be unspoken, and even out of consciousness. Children who are targets of sexual or physical abuse are particularly susceptible in this regard. If they confuse their own sexual stirrings with feelings of affection for the offending parent, then it is difficult for them to not feel culpable. If their behavior is difficult or provocative, then a cause and effect link is established between that behavior and the consequences (abuse becomes "punishment"). Even if the child does not know why he or she is targeted for abuse, it is likely that reasons will be invented. Sympathetic interviewing of the child can bring such fantasies to light.

The adult victim is also prone to self-blame. In the course of therapy, the abused spouse will readily reveal that he or she may in some way be to blame for the violence. Most of the abused wives in this study admitted to feelings of "deserving" their husband's wrath. This admission of guilt is usually tied to some awareness of their own hostility towards the husband. Inquiries usually elicited references to being overly critical, or demanding, or sexually withholding. Not surprisingly, the proclivity for assuming blame by victims is often encouraged by the offender in order to lessen his or her guilt, and a vicious cycle is thus maintained. An early goal of treatment that is even possible to initiate during the evaluation phase is to counter the tendency for assumption of blame by any family member. The therapist may be the first person to ever present this perspective, since violence is generally viewed as polarity of right and wrong.

Involvement of Family Members

An accurate and thorough evaluation of family violence is best assured by seeing the whole family together. This is particularly important in cases of child abuse and is advisable in cases of marital violence. Sometimes it is best to start with the couple first and involve the children at a later point. Even when the violence is confined to marital discord, the children play complicated roles in the relationship between the parents.

Sometimes the role of the child may unwittingly reinforce the violence. An example is the child who behaves provocatively when one parent is abusing the other parent. This child is sacrificing himself or herself by drawing attention away from the parent-victim. Another example is the child who adopts the role of mediator between the parents or champion defender of one of the parents. The child may either exacerbate the anger of the violent parent, or else the parents learn to rely on the child to mediate, thus neutralizing their own motivation for dealing with the situation.

While it may make sense to meet with the couple only for a while, it is inadvisable to meet with either spouse alone. This is the exception rather than the rule in most clinical settings, where only one partner is usually seen or where they are seen separately. The conviction that it is not advisable to meet with the spouses separately comes from considerable experience in working with violent families. The couples in the study invariably adopted defensive and blaming stances towards each other, and their relationships with others including their children were strongly motivated by manipulative efforts to win allies. The therapist places himself or herself in a precarious position by meeting with only one spouse. Even if the therapist can resist being drawn into an alliance with that person, he or she may be encumbered with unwelcome information in the form of secrets that can jeopardize further work with the family. Common examples include confidences about affairs, secret plans for marital separation, and unpleasant "facts" about the other spouse that he or she would never admit. The very fact of meeting with one partner pushes the absent partner into a defensive posture, since he or she knows that the spouse is likely to paint a one-sided picture. Frequently there is pressure from one partner wishing to be seen alone, but in the experience of the clinic therapists, the therapists' insistence on meeting only with both at the same time is eventually accepted with equanimity as the couple recognizes the therapist's intention of maintaining impartiality.

However, one exception obtains in ruling against separate sessions. A child may need to be seen separately for a while if he or she is fearful of opening up because of retribution for speaking openly with the parents present. Sometimes the child's fears are well grounded. The young child who has been sexually abused or severely beaten is in particular need of support and reassurance, and this may require several private meetings with the therapist. Again, the therapist must be aware of the family's inclination to operate on the basis of adversarial relationships. It may be important to reassure the parents that the child should have opportunities to talk privately with the therapist, but that the therapist will keep an open mind and not take sides.

Structuring the Treatment

Several meetings with the family may be required in order to gain a clear understanding of the violence, but the evaluation seldom needs to be extended beyond two or three meetings. If further treatment is indicated, a clear-cut contract should be established with the family. This is particularly important with a violent family. They characteristically act out impulses and have difficulty in adhering to the discipline of fixed meeting times and appropriate verbalization of their problems. The therapist must take charge from the outset of the structure and process of treatment. This increases the feeling of safety of the family (the therapist demonstrates benign power), and it reduces the risk of the therapist being manipulated by the family. Issues such as duration of therapy, meeting times, fees, and membership at sessions should all be spelled out clearly and agreed to. Rules relating to the violence itself (such as no physical violence being permitted during sessions and agreement to prohibit violence at home) may be necessary. An immediate cessation of violence is crucial. Treatment strategies can then be developed to ensure that violence is no longer called for when conflictual situations arise.

Treatment Goals

We have touched on some of the objectives in working with violent families. The most important short-term goals for the therapist are the involvement of family members and the immediate cessation of violence. The therapist must make contact with all family members and involve them in order to arrive at an accurate and thorough evaluation of the family and its problems and also to formulate the most effective treatment contract. As we have seen, the therapist has to recognize and skillfully counter the resistances and effect positive working alliances with the family members. The therapist must also insist that violence cease as soon as he or she has contact with the family. Mention has been made of crisis intervention, techniques to ensure that the violence stops, and the explication of rules as an advisable measure for discouraging further violence.

If the therapist believes that there is still a likelihood of violence, he or she might introduce an agreement with the family whereby a clearly understood negative consequence would follow any violent act. In our experience an excellent consequence involves one partner having to leave the home for a period of time should violence occur or be threatened. The effectiveness of this strategy has been corroborated in discussions with other colleagues who have used it. At the Family and Marriage Center, the therapists established an understanding with the family that a particular person would leave the home for a fixed period of time (usually at least two days), and arrangements had to be made for an appropriate place to be used in such an event. In cases of spouse abuse, we helped the couple decide which of them would leave or be required to leave. In cases of child abuse, the abusive parent was the one who had to leave. The implementation of a separation consequence seems to work well for two reasons. First, the therapist assumes responsibiliity for the suggestion so that it is not seen as a threat or ultimatum made by one family member. Second, this particular consequence touches on an issue of particular significance. The couples in the clinic population seemed unusually dependent in their relationship with each other. Any type of separation was threatening, and so the consequence of being separated for a period of time carried great weight. It must be appreciated that these interventions are stopgap measures that are sometimes sufficient to resolve a crisis or even resolve difficulties in a family where violence has only become a recent phenomenon. However, most families in which violence occurs have long-standing difficulties, and an adequate period of therapy is required in order to effect any long term changes. In the clinic, the most violent families required at least six therapy sessions, with most of the families being seen for periods ranging from two to five months.

Long-term goals involved the modification of the family system itself. Only by altering the interactional patterns within the family could enduring changes be achieved, including the permanent extinction of violence. In order to learn the interactional sequences for each family, the therapist obtained detailed reports from family members about significant incidents that occurred at home and also carefully observed the enactments of important interactions during the sessions. The interactions of most significance obviously concerned those in which anger was generated, particularly when it seemed likely to escalate into violence. By carefully observing and monitoring the complex interactions, the therapists were able to discover what incidents seemed likely to trigger violent reactions, and we could note what reactions seemed to heighten or diminish the anger of the persons concerned. It became clear that these families had extremely inefficient patterns of communication. When emotions were running high, members of these families simply did not hear each other. More often than not they spoke simultaneously or allowed themselves no time to consider the import of statements made to them. Communications were generally defensive. The families showed an extraordinary inability to use communication for problem solving. Consequently, much of the therapeutic emphasis was on restructuring the interactional sequences through intervention at the level of communication. In most cases we literally had to train members of these families in more effective forms of communication.

Other long-term goals for therapy seemed applicable to those violent families. The structure of these family systems tended to extremes, as reflected in the boundaries between parents and children being either too unyielding or too permeable (Minuchin, 1974). In the former case, the disengagement between the parents and children made for extreme difficulty in creating the cooperation and empathy necessary for change. In families with weak boundaries the children, or a particular child, was usually overly involved in an alliance with one parent against the other parent. The treatment goal was to neutralize the child-parent tie by replacing it with the more appropriate marital dyad.

Many of the parents treated came from homes in which they themselves had been abused as children. During the course of therapy, it became important to resolve difficulties that were generated in their families of origin that seemed to be perpetuated in their current family situations. On occasion this was effected directly by involving members of the family of origin in treatment sessions.

It is characteristic of abusive parents and their partners that they struggle with feelings of inadequacy and poor self-esteem. A positive relationship with the therapist often provided a corrective experience for these parents. Many of them had never known a significant relationship with someone consistent, warm, and accepting. Once they overcame their initial resistance, these couples were able to maintain ongoing contact with the therapist and incorporate healthy aspects of that relationship. With the help of the therapist, these adults were often able to gain increased self-confidence, establish appropriate means of gratification, and learn to communicate effectively with each other. In concert with these changes, the incidence of interactions leading to violence was dramatically diminished and replaced by more appropriate methods of resolving conflict.

REFERENCES

Bakan, D.: *Slaughter of the Innocents*. San Francisco, Jossey-Bass, 1971.

Barnhill, L.R.: Clinical assessment of intrafamilial violence. *Hospital and Community Psychiatry, 31*:543-546, 1980.

Elliott, F.A.: Neurological factors in violent behavior (the dyscontrol syndrome). *Bulletin of the American Academy of Psychiatry and the Law, 4*:297-315, 1976.

Gelles, R.: Abused wives: Why do they stay? *Journal of Marriage and Family, 38*:659-668, 1976.

Gelles, R.: no place to go. The social dynamics of marital violence. In Roy, M. (Ed.): *Battered Women: A Psychological Study*, New York, Van Nostrand Reinhold Co., 1977.

Harbin, H.T.: Episodic dyscontrol and family dynamics. *American Journal of Psychiatry, 134*:111-116, 1977.

Lystad, M.H.: Violence at home: A review of the literature. *American Journal of Orthopsychiatry, 45*:328-345, 1975.

Minuchin, S.: *Families and Family Therapy*. Cambridge, Mass., Harvard University Press, 1974.

Minuchin, S., and Fishman, H.C.: *Family Therapy Techniques*. Cambridge, Mass., Harvard University Press, 1981.

Pagelow, M.: *Preliminary Report on Battered Women*. Paper presented at Second Annual Symposium on Victimology. Boston, September 1976.

Pinderhughes, C.: Managing paranoia in violent relationships. In Usdin, G. (Ed.): *Perspectives on Violence*. New York, Brunner/Mazel, 1972.

Rosenbaum, A., and O'Leary, K.D.: Marital violence: Characteristics of abusive couples. *Journal of Consulting and Clinical Psychology, 49*: 63-71, 1981.

Roy, M. (Ed.): *Battered Women: A Psychosociological Study of Domestic Violence*. New York, Van Nostrand Reinhold Co., 1977.

Saunders, D.G.: Marital violence: Dimensions of the problem and modes of intervention: *Journal of Marriage and Family Counseling*, 1977, pp. 43-52.

Segal, J.: Child abuse: A review of research. *In Families Today*, NIMH Science Monograph, Vol., I. Washington, D.C., National Institute of Mental

Health, 1979.

Shapiro, R.J.: A family therapy approach to alcoholism. *Journal of Marriage and Family Counseling, 3*:71-78, 1977.

Shapiro, R.J. and Budman, S.HJ.: Defection, termination, and continuation in family and individual therapy. *Family Process, 12*:55-67, 1973.

Spinetta, J., and Rigler, D.: The child-abusing parent: A psychological review. *Psychological Bulletin, 77*:296-304, 1972.

Steinmetz, S.K., and Straus, M.A. (Eds.): *Violence in the Family*. New York, Harper and Row, 1974.

Straus, M.A.: A sociological perspective on the prevention and treatment of wifebeating. In Roy, M. (Ed.): *Battered Women: A Psychosociological Study of Domestic Violence*. New York, Van Nostrand Reinhold Co., 1977.

Straus, M.: Victims and aggressors in marital violence. *American Behavioral Scientific, 23*:681-704, 1980.

Straus, M.A., Gelles, R.J., and Steinmetz, S.K.: *Behind Closed Doors: Violence in the American Family*. New York, Doubleday/Anchor, 1980.

Symonds, M.: The psychodynamics of violence-prone marriages. *American Journal of Psychoanalysis, 38*:213-222, 1978.

Walker, L.: *Battered Women and Learned Helplessness*. Victimology, 1978.

Chapter 8

FAMILY VIOLENCE TOWARD ELDERS*

SUZANNE K. STEINMETZ

WHEN problems of elder abuse are discussed, there is a tendency to suggest that in the past the family provided love, support, and care to their aging family members that are not provided in current American society. This assumed lack of caring is seen as an indication of the decline of the family. Therefore it is important to put the problem of elder abuse in a proper historical perspective. In the past, families were not confronted with a similar experience.

The three-generational family that is idealized in the television series "The Waltons" was for the most part not the prevailing pattern of family residents. Those who moved west in earlier times were the young and the healthy; the elderly stayed at home.

Today, for the first time in history, there is a larger number of dependent elderly who rely on their kin for prolonged physical, emotional, and financial aid. Aging children and their parents are faced with this emerging family form without historical precedents or role models for dealing with these dependent, and often disabled, family members. Abuse of the elderly is a result of more complex factors than simply the decline of the family.

This chapter will explore the physical, social, economic, and

*The author expresses appreciation to Marge Murvine, Nancy Pegan, Joan Simpson, and Cathy Sullivan for their assistance in technical editing, chapter preparation, and editorial comments.

emotional factors that contribute to the phenomena of (1) increased elders living with their children, (2) increasing incidence of violence against elders by their children, and (3) intervening in this serious family situation.

SOCIAL AND ECONOMIC FACTORS CONTRIBUTING TO ELDER ABUSE

INCREASING DEPENDENT ELDERLY POPULATION. The advent of antibiotics in the early 1940s and major medical, public health, and nutrition advances in the 1950s resulted in a greater number of people reaching the vulnerable age of seventy-five years or older. Although these health advances have helped more people survive illness and epidemics, many of the surviving elderly are left with varying degrees of physical disability and chronic diseases resulting from heart attacks, strokes, arthritis, diabetes, and cancer. Therefore, the current elder population is larger in numbers and more physically incapacitated than the previous "older" generations.

The last quarter of the twentieth century can best be described by its shifting age structure. Not only will one out of every five persons be sixty-five or older by the close of this century, but the greatest increase will be among the very oldest citizens. Between 1960 and 1970, those citizens seventy-five years and older increased at three times the rate of those in the sixty-five to seventy age-group. Between 1970 and 1976 the population between forty and sixty-four years old increased just under 2 percent. However, those eighty-five years and older increased by nearly 40 percent (U.S. Bureau of Census, 1977). During the last quarter of this century, people under sixty-five will increase by 21 percent; those between sixty-five and seventy-five by 23 percent; and those seventy-five years and older by 60 percent. It is this last group, those seventy-five and older, who are the most vulnerable to physical, mental, and financial crisis requiring the care of their family and society (Brody, 1978).

The trend towards increased numbers of elderly living longer has been well documented (Brody, 1978; Busse, 1977; Clark and Spengler, 1978; Samuelson, 1978; Tobin, 1978). A sizable number of persons over sixty-five years old have one living parent or more than one. Furthermore, about one in ten older persons are parents of a child over sixty-five (Butler and Lewis, 1977; Townsend, 1968).

About one-half of all persons over sixty-five who have living children are members of a four-generational family. This is the century, not only of old age, but of multigenerational families, often several generations of near elderly, elderly, and frail elderly women. Townsend's (1966) prediction that the family of the future could conceivably include a generation of frail elderly has become a reality.

Table 8-I

Shifts in Increases to Older Age Groups 1960-1976, Projections 1976-2000

Years	Ages	Increases
1960 – 1970	75 +	3 × rate of 65 to 75
1970 – 1976	40 – 64	2%
1970 – 1976	85 +	40%
1976 – 2000 (projected)	65	21%
	65 – 75	23%
	75	60%

DECREASING YOUNGER POPULATION. Another demographic factor that contributes to the vulnerability of elders is the decreasing size of the younger generation. While the aging population is growing, fewer younger kin will be available to provide support for their elders (Treas, 1977).

The birth rate is declining, and while women are marrying at a younger age, they are having fewer children and often putting off childbirth until later in life; thus, there will be fewer members of the younger generation (Brody, 1978; Treas, 1977). Declining birth rates restrict the older generation's access to younger kin, which they may count on for assistance (Treas, 1977).

In addition to the declining birth rates, later marriages restrict and narrow the average span of years between generations. Thus, we find families in which there are several members still living into advanced age while there are relatively few members of the child and grandchild generations available to provide assistance.

INCREASED LONGEVITY BEYOND PRODUCTIVITY. Another condition that contributes to the elder problem and increases the risk for abuse is that elders are living long beyond their economically productive years. Economically productive is defined as maintaining full-time employment. Even with the extension of the mandatory retirement age from sixty-five to seventy, increasing numbers of people now face a decade or more of lower fixed incomes. This means that more American elders will live longer with less income and without the status that comes with the identity of a work role. Therefore, this growing retired population has less status, power, and prestige that is associated with the economically productive member of society.

These losses often cause elders to try to use force or manipulate family members who have power over them and therefore contribute to their own abuse. (Steinmetz, 1980; 1981).

GENERATIONAL INVERSION. Generationally inverted families in which the elderly parent is dependent on the child generation for emotional, financial, physical, or mental support are no longer unique. They are increasing as a result of greater longevity and increasing numbers of physically and financially dependent elders. In these families it is not just role reversal, but the entire set of generationally linked rights, responsibilities, and obligations which is reversed (Steinmetz, 1979).

Today it is not uncommon for one or two brothers or sisters to bear the responsibility for four or five family members over seventy-five years of age who are no longer able to live independently. The existence of multiple generations featuring generationally inverse families is a growing phenomena, and the impact of "parent caring" on the middle-aged offspring is acknowledged (Silverstone and Hyman, 1976; Shanas, 1979; Archbold, 1980). The question of who takes care of the caretakers when the caretakers need taking care of needs to be raised. The impact of elder dependence on children over extended periods needs to be considered.

While extending the life expectancy has been a focus of biomedical research, the issue of quality of life has been minimally addressed. The problems created by increased longevity are not confined to the elderly, but encompass the whole family life cycle.

Middle-aged children often are unable to cope with problems arising from within their own nuclear families (Kirschner, 1979; Silverstone and Hyman, 1976). The additional burden of shouldering a parent's problems becomes a tipping point with the potential for abuse and neglect (Rathbone-McCuan, 1978; Steinmetz, 1978; 1980; 1981).

The change in the role of the child from being cared for to that of caretaker may build feelings of resentment and misapprehension in both generations (Hooker, 1976; Knopf, 1975; Silverstone and Hyman, 1976). Feelings of love and respect easily can turn into guilt, hatred, and disappointment as children attempt to function in their new roles of care giver (Cohen and Gans, 1978; Knopf, 1975). Unresolved conflict between parents and adolescent-age children often continues throughout the life cycle (Boszormenyi-Nagy and Spark, 1973; Brody, 1966), with the result that contact may remain at the level of obligatory vacation or holiday visits during the child's adulthood. In such unresolved conflicts it is unlikely the child will shoulder the responsibility of caring for an elderly parent with open arms and a warm heart. Consequently the motivation to care for the older kin may not only be out of love and concern but also out of a sense of responsibility, duty, or guilt.

When the child generation is responsible for two or more older kin, the pressures and strains, which vary with the degree of dependency needs of the elderly persons, can be severe. This problem is further intensified because the caretaker is often elderly. Thus the elderly caretaker in addition to preparing for his own retirement on a fixed income and facing increasing health problems must often bear the heavy responsibility of caring for a still older parent or kin.

STRESSES THAT CONTRIBUTE TO ELDER ABUSE. There are a number of stresses that seem to be related to conflict and violence in generationally inversed families. As the economic, physical, social, and emotional dependency needs of the vulnerable elderly increase, the potential for abuse increases unless adequate resources are available (Blenkner, 1965; 1969). Economic dependency with the loss of economic power produces loss of control, self-esteem, and prestige for the elderly person as well as an economic drain and conflict over competing goals for the utilization of limited resources within the caretaking family (Steinmetz, 1980).

Physical dependency also becomes a problem for the caretaker (Knopf, 1975). Physical deterioration may be evident through loss of hearing, failing vision, or decreased strength (Hooker, 1976; Knopf, 1975). Severe or chronic illness, which often accompanies aging, places additional burdens on the caretaking family. Medical costs frequently are not compensated or at best may be undercompensated by public and private health insurance. Medical costs, therefore, compete with other expenses (such as children's education, weddings, or providing for their own retirement) incurred by the caretaking family.

Social, psychological, and emotional dependencies must also be negotiated. Foulke (1980) found that physical dependencies were easier for caretakers to deal with and produced less stress than did social-emotional dependencies. Most often it was the decision making associated with emotional dependencies that was stressful for care givers. The increased amount of personal time needed to care for a dependent elder often totally absorbs any time available to fulfill one's own needs. Furthermore, any attempt to reserve personal time is likely to be viewed by the elderly kin as an indication that the care giver is rejecting him or her.

Control over one's environment and lack of privacy pose additional potential conflicts for both generations (Foulke, 1980). To have a smooth running home, one assumes that all members must function interdependently. Yet, it is often difficult for an older person who has been transplanted from his or her home to find an appropriate role in the new setting. Since this problem is predominantly faced by women (Brody, 1979; Hess, 1979; Morgan, 1969), it takes on an additional dimension: rivalry between mother and daughter over appropriate ways to manage households, husbands, and children (Farrar, 1955; Johnson, 1978).

RESEARCH DESCRIBING THE EXTENT OF THE PROBLEM. Abusers research has shown that the most frequent abusers of the elderly are family members (Block, 1979; Douglas, 1979; Steinmetz, 1978; 1980). Thirteen percent of the service providers who responded to a mail survey reported abuse; however, 88 percent were aware of the problem of the elder abuse, even if they had no cases to report (Block, 1979). Seventeen percent of respondents from a mail survey of professionals reported physical abuse of an elder, and 44 percent reported verbal-emotional abuse (Douglas, Hickey and Noel, 1980).

A mail survey, sent to over 1,000 medical people, social service professionals, and paraprofessionals, was conducted by the Legal

Research and Services for the Elderly in Boston, Massachusetts (O'Malley et al., 1979). These researchers note that although 183 reports of elder abuse were received, it is possible that different professionals were reporting the same case. They found that in 70 percent of the reports, the abuse occurred at least twice; in 75 percent of the reports, the victim lived with the abuser; and in over 80 percent of the reports, the abuser was a relative. These researchers suggested that abuse, like charity, begins at home. Nearly three-fourths were experiencing some form of stress, such as alcoholism, drug addiction, medical problems, or long-term financial problems. However, it was also noted that the elderly victim was a source of stress to the abuser primarily because of the physical and emotional or financial care required. Most studies found that although abuse occurred in all age-groups, it tended to be concentrated among elders seventy-five years or older. Furthermore, a greater proportion of the victims were women (80 percent in the O'Malley 1979 study). Therefore, it may be the elders' frailty, like that of an infant, that results in abuse acts producing visible, serious injury.

VICTIMS OF ABUSE. Family Services Association of greater Lawrence, Massachusetts, also collected data through a specialized program funded by Title III under the Older American Act. During a twelve-month period (March 1, 1978 – February 28, 1979), eighty-two cases were referred to this project. Client's ages ranged from sixty to ninety years old, with about half between eighty and ninety-nine years of age. In one three-month period, December 1978 until February 1979, fifty cases were handled. Of these, eight were suspected of abuse by a family member, four were suspected of being physically abused by a nonrelative, and three were referred for possible neglect by a family member who was caring for the physically dependent elder. However, a follow-up of these cases revealed that twenty-one elders were experiencing harm or were seriously threatened with harm by the actions of individuals upon whom they were dependent (Langdon, 1979).

During a single year, in 1978, Baltimore City Police Department reported 149 assaults against individuals sixty years or older. Nearly two-thirds of these assaults (62.7 percent) were committed by relatives other than spouses (Block, 1980).

In the first eight months after passage of the Connecticut Elderly Protective Service Law (June 1978 to January 1979), eighty-seven cases of physical abuse, 314 cases of neglect, sixty-five cases of exploitation, and eight cases of abandonment were reported (Block, 1980). By April 1979 the total number of reported cases was 937, which included 651 neglect cases, both self-neglect of the elderly as well as neglect by the caretaker; 166 cases of physical abuse (a majority of which had been inflicted by grown children of the abused victim or by a spouse); 127 cases of exploitation; thirty-two cases of abandonment; and eighty-nine cases needing other kinds of assistance. Law and Kosberg (1978) found that over three-fourths of their abused elderly cases involved physical abuse and over half involved psychological abuse. Data from the above studies were obtained from third parties, for example, social service delivery professionals, police, and protective or social workers.

PROFILE OF DEPENDENT ELDERLY AND CARE-GIVING "CHILDREN." Steinmetz (1980-1981) interviewed adult children who were presently (or within the last three years) caring for a dependent elderly parent. Based on preliminary data of sixty elderly, the following profile emerged: The average age of the dependent elderly was just over eighty with an age range of sixty to ninety-nine years. The average age of the care-giving "children" was forty-eight with a range of twenty-three to sixty-five years of age. The average age of care givers was somewhat lower by several instances of a missing generation, that is, a twenty-three-year-old grandchild caring for a seventy-nine-year-old or a thirty-nine-year-old caring for a ninety-nine-year-old grandparent. However, 39 percent of the care givers were over fifty years old, and 18 percent were sixty or over. Thus 57 percent of the care givers were elderly or rapidly approaching this stage themselves. Most respondents were women, and their husbands tended to be still two to three years older.

ANALYSIS OF RESEARCH ON ABUSE OF ELDERS—VICTIMS AND CARE GIVERS. Preliminary analysis revealed some other interesting aspects of family violence. The victims are doubly victimized since they are not only dependent on the abuser for basic survival needs, but bear the stigma and guilt of having raised a child who would mistreat them if they seek help to alleviate the violence.

The overwhelming majority of care givers are women, and likewise they comprise the overwhelming majority of vulnerable elderly. Women face a double jeopardy: They bear the stresses and strains of caring for an elderly woman and they face the high probability of being in the same situation (Brody, 1979; Block, 1979; O'Malley, 1980; Steinmetz, 1980; 1981).

Table 8-II

Profile of Dependent Elders and Care-giving "Children"

	Average Age	Age Range			
Dependent Elderly	80	60-99			
			% over 50	% over 60	Total % over 50
Care-giving "Children" (predominantly women)	48	23-65	39	18	57

One fifty-eight-year-old respondent in our study blamed her divorce on having to care for her demanding, selfish, eighty-two-year-old mother. She noted that this was one of the contributing factors. Her husband had "just had it up to here. One day he just left." This care giver later noted that her mother would not offer to contribute to household costs: "I am making a woman's salary and keeping a big house. This is an obligation that I think she should partly assume. She doesn't feel that way. I am her daughter, she gave me life and she provided for me when I was young and couldn't do it myself. This obligation is now on my shoulders."

Another unique characteristic of this group of individuals is that the care givers are often elderly themselves, by the standard definition sixty or older, and yet they are caring for a still older dependent (Foulke, 1980; O'Malley, 1979; Steinmetz, 1980; 1981).

An additional characteristic of the care givers is that they are often caught in the middle between two or more generations. At the very time that their own family income is leveling off, retirement plans are imminent, and college and wedding plans of their children are still being paid for, this middle generation often has to assume the cost of caring for their elderly parents (Cohen and Gans, 1978; Silverstone and Human, 1976).

The value system is also strained. Where do these middle-aged care givers put their priorities? Should they give priority to the parents who reared them or their children who may still need emotional and financial support? Caught in this dilemma, the middle generations often find that there is no physical, psychic, or financial cushion for themselves.

These various issues are of major importance because they are dilemmas that most of us will face first as a care giver and later as we grow older and become dependent.

The effect of being caught in the middle is evident in a comment made by one of the sixty-year-old respondents regarding her eighty-four-year-old mother. She notes, "I don't want to consider my mother a burden. I would be glad to continue to care for her if she were not unpredictable and I could. This is the selfish part—I want to do some of the things I like to do because I am not very young either."

VIOLENCE AS A METHOD OF CONTROL IN THE FAMILY. Violence is often the method of last resort for both caretakers and elders when it is perceived that no other method will work. As a result of conflicting demands, learned or reactive, abusive adaptive responses became the method of last resort.

In a study of methods used by care givers and elderly patients to resolve conflict, Steinmetz (1981) revealed that violence is used by both care givers and the elderly parent.

Table 8-III reveals that elders also use violence to gain control. The relatively lower physical, financial, and emotional resources of the elderly parent may account for the high levels of violence that this study revealed. However, age-related disease and medication that alter personality must also be considered. The additional problem of double-direction violence needs more consideration in research. While violence perpetrated on elders has been sensationalized in the media, violence by elders on their middle-aged or older children has remained hidden (Steinmetz, 1980; 1981). The authoritarian father who rules his children with an iron fist and used beating when his authority or control was questioned unfortunately still resorts to these techniques at age ninety. These elders, finding control over the children to be more difficult, often resort to temper tantrums and physical outbursts. It is not difficult to understand why these elders would resort to physical violence when you realize that they have no other mechanism, such as money, prestige, mobility, or independence with which to assert their will and gain their wishes. They must depend on manipulations or physical control if their children are unwilling to meet their needs or their demands.

Table 8-III

Methods Used by Care-Giving Adult Children and Their Elderly Parents to Resolve Conflict

Methods	Parent-Child	Child-Parent
Screamed and yelled	43	40
Used physical restraint	—	6
Refused food medication	16	—
Forced feeding or medication	—	6
Threatened to send to nursing home	—	6
Threatened with physical force	—	4
Call police or others for imagined threats	10	—
Pout/withdraw	47	—
Hit or slapped	22	3
Manipulate/cry/used physical or emotional disability	32	—

GENERATION INVERSION. The process of generational inversion itself seems to cause some problems. Some parents never understand that their children are adults. This study revealed that 63 percent of the care givers reported that their elderly parents did not respect their privacy. In other cases, the elderly parent is unable to relinquish power. One woman in her late sixties was unable to leave the home to be interviewed because her ninety-four-year-old father felt that it was her place to remain at home and answer his demands. When she would leave, he would violently attack any caretaker left with him and would turn the room into shambles. Another respondent noted that "her mother was raised to honor thy father and thy mother, parents are right and always are up until the hour of death, you don't talk back. One day she told me I was talking back to her. Here I am a grandmother talking back!"

INTERVENTIONS TO PREVENT ELDER ABUSE. Because the decision to have an aging parent come live with an adult child is often made during a period of crisis, this decision is often based on haste, guilt, a sense of responsibility, and love, rather than a careful evaluation of all options and an acknowledgement of what is best for the elder, the adult child, and the family. Later, feelings of loss of privacy or personal space, personal time, physical energy, and financial resources may create the conditions for eventual abuse (Burnstein, 1978).

An examination of in-depth interviews with adult children caring for an elderly kin (Steinmetz, 1982*b*) revealed that this care giver often had the kin move in under the previous rules of "guest" status. Having all family members bow to the wishes of a guest, that is, rising early on the weekends to fix breakfast when the family prefers sleeping in, always asking the guest what he or she wants to eat and fixing his or her favorite regardless of the family's taste, and constantly reminding the kids to play quietly may be possible for a week-long or even a month-long visit. This alteration of the care-giving family's life-style often becomes unbearable when continued for long periods of time, especially when the family realizes that this situation is permanent. The elder's demands often become stressful to the family and are interpreted as selfish. However, any attempt to change this routine is met by the elder as an indication that the care-giving family no longer wants them. They feel that something is being taken away from them when they have already lost so much, for example, spouse, own residence, friends, and autonomy over their own environment. This response increases the guilt and the stress felt by the care givers and is likely to intensify their resentment. Unfortunately, the decision to assume the responsibility for an elderly person is often made devoid of the knowledge of the tremendous amounts of responsibilities and adjustments that will be required.

Obviously, an open discussion of both the family's and elder's life-style and negotiation of the degree of accomodation of each other's demands should be undertaken before a decision is reached. The following section presents some ways for helping care-giving families to have a more realistic approach to making the decision to care for an elder.

COUNSELING CARE-GIVING FAMILIES AND THEIR ELDERLY KIN. The counseling of families who are caring for elderly can help families anticipate and provide rational care. Counseling will need to be concerned with three major areas: decision making regarding the assumption of the care-giver role, counseling the family while care giving, and helping the family address the need for alternatives when the cost of caring for the elder outweighs the benefits derived from this role. Ideally, counseling should begin with the entire family before any decision is reached. However, the ideal situation rarely occurs. More often the decision to care for an elder is made hastily, following a crisis, such as severe illness, hospitalization, or death of a spouse, and with little emotional, psychological, or financial preparation.

HELPING FAMILIES MAKE AN INFORMED DECISION. One of the major considerations for a care-giving family is resources. While social-emotional responsibilities, (i.e. being the elder's total social life, never having any privacy, and always putting the elder's needs before those of the rest of the family [Steinmetz, 1982*a*]) appear to be the most burdensome, the financial obligation, especially since many care-giving families are facing retirement, is often devastating.

Financial eligibility for services when they are available creates additional obstacles. In order to be eligible for benefits, it is often necessary to spend down all the family assets resulting in the creation of pauperized widows. Furthermore, while an elder parent may be eligible when living alone, when the parent moves in with an adult child, the total family income is considered. This frustration was exhibited by one respondent attempting to get help for her eighty-seven-year-old mother:

> Went to Social Security to put her on Medicaid. They said "how much Social Security does she get?" I told them $160. They told me "you know your mother has to pay her fair share..." They said "you have to add up all of your income"; if you divide four into ($1200) the total family income, that is $300 a month in order for her to be eligible for Medicaid. I made them explain it and go over it four or five times. I said, "Look, my mother doesn't have $300 a month, where is she going to get the other $140 a month to pay her fair share." I did a work-up of my bills, electric, heat, all of the necessary items. They determined that

> she was not eligible and told me she could get food stamps. What good does that do, none; not for the medical problems we were facing. It is a horror story, I'll tell you.

The respondent noted that her mother had Blue Cross/Blue Shield, but in order to be eligible, she had to go directly from the hospital to a nursing home. Because she required custodial care, nobody would take her into a hospital and no one would cover the cost of in-home help.

There is a need for more services to help these families. Difficulty in obtaining services or lack of services further hinders healthy resolution of intergenerational problems. One respondent related the problems encountered in getting help for her eighty-nine-year-old father: "We could not get help from Medicare, Medicaid or Blue Cross. Everything fell onto us financially . . . because he required custodial care. I think I called about thirty people in the state of Delaware trying to get information. It was very frustrating . . . Social Security was over the cut-off amount. He didn't have a suitable income as far as pension . . . . Here was a man who did for others all of his life and when it came his turn to try to get some help, there was none."

Unfortunately, in penny-wise, pound-foolish fashion, the current fiscal and social policies have reduced and in many instances eliminated many of the services that would have enabled families to care for the elders at home, resulting in the government being forced to assume a large portion of the cost of institutionalization.

The counselor must often help the family deal with their actual ability to care for the elder aside from their emotional feelings of guilt, duty or responsibility, love, obligation, or any deathbed promises.

CHECKLIST FOR FAMILIES CONSIDERING CARETAKING OF ELDERS. The following checklist (Steinmetz, 1982*b*) is helpful for initiating discussion as well as making clients be aware of the range of changes that might occur. While there is no magical score ratio of yes/no answers, in fact a no answer does not necessarily mean a negative score (e.g. is there marginal conflict?). Having the clients provide a verbal or written response requires that they carefully consider the question. Answers that indicate a potential problem can then be discussed and possible solutions can be suggested.

A CHECKLIST FOR FAMILIES WHO MAY ASSUME THE CARE OF AN ELDER*

Your Family Situation

Is the family strong enough to withstand the additional stress? Yes___ No___
Is there marital conflict? Yes___ No___
Will there be conflicts because of small children? Yes___ No___
Is there another family member who has a serious illness, emotional, mental or physical handicap? Yes___ No___
Is the caretaker(s) employed? Yes___ No___
Who will take care of the elder while you work? ___________

Your Financial Situation

Is there adequate income for an alternative to taking the adult in the home? Yes___ No___
Are there other relatives who can contribute financially? Yes___ No___
Is it near activities enjoyed by the elderly such as church, senior center and shopping area? Yes___ No___
Will the elder be able to visit old friends and the neighborhood? Yes___ No___
(Is the distance so great that the elder will never be able to go home on a visit?) Yes___ No___

The Elder's Level of Dependency

Will this person be financially dependent on you and how much? Yes___ No___
Will this person be dependent on you for most of his social life? Yes___ No___

---

*From Suzanne Steinmetz, Family care of elders: Myths and Realities. In Stinnet et al.: *Family Strengths*, Vol. 5, 1982*b*, Lincoln, Nebr., University of Nebraska Press. Courtesy of Steinmetz.

Does the elder person have some loss of mental capabilities (gets lost, confused, senile)? Yes___ No___

Does the elder have a source of income? Yes___ No___

Does the elder have any savings, property, investments? Yes___ No___

Your Home

Is there enough physical space? Yes___ No___

Will the elderly person have his own bath? Yes___ No___

Will the elderly person have a wing or a section of the house to call his? Yes___ No___

Is your house barrier free? How much will it cost to remove barriers if they are present? Yes___ No___

(Are there guard rails on steps, by the toilet and in tub; can your halls and ramps accommodate wheel chair or walker; is the bathroom easily accessible to elderly; are there uneven floors, interior and exterior steps, floor to ceiling windows?)

Are there areas to protect the privacy of the children (own bedrooms, or family room for parties)? Yes___ No___

Elder's Health Status

Is the elder in good physical health for a person that age? Yes___ No___

Does the elder have some loss of mobility (needs help with stairs, getting out of chairs, needs walker, is bedridden)? Yes___ No___

Does the elder have a chronic illness or physical problem? Yes___ No___

Is the elder experiencing loss of sight or hearing? Yes___ No___

Can the elder provide for their own personal care (bathing, grooming, personal laundry)? Yes___ No___

Can the elder help with light housework (dishes, cooking, taking care of their room, dusting)? Yes___ No___

Your Capabilities

Can you care for the physical and emotional needs of this person? Yes___ No___

Did you ever have an elder living in your home when growing up? Yes___ No___

Will you have to give up a job, schooling, or social activities to care for this person? Yes___ No___

Are there relatives who will share the burden (take the elder for vacations for short periods of time)? Yes___ No___

Do you honestly have positive feelings towards this person? Yes___ No___

(If you have never gotten along or seen eye to eye, why will it be different now)?

Will you still be able to maintain your own identity, express your opinions, interact with your spouse and rear your children the way YOU think best if the elder moves in? (Remember once a daughter, always a daughter . . . mother is always right. Is this a problem? Can you deal with it?) Yes___ No___

Do you know what resources are available in your community which might help? Yes___ No___

EDUCATION AND ROLE PLAYING. Along with a discussion of the family's ability to care for the elders is the need to educate them about care of the elderly. Unfortunately while we have had formal education, experience, and "how-to" books on everything from child rearing, sex, driving, and home repairs, few of us have had either formal courses, read books on the care of the elderly, or have experience.

Previous education has come from baby-sitting classes in child care in junior and senior high school, books, magazine articles, and TV talk shows, as well as having our parents as role models. While most mothers embark upon the rearing of a newborn infant with at least minimal information on day-to-day care, most of us have no information on the care of the frail elderly individual, who has special dietary needs and physical requirements. There is no Doctor Spock book on the care, feeding, and discipline of one's elders. This lack of knowledge regarding the processes of normal aging and awareness of developmental changes can lead to inaccurate assessment of the elder's needs. For example, the daughter who has never been able to please her mother may view her mother's comments about tasteless meals as further indication of her inability to accommodate her mother. It will certainly be easier for the daughter to understand and cope if she realizes that because of the aging process and the decline in the sensitivity of the taste buds, the food may indeed be quite tasteless to the mother. It is a result of the mother's advancing age, not the daughter's level of competency in the kitchen, that is the source of the problem.

What is the best way to prepare families to adequately deal with this new role? Obviously reading books and articles increases our knowledge of the process of aging. However, book knowledge is quite different than hands-on experience. One way to gain insight into the potential impact that caring for an elder kin might have on the adult children and their family is through role playing.

Role playing has the advantage of allowing the participant the opportunity to experience an activity without the responsibility of being forced to permanently live with a decision or set of events. The role-playing activity "What are we going to do about Momma?" was first developed as a college classroom activity. It has been used extensively in staff training as well as with adult groups interested in the problem of caring for a parent. It has also been used with junior and senior high school students.

There are three major advantages to this game. First, the rules are easy to understand; therefore the game is appropriate for a wide age range of people. Second, the handing-out of cards assigning characteristics helps the players get into the game with a minimum of inhibitions. It is not necessary to be familiar with the techniques of psychodrama therapy to successfully direct the activity. Third, by assigning other participants the general role of friends, neighbors, and other relatives, a larger group can participate and provide comments, criticisms, and suggestions to the "family."

The directions are given in skeleton form. Each user will want to tailor the categories to his or her particular clients' needs. For example, if one works almost exclusively with one specific ethnic group, then the cards on religion and ethnicity of the elderly may not be appropriate. However, a player may want to develop a set of cards for "in-laws" that includes not only that ethnic group but others. This allows for discussion of how the elder might feel moving in with the outsider daughter-in-law or how that daughter-in-law might feel having been an outsider for twenty-five years and now being asked to care for Momma.

Another adaptation would be to use the names of actual services in your area. Thus, instead of *family counseling*, the cards might read *Northside Catholic Services, Family Services of Eastland,* or *Westland Family Growth Center, Inc.*

WHAT ARE WE GOING TO DO ABOUT MOMMA?*

This is a decision-making game with the goal of finding an alternative when an aging parent can no longer live independently.

Objectives: Through role playing, providers can learn to come to a group (family) decision on what arrangements are to be made for an elderly parent who can no longer live alone.

Procedure: 1 – Select players, four to six players works best.

2 – If large group is present, the remaining audience is told that they are to be other family members, friends, and neighbors and should feel free to offer advice.

3 – Players randomly draw cards from within each category. The order can be changed as the progression of the role playing warrants.

4 – At different point in the game, the moderator can ask players to review their cards; provide a decision based on the facts they have; ask for audience (family, friends, neighbors) comments. At the decision-making point, ask the family how the decision will be enforced; ask what the contingency plans are if elder's condition changes.

Materials: Three-by-five-inch file cards; different colored cards are helpful. One side of the card has a number (1 = 1st cards)

*Courtesy of Steinmetz.

and category (family members). The other side contains one of a range of items within the category (son, daughter, brother). Feel free to add or delete items to fit the special characteristics of your target population.

Items in the category Social Services can be general (counseling, home visiting, day-care center) or specific to your area (Family Services of Delaware, Harrisburg Home Care, Inc., East Side Day-Care Center).

Front of Card	*Back of Card (1 item/card)**	*Number of Cards*
1 sex of elderly	male; female	one card
2 family members:	niece, nephew of elderly; son, son-in-law, daughter, daughter-in-law of elderly; grandson, granddaughter of elderly; brother, brother-in-law of elderly; sister and sister-in-law of elderly (After these cards are selected, arranging players by family units and generations is helpful, i.e. brother-in-law of elderly and sister = elder's generation; son, niece, and daughter-in-law = child's generation; grandson = grandchild's generation.)*	one per player
3 family social class:	welfare, working class, middle class, upper middle class, very wealthy*	one per player**
4 family structure:	couple with adult children and grandchildren; couple with no children; couple with children nearing college and marriage; single individual; couple with adolescent-aged children; couple with small children	one per player**

*Add several cards of the same items so that it is possible for more than one player to have the same item, for example two players are daughters and two are working class.

**If family members contain a husband/wife or parent/dependent child as players, then only one card/unit is given.

5 housing:	floor-to-ceiling windows; hazardous steps inside and/or out; architectural barriers; cramped living space; no central heat; inadequate bath; expandable ranch house; split level; many steps*	one per player**
6 health of elder:	nonambulatory; intermediate care; healthy; ambulatory; skilled medical care; chronic health problems under control	one card
7 proximity of kin:	lives in same town, one block from elder; lives in same town, next door; lives out of state less than 300 miles away; lives in next town, fifteen minutes away; lives in same state an hour or more away; lives in large city several hours away; lives out of state 1,500 miles away; lives out of the country	one per player
8 religion of elder:	Quaker; Methodist; Christian Scientist; Roman Catholic; Jewish; atheist; Baptist	one card
9 ethnicity of elder:	no ethnic ties; Spanish speaking Anglo-Saxon; Oriental; Greek; North American – many generations (WASP); native American; black	one card
10 special family conditions:	wife employed or continuing education; marital harmony; compatible values and life-styles; positive emotional feelings; marital discord; already responsible for one elderly kin; incompatible values and life-styles; negative emotional feelings towards elderly kin; positive emotional feelings; family member has serious illness*	two cards per player
11 elder's characteristics	constantly talks; frugal; always worries; likes to argue; complains constantly; favors one child over another; demands a lot of attention;	one or two cards per player

	good natured; constantly criticizes; very neat; makes comparisons; sickly; feels sorry for self; happy go lucky; considerate; likes to joke (practical joker); family cannot do enough; is never satisfied; has a favorite child; always wants his or her own way	
12 resources of elderly:	none; social security; social security and small pension; meager; wealthy; small pension; adequate (middle class); owns property; railroad retirement pension	one card
13 social services:	Meals on Wheels; telephone reassurance; Lions Club; chore service; dietician—help with special diets and meal planning; homemaker service; social worker outreach; vocational rehabilitation; foster homes for the elderly; Cancer Society (free beds and other equipment); senior centers; RSVP; geriatric day care; occupational therapy; church visitation; respite care*	two or three cards per player
14 elderly's preference:	live independently (in-home services); to the nursing home; go to retirement home; wants to live with children; elder doesn't care	one card

COUNSELING THE CARE-GIVING FAMILY. In addition to education, there is a need to provide families who are assuming the care of an elderly person with ongoing counseling. Very often the adolescent-parent conflicts of forty years earlier that served as the impetus for the child to leave home remain unresolved. In many families, the only contact is the obligatory Christmas or Easter visit during which relations are strained and filled with guilt, resentment, and tension. Given this background, it is easy to understand the emotions that the adult child feels when faced with the realization of assuming full-time responsibility for this parent.

Even when the relationship is a positive one, the inversing of the generations and the ensuing responsibilities and obligations often require third-party mediation. The older person may need help in understanding that the care-giving family's desire to have some time to itself is not a sign of rejection. A counselor may help the elder to understand that he or she can't expect to always be the center of attention, and in some cases, the elder's personal demands may have to be secondary to those of the care-giver family.

It is difficult, especially if the older person is a woman, to realize that she is not the head of this household and that she really has no legitimate right to order her daughter or daughter-in-law to do things her way. At the same time, the daughter, who may feel ambiguity about her role as a child versus her role as a care giver, needs support in setting down certain guidelines. This is necessary to avoid disruption of family harmony. Counseling can help both parties with understanding and accepting their new role relationships.

Support groups should be set up for middle-aged children who have the responsibility of caring for the elderly individual. In addition to the recognized benefits of peer counseling, these groups provide contact with other care givers experiencing similar problems. Very often this decision is made in the atmosphere of guilt—the obligation to the parent. A rational discussion of pre-care-giving responsibilities and how well they can now be met since the elderly person moved in must be considered. Because of the cultural ideal of providing care for one's parent at all costs because of love, honor, and respect, there is reluctance to express the frustration and trapped feelings that care givers often feel.

Sometimes it is not socially acceptable to mention that one resents the amount of financial, physical, or emotional drain on the resources that is encountered when one assumes the responsibility for an elderly parent. If there were support groups where care givers could share not only their common problems but the mechanisms used in resolving these problems, this would help alleviate some of the guilt that is expressed by these individuals. They would also not be as likely to be met with statements such as "How can you be so unfeeling," or "You owe your whole life to your parent," which is the response often offered people who have not been in a similar situation.

CONCLUSION

Families need help to locate additional resources if they assume the care of an elderly person. While the best place for an elderly person to live may be with the kin, there has to be recognition that without some additional resources, the prolonged and severe types of dependency that may result are more than many families can cope with alone.

Counselors of care givers also need to recognize that this family may consist of a couple (or an individual) who not only feel responsible for their own children and grandchildren, but are likely to be in the process of making plans for their own impending retirement. Thus, the care giver's statement "I'm all Aunt Jane has" should alert the counselor to explore family resources and alternative options with the care giver. If Aunt Jane has no resources or other family members to help with the care, can the care giver absorb this additional burden and at what cost? This discussion must include a careful analysis of the constantly changing Medicaid, Medicare, and Social Security regulations. In some instances, Aunt Jane may receive better, more comprehensive care if she doesn't move in with the care giver. While making an economically sound decision based on financial ability, social policy and federal regulations may seem devoid of caring, love, and a sense of responsibility (and guilt). Responsibility and love wear thin after years of financial and physical stress. A happier healthier relationship in which the care giver makes frequent visits to the nursing home and the elder comes home during holidays and vacation is far better for everyone.

The population of people sixty-five and older is growing. The cost of living is increasing, and there is a greater demand for alternative housing for the elderly. The result is a lack of housing at an affordable price for the elderly people who are unable to live totally independently.

With the higher cost of living a greater percentage of income will be needed to cover the basic necessities, and thus a smaller amount will be available for those things that we might call luxuries, for example, additional cars, vacations, and single family homes with room to expand. How this is going to impact on the family caring for an elderly person is not known. However, one can predict that the smaller the amount of money available for luxuries, the smaller the amount of money there will be to provide elder sitters or housekeepers, or some of the other resources that might help to alleviate the stress.

The final factor that needs to be considered is that the working woman is a growing phenomena with many women returning to work after the children have left the home in order to meet some of the additional expenses and maintain the standard of living they have enjoyed. We find in some cases that women are faced with the question, "If I work, who will take care of Mother?" and yet, "If I don't work, how can I meet my monthly bills?" With the increasing conflict among the needs of their elderly parent, the help they want to provide for their children, and fulfillment of their own goals, we can predict an increase in the amount of stress and the use of violence by children to control their elderly parents unless adequate support systems are available.

As these problems grow, the need for counseling to facilitate the adjustment of the elderly, the care givers, and their families to these unfamiliar sets of roles and responsibilities is crucial if we are to embrace this emerging stage as a family challenge encompassing growth and family solidarity rather than a potential arena of conflict and violence.

REFERENCES

Archbold, Patricia: Impact of parent caring on middle-aged offspring. *Journal of Gerontological Nursing, 6*:79-85, February, 1980.

Blenkner, Margaret: Social work and the family relationships in later life with some thoughts of filial maturity. In Shanas, E., and Streib, G. (Eds.): *Social Structure and the Family*. Englewood Cliffs, N.J., Prentice Hall, 1965.

Blenkner, Margaret: The normal dependencies of aging. In Kalish, Richard, (Ed.): *The Dependencies of Old People*. Ann Arbor, Mich., University of Michigan Institute of Gerontology, 1969.

Block, Marilyn, and Sinnet, Jan P. (Eds.): *The Battered Elder Syndrome: An Exploratory Study*. College Park, Md., Center on Aging, University of Maryland, 1979.

Boszormenyi-Nagy, Ivan, and Spark,, Geraldine M.: *Invisible Loyalties Reciprocity in Intergenerational Family Therapy*. Medical Department, Hagerstown, Md., Harper and Row, 1973.

Brody, E.M.: The aging family. *The Gerontologist, 6*:201-206, 1966.

Brody, Elaine: The aging of the family. *Annals AAPSS, 438*:13-26, July 1978.

Brody, Elaine: Women's changing roles, the aging family and long-term care of older people. *National Journal*, October 1979, pp. 1828-1833.

Burston, G.R.: Do your elderly parents live in fear of being battered? *Modern Geriatrics*, November 16, 1978.

Busse, Ewald, W.: Theories of aging. In Busse, Ewald, and Pfeiffer, Eric (Eds.): *Behavior and Adaptation in Later Life*, Boston, Little Brown and Company, 1977.

Butler, Robert N., and Lewis, Myrna: *Aging and Mental Health*. St. Louis, C.V. Mosby Co., 1977.

Clark, Robert and Spengler, Joseph: Population aging in the twenty-first century. *Aging*, January-February 1978, pp. 7-13.

Cohen, Stephan A., and Gans, Bruce Michael: *The Other Generation Gap: The Middle-Aged and Their Aging Parents*. Chicago, Follett Publishing Company, 1978.

Douglas, Richard: *A Study of Neglect and Abuse of the Elderly in Michigan*. Paper presented to the 32nd Annual Meeting of Gerontological Society. Washington, D.C., November 1979.

Douglas, R., Hickey, T., and Noel, C.: *A Study of Maltreatment of the Elderly and other Vulnerable Adults*. Final report to the U.S. Administration on Aging and the Michigan Department of Social Services, Ann Arbor, Mich., November 1980.

Farrar, Marcella: Mother-daughter conflicts extended into later life. *Social Casework, 45*:202-207, May 1955.

Foulke, Sarah R.: *Caring for the Parental Generation: An Analysis of Family Resources and Support*. Unpublished master's thesis, University of Delaware, Newark, Del., May 1980.

Hess, Beth: Family myths. *New York Times*, January 9, 1979, p. A19.

Hooker, Susan: *Caring for Elderly People: Understanding and Practical Help*. London, Routledge and Kegan, Paul, 1976.

Johnson, Elizabeth: Good relationships between older mothers and their daughters: A casual model. *The Gerontologist, 12*:209-216, 1978.

Kirschner, Charlotte: The aging family in crisis: A problem in living. *Social Casework, 60*:209-216, April 1979.

Knopf, Olga: *Successful Aging, the Facts and Fallacies of Growing Old*. New York, The Viking Press, 1975.

Langdon, Brian: Statement presented at the House of Representatives Select Committee on Aging (96), June 23, 1979, Boston, Mass. Washington, D.C., 1980, pp. 16-21.

Law, Elizabeth, and Kosberg, Jordan: *Abuse of the Elderly by Informed Care Providers: Practice Research Issues*. Paper presented at 31st Annual Meeting of the Gerontological Society, Dallas, Tex., November 1978.

Morgan, Mildred: The middle life and the aging family. *The Family Coordinator, 29*:37-46, 1969.

O'Malley, Helen: Testimony presented at the House of Representatives Select Committee on Aging (99-6), June 23, 1979, Boston, Mass. Washington, D.C., 1980, pp. 12-26.

O'Malley, Helen, et al.,: *Elder Abuse in Massachusetts: A Survey of Professionals and Paraprofessionals*. Boston, Mass., Legal Research and Services for the Elderly, 1979.

Rathbone-McCuan, Eloise: *Intergenerational Family Violence and Neglect: The Aged as Victims of Peactuated and Reverse Neglect Paper*. Paper presented to 11th International Congress of Gerontology, Tokyo, Japan,

Renvoize, J.: *Web of Violence: A Study of Family Violence*. London, Routledge and Kegan, Paul, 1978.

Samuelson, Robert J.: Aging America—Who will shoulder the growing burden? *National Journal, 43*:1712-1717, November 28, 1978.

Shanas, Ethel: The family as a social support system in old age. *The Gerontologist, 19*:169-174, April 1979.

Silverstone, Barbara, and Hyman, Helen Kardell: *You and Your Aging Parent*. New York, Parthenon Books, 1976.

Steinmetz, Suzanne K.: Dependency, stress and violence between middle-aged caregivers and their elderly parents. In Kosberg, J.I.: *Abuse and Maltreatment of the Elderly*. Littleton, Mass., John-Wright PSG, Inc., 1982.

Steinmetz, Suzanne K.: Elder abuse. *Aging, 315-316*:6-10, January-February 1981.

Steinmetz, Suzanne K.: *Elder Abuse: Society's Double Dilemma*. Hearing Senate Select Committee on Aging (97), Washington, D.C., May 28, 1980.

Steinmetz, Suzanne K.: Family care of elders: Myths and realities. In Stinnet et al.: *Family Strengths*, Vol. 5 Lincoln, Nebr., University of Nebraska Press, 1982*b*.

Steinmetz, Suzanne K.: Prepared statements. *Elder Abuse: The Hidden Problem*. Briefing by the Select Committee on Aging, U.S. House of Representatives (96), June 23, 1979, Boston, Mass. Washington, D.C., 1980, pp.7-10.

Steinmetz, Suzanne K.: The politics of aging, battered parents. *Society*, July-August 1978, pp.54-55.

Tobin, Sheldon S.: The future elderly: Needs and services. *Aging, 279-280*:23-46, January-February 1978.

Townsend, Peter: The emergence of the four-generation family in industrial society. In Neugarten, Bernice L. (Ed.): *Middle Age and Aging*. Chicago, University of Chicago Press, 1968.

Treas, J.: Family support systems for the aged: Some social and demographic considerations. *The Gerontologist, 17(6)*:486-491, 1977.

U.S. Bureau of Census. *Current Population Reports*, No. 643, Tables 2 and 5. Washington, D.C., U.S. Government Printing Office, 1977.

Chapter 9

MANAGING VIOLENCE IN AN INPATIENT SETTING

CYNTHIA ALLEN HART, JUDITH BROAD AND SHARON TRIMBORN

INTRODUCTION

THE commission of violent acts by patients is a recurring, although infrequent, problem in acute care psychiatric hospitals. The emotion generated in staff and patients by these actions is substantial, almost always negative, and capable of provoking deleterious effects on patient care. For nursing staff members, high levels of fear and anxiety caused by their close, ongoing contact with acutely ill psychiatric patients who possess the potential for violent behavior may lead to low morale and even termination of employment. Obviously, there is a need to assist all psychiatric staff members who work in acute care settings to maximize their ability to prevent and/or intervene effectively in incidents that involve violent patient behaviors. Staff members best able to do so are those who (1) understand antecedent variables associated with the occurrence of violent behavior; (2) utilize their understanding to systematically assess patients regarding their violence potential; (3) employ prevention strategies (violence precautions) early when patients are judged potentially violent; (4) intervene decisively utilizing strategies that are known for their effectiveness in reducing violence; and (5) possess self-awareness of their own fears, anxieties, and usual coping strategies.

The present chapter will address these five areas. For a complete discussion of the theoretical explanations for the genesis of violence, the reader is referred to other chapters in this text.

ASSESSMENT OF VIOLENCE POTENTIAL

A systematic assessment of violence potential includes diagnostic categories associated as high risk for violent behavior, personality characteristics of violence-prone individuals, environmental variables associated with assaultive behavior in institutional settings, and general violence indicators.

Operational Definition of Assaultive Behavior

While the dynamics differ within each of the diagnostic categories to be described, there are common forces that operate in association with violent or assaultive patient behavior. An operational definition of assaultive behavior that incorporates these forces is presented to facilitate understanding of how such behavior is generated and also to encourage the design of deliberative intervention strategies for use prior to the actual assault (*see* Figure 9-1).

According to the dynamics outlined in Figure 9-1, aggressive behavior serves as a defense against anxiety (Sullivan, 1953). In addition, the behavior is reinforced since it serves to reduce anxiety and to increase the individual's sense of power and control (Lion, 1972). As is discussed later, it becomes important for the patient to be helped to manage his or her anxiety through constructive channels. It is equally important for the staff to appreciate the discomfort experienced by the patient in response to the feelings of anxiety and helplessness and to implement interventions to decrease the negative feelings.

The potential for assaultive behavior in patients that is directly related to mental illness exists primarily during the acute phase. Even then, with proper management, most patients can and want to be helped to stay in control.

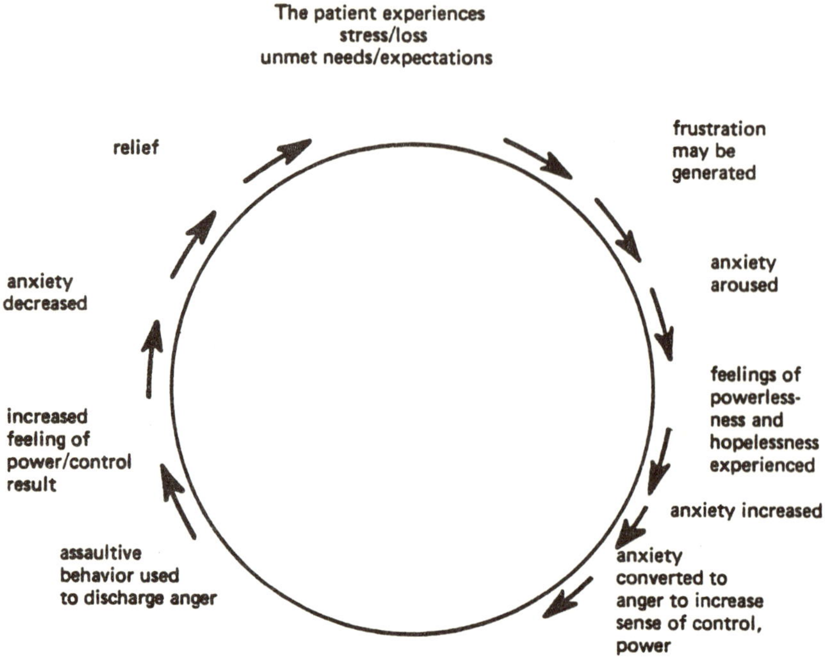

Figure 9-1. Operational Definition of Assaultive Behavior (Drawn from theories presented in J. Clark, Nursing intervention into the aggressive behavior of patients, in S.F. Burd and M.A. Marshall (Eds.), *Some Clinical Approaches to Psychiatric Nursing*, New York, MacMillan Information, 1963; and J.R. Lion, *Evaluation and Management of the Violent Patient*, Springfield, Ill., Charles C Thomas, Publisher, 1972.)

Diagnostic Categories Associated as High Risk for Violent Behavior

When staff members are asked to identify factors associated with violence among hospitalized psychiatric patients, they often respond by indicating certain psychiatric diagnostic categories. There are types of patients more prone to violence because of their psychiatric conditions than others. The following categories of psychiatric patients are generally considered high risk for violent behavior:

1. Acutely psychotic patients who threaten violence, have persecutional delusions or other violent fantasies and/or are confused, agitated, and frightened are at risk for violence. Because of hallucinations and delusions, these patients may tend to misidentify persons in the environment (at times confusing them

with significant others) or to misinterpret the motives underlying actions of the staff or other patients.

2. Psychotic patients who show little regard for people and who have shallow affect may respond with violent behavior (Lion, 1972).
3. Excessively controlled, inflexible people, such as those with obsessive-compulsive or schizoid qualities, who have decreased responsiveness to emotional stimuli often respond with violent outbursts under severe stress. (Lion, 1972).
4. Patients diagnosed as having character disorders. This group is, according to Lion (1972), the largest source of violent patients. Their need for immediate gratification, their inability to control impulses, and their insensitivity to others' feelings put them at risk. Many of these patients possess the personality characteristics of violence-prone individuals discussed in the next section. They may be admitted to a psychiatric setting after having been involved in a violent episode.
5. Patients experiencing an acute episode of an affective disorder may become involved in violent behavior (Halleck, 1971; Hudgens, 1965; Lion, Bach-Y-Rita, and Ervin, 1969). Aggression may be manifested by an inwardly directed, aggressive act, as in self-destructive behavior or as violence towards others. The staff may be less likely to recognize the intent of some patients to produce self-harm through the provocation of violent behavior. In contrast, manic patients who are irritable, hyperactive, and intolerant of frustration are usually recognized by staff as likely to respond negatively, sometimes violently, when attempts are made to structure their behavior.
6. Patients who abuse alcohol and drugs, especially amphetamines and phencyclidine (PCP) (Fauman and Fauman, 1979), are prone to increased violent behavior. Alcohol and drugs impair judgment and reduce internal controls over feelings and behavior (Lion, Bach-Y-Rita, and Ervin, 1969). As inhibition is reduced, these patients may engage in disruptive or destructive behavior.
7. Organically impaired patients with poor impulse control may demonstrate violent behavior. For patients with degenerative organic disease, the onset of destructive behavior may be com-

pletely out of character with the patient's previously normal level of self-control. For moderately retarded or brain-damaged individuals, the destructive behavior may be generated only when frustration or stress is encountered (Lion, 1976).

Personality Characteristics of Violence-Prone Individuals

In addition to violent patient behavior triggered during an acute phase of mental illness, violent acts are committed on a psychiatric unit by patients with antisocial behavior patterns. These patients may or may not exhibit other forms of mental illness associated with their hospitalization. Generally, these individuals will present a childhood history that includes some of the following characteristics: emotional deprivation, parental brutality, abandonment, or seductiveness (Goldstein, 1974); nocturnal enuresis, pyromania, and cruelty to animals (Hellman and Blackman, 1966); and fighting, inability to get along with others, temper tantrums, and school problems (Justice, Justice, and Kraft, 1974). As adults, they usually report previous involvement in violent behavior including family fights and self-directed violence. It is not uncommon for them to misuse drugs and alcohol, to engage in reckless driving, and to own and use weapons. Interpersonal difficulties with their spouses are common, as are problematic relationships with coworkers and supervisors, which result in frequent job changes (Lion, 1972).

Males under forty are most frequently initiators of assaultive behavior (Mikolejczak, 1978). These men are viewed as compensating for feelings of helplessness and dependency needs by assuming a "macho" posture (Halleck, 1976). Problems with sexual identity and sexual functioning are frequent and are thought to lead to feelings of inadequacy and subsequent overtly aggressive behavior (Halleck, 1976).

According to the importation theory (Guenther, 1978), violence as a way of life is imported to the hospital. Patients bring with them the values, goals, and behavior patterns they were taught in the community. If patients such as those described above have learned to use assaultive behavior as a problem-solving technique or coping mechanism, such behavior will be activated in the hospital when circumstances generate the need.

It is important, therefore, that staff members assess the potential for violence in relation to the patient's diagnosed mental illness as well as in relation to his or her personality and life-style.

Environmental Variables Associated with Assaultive Behavior in Institutional Settings

When a patient is admitted to a psychiatric hospital, he or she is brought into contact with a wide variety of other disturbed patients who may wittingly or unwittingly be provocative (Kalogerakis, 1971). Consequently, it is important that the physical environment allow for adequate open space so that patients can move about freely, especially if agitated or upset, and so that distance can be maintained between those patients who provoke each other. Some evidence now exists that patients with a history of assaultive behavior should not be housed together on the same unit. It may prove difficult to set nonviolent norms if several patients adhere to standards in which violent behavior is condoned or at least acknowledged as an inevitable occurrence.

Adequacy of available and well-qualified staff is viewed as an important variable in the prevention of patient violence. As mentioned earlier, violence-prone patients are often anxious and are feeling helpless and powerless while experiencing a low frustration tolerance. Frequent assessment of the violence-prone patient's condition, monitoring of the environment, and consistent supportive interactions are important staff functions throughout the patient's stay, but especially during the first forty-eight to seventy-two hours after admission, since that is the time during which many episodes of violent patient behavior tend to occur.

Because boredom is also associated with the occurrence of violent behavior in some patients, staff members are also important in helping these patients to structure their time and to create relevant, interesting activities in which to participate.

In addition to its physical characteristics, the institution is viewed by some as contributing to violence as a result of its social structure and process. The structure can easily be perceived as coercive and regimented in which clients "perceive themselves, on the basis of real or imaginary criteria, to be deprived of ordinary social prerequisites" (Guenther, 1978, p. 463). Locked doors, limits, and restrictions on visiting hours all serve as reminders to the patient of his or her lack of control. The resulting feelings of helplessness before rather powerful authorities, who may be perceived as controlling his fate, can exacerbate the patient's already existing feelings of hopelessness, powerlessness, decreased self-worth, and possibly, transference reactions involving resentments stemming from earlier experience (Kalogerakis, 1971). These feelings may serve as precipitants of increased anxiety and subsequent violent behavior. Again, staff members are important in facilitating the patient's expression of these feelings through constructive channels. Various interventions, which are described later, also can be used to increase the patient's involvement in his or her own care, thus raising the person's sense of control.

While the hospital contains elements that serve to provoke the occurrence of violent behavior, its structure can also be viewed as reducing the occurrence of assaultive behavior. Since violent behavior is most often directed at family members or friends, the context in which violent feelings are likely to erupt is changed by admission to a hospital (Kalogerakis, 1971). The attention given patients by the staff along with a structured routine serves to reduce anxiety. In addition, the absence of readily available weapons helps to limit the possibility of violence.

General Violence Indicators

Patients at risk for violent episodes can be identified during the initial screening interview on an inpatient unit or in the emergency department through use of violence indicators. In a large university medical center psychiatric wing, psychiatric nursing administrators initiated the formulation and implementation of violence precautions, which include violence indicators commonly referred to in the literature and interventions to prevent and/or deal with violent episodes. When used, violence precautions increase the likelihood that violence can be prevented and/or managed more effectively. Patients who have demonstrated one or more of the indicators are generally placed on violence precautions. The violence indicators include the following:

1. *Known history of violent behavior on previous admissions*. This is ascertained through a review of old records, a report by the pa-

tient and/or family, and staff familiarity with the patient during past hospitalizations or outpatient care.

2. *Presentation to a health care facility following a violent episode.* In such instances, the patient is generally brought to the emergency department by family or by the police who readily share the violent episode as precipitating their actions to secure psychiatric care for the patient.
3. *Actual assault/violent behavior during the initial assessment in the emergency room or on an inpatient unit*
4. *Verbal threats of physical assault.* The patient may have threatened to harm family, friends, or associates prior to being seen by a health care provider or during the initial assessment may have threatened to harm relatives, staff, or others. Relatives may seek help for the patient because of verbal threats, or the patient may present on his or her own, fearing loss of control.
5. *Decreased tolerance for frustration and poor impulse control.* In general, this information may be obtained by history and through patient-staff interaction and observation.
6. *Acute manifestations of agitation and persecutory delusions.* The fearful, suspicious patient has a potential for violence, along with the hypomanic-manic patient who is agitated and pressured. Observations by staff during the initial interview are usually sufficient to make this evaluation.

STAFF AND VIOLENT BEHAVIOR

Nursing staff members are the largest source of mental health providers at inpatient psychiatric facilities. Nurses interact with potentially violent or violent patients over a twenty-four-hour period each day of the week. The quantity and quality of nursing staff members are viewed as salient factors in the prevention of patient violence in inpatient settings. Studies indicate that appropriate kinds and numbers of staff are important variables in the management of patients and their environment (Stanton and Schwartz, 1954). Although mental health providers may be knowledgeable about environment, interpersonal, and intrapsychic antecedents to violent behavior, practitioners studying violence (Lion and Madden, 1976) also encourage the staff to examine their own behavior as possible antecedents to patient violence. For example, patient assaults on therapists are frequently related to emotional responses and subsequent behaviors of the therapists (Whitman, 1978).

Just as patients import values and behavior patterns to the inpatient experience (Guenther, 1978), staff members also bring past experiences and learned behaviors to the staff-patient relationship. For example, staff often respond to having their competency or authority challenged in the same manner as they were responded to when they challenged their own parent's authority. These countertransference reactions of the staff frequently result in authoritarian and punitive approaches with patients (Lange, 1966; Lion and Pasterna, 1973).

The ability of the staff to prevent and intervene effectively with violent patients can be affected by their lack of self-awareness of patient behaviors that cause them to become afraid or angry. Self-awareness of their own emotional responses and behaviors can help staff develop a vigilance that allows them to modify their own emotional responses to violent behavior and to develop more rational approaches for managing violent behavior of patients (Haber, 1979). Strong reactions to hostile patients are normal, but they can cause staff to employ nontherapeutic defense mechanisms to cope with these reactions, such as denial, withdrawal, reaction formation, displacement of anger, and acting-out (DiBella, 1979).

Beck presents a cognitive model for identifying situations that commonly make people angry and afraid. He states that ". . . a common factor for arousal of anger is the individual's appraisal of an assault of his domain, including values, moral code, and protective rules" (Beck, 1976, p. 71). He explains that if a danger element exists, fear and anxiety are the initial responses that can be transformed into anger. The focus of this section will be on self-assessment of the response of the staff to angry behavior and the development of deliberative interventions.

Self-Assessment Approach to the Prevention and Management of Violence

Inpatient staff often do not have the opportunity to assess or predict violence when approaching patients in the emergency room or hospital units. However, staff can assess their own response patterns to patients who are potentially or overtly violent. The staff member is always the constant variable in the interpersonal interaction with the patient. Therefore, the staff must learn to anticipate how they will react to threatening behavior.

Because staff members as well as patients are capable of angry responses and violence, it is important that staff members assess this potential in themselves by looking at their lives and past responses to confrontation. Steinmetz (1978) reminds us that behavior of both patients and the staff is learned at the knees of parents, and the parents' past behavior predicts whether the children will respond to frustration with violence.

The goals of self-assessment are (1) to prevent the possibility that a staff may unwittingly contribute to a violent episode, (2) to actively avoid a violent patient-staff experience, and (3) to provide alternatives so that the patient can deal more functionally with situations of powerlessness and helplessness. As mentioned earlier, the patient will use violence to handle feelings of powerlessness because the process becomes reinforcing when anxiety is reduced and power is experienced briefly. When staff become aware of their emotions and behaviors, they can begin to modify their own intense emotions. When staff learn to manage their own emotions, they model rational behaviors and demonstrate more effective approaches for negotiating.

Reactions of Staff to Angry or Violent Behavior

The ability of staff to intervene effectively in regard to threatening behaviors depends on their awareness of what makes them afraid and angry and their responses to their own fear and anger. Keeping a daily journal (*see* Table 9-I) of responses to fear and anger can help staff track their response patterns.

What makes the staff in a psychiatric hospital, or anywhere, afraid? Fear is a natural, inevitable response when bodily harm is possible. Fear is not a weak response because the anxiety triggered by a fear response signals danger, and therefore, is protective. Physiological responses such as palpitations and gastric uneasiness are important clues to potential danger. It is important for the staff to heed these somatic signals of anxiety or "gut reactions" resulting from fear for three reasons: (1) The unchecked excess anxiety can diminish ego functioning and interfere with rational interventions; (2) it is likely that the patient will pick up on this fear and anxiety

Table 9-I

Staff Journal Recording
Daily Responses to Fear or Anger

Date	Person	Behavior	My Reaction
4/6/82 PM			
4/7/82 eve.	M.P.	Refused medications	Irritation
4/8/82 PM	M.P.	Criticism of care	Defensiveness
4/8/82 eve.	M.P.	Criticism of personal activities	Flushed skin pounding heart; 2 hours later—angry feelings
4/9/82 AM	C.P.	Shoved me	Rational response: helped patient focus on source of anger. One hour later, recognized my anger over this unprovoked attack on me.

and deduce that the staff will not be able to control the patient's violent urges; and (3) fear and anxiety can be transformed into anger or rage, and the staff will be at risk for loss of control.

Sullivan (1953) states that anxiety triggered from fear based on reality or distortion is transformed into anger as a security operation to reduce the agonizing anxiety. Anger is usually more comfortable than anxiety. Past experience, perceptions, thoughts, and feelings that the staff import to work often facilitate the transformation of anxiety into anger rather than into a less restrictive emotional state or a more creative approach to the interpersonal interaction.

According to Aaron Beck (1978), situations leading to anger are common to all, regardless of personality. All individuals become angry when unpleasant experiences encroach on personal safety, individual standards, self-esteem, and human needs. However, how the individual appraises and handles the situation depends on personality structure and past experience. Other variables affecting the anger response are how unreasonable or improper the offense seems to the recipient of the offense and how likable the offender is perceived (Beck, 1978, p. 73). If the offender seems to be a nice person to the recipient, sadness and depression can result in lieu of anger.

Therefore, feeling sad during a conflictual encounter can be a warning to the staff that a threatening act has been experienced.

Beck categorizes common situations that cause anger as assaults on the personal domain or the self-space of the individual. Beck theorizes that when the self or one's territory is threatened or attacked verbally or physically, a judgment is made and action is taken according to the perception of the situation.

Assaults on the Personal Domain

Assaults on the personal domain that anger everyone are classified as (1) direct and intentional assault, (2) direct and unintentional assault, (3) violation of an individual moral code or a rigid idiosyncratic code, (4) violation of laws, standards, and social mores, and (5) indirect assault on the self-esteem.

DIRECT AND INTENTIONAL ASSAULT. Direct and intentional assault provokes the angriest feelings of all the categories of assaults on self-space. At the time of the assault, it is difficult to assess whether a direct physical assault like a kick or a punch in the nose is intentional or unintentional. However, it is important for the staff to try to immediately evaluate the intentionality. In most cases, a direct assault on the staff is related to confusion, a transference reaction, displacement, or a paranoid delusion. Staff will need to ascertain whether the patient distorted the identity of the staff member attacked and therefore did not rationally intend to attack.

DIRECT AND UNINTENTIONAL ASSAULT. The direct assault will always anger the recipient, even if it is accidental or unintentional, for example, injuries due to swinging arms and legs or confusion about a staff member's identity. Most of the time, however, if the staff's bodies are touched in a rough manner, they will react with anger and caution is in order. Effective responses that limit out-of-control behavior are discussed later in the chapter.

VIOLATION OF A CODE. Staff members carry around learned codes as to how people should look and behave. They harbor the arbitrary "should, oughts, and musts" as described by Ellis (1962). The staff can automatically become angry at macho men, seductive women, racial differences, alcoholics, drug addicts, child abusers, and those who are deviant in appearance. Violations of personal codes can cause the staff to respond to others automatically and insensitively. A recent study indicates that it is easy for most people to recognize nonverbal cues that reveal how other people are feeling. However, the findings also demonstrate that people are often insensitive to the feelings of others and are unable to respond to their distress. They are insensitive and unable to respond not because they are unable to identify others' feelings or behavior, but because they make a decision not to respond based on a judgment about how others behave or "ought" to behave in certain situations (Christensen and Farina, 1981)

VIOLATION OF LAWS, STANDARDS, AND SOCIAL MORES. Staff members often react angrily to patients who are transferred from jail and have committed crimes such as rape, incest, or spouse and child abuse. Obscene language and shared confidentialities concerning stealing and cheating also can violate the staff's sense of basic behavioral standards. Violating behaviors call up learned responses to violations of laws and standards (e.g. a staff member thinking, "They ought to be punished."). Therefore, seclusion could be judged as a suitable intervention for any threatening behavior when the patient's behavior assaults a personal behavioral code of the provider.

INDIRECT ASSAULT ON THE SELF-ESTEEM. Patients who are concerned for their own safety often challenge the authority and competence of staff members. Patients often transfer negative feelings from significant others who were responsible for their care in the past to present care providers. Fearful patients, especially adolescent and manic-depressive patients, are clever at identifying the weakest features of staff, such as physical deficits, age extremities, and skill deficiencies. Insults and obscenities concerning sexual identity are common (Madden, 1978). An important facet of self-assessment is to recognize weaknesses and to identify the feelings and coping mechanisms used to deal with an attack on self-esteem. When staff members become frustrated and fearful, they too are drawn into the same dynamics demonstrated in the operational definition of assaultive behavior (Fig. 9-1) and can seek relief from anxiety, powerlessness, and anger by reacting to the patient with assaultive behavior.

STEREOTYPICAL RESPONSES TO VIOLENCE. Male nursing staff members often respond to hostile or violent patients with automatic responses that are derived from the stereotypical role of masculine authority and are based on an intent to use force as the only available intervention (Levy and Harticollis, 1976; Foster, 1976). According to Whitman (1976), confrontation is the most widely used technique to resolve conflict. Most interventions are punitive, and few are based on theory or a plan to ameliorate a disruptive situation. Levy and Horticollis (1976) studied threatening incidents and staff responses on two twenty-bed psychiatric units with similar populations for one year. One unit was staffed with a traditional male-female nursing staff, and the second unit was staffed with females only. The male-female nursing staff reported thirteen violent incidents. The all-female unit did not report any violent incidents, although threatening verbal behaviors and crises were experienced. The researchers questioned if male nursing staff members increased the probability of violence, since the male's formal or informal role of masculine authority is based on the intent to use force when dealing with the violent person. In addition, the researchers wondered if the female staff contributed to stereotypical responses to violent behavior by relying on male staff to confront these patients rather than planning alternative deliberative approaches. The authors also emphasized the role of the male staff members in provoking physical violence with patients when these males are employed specifically to physically enforce rules and to set an expectation for the use of force.

Other Stereotypical Attitudes Affecting the Role of Staff

Rosenhan (1980) notes that psychiatric diagnostic labels attached to patients can set an expectation in staff members for patient behavior. He reports on mentally healthy individuals who were admitted to psychiatric facilities with false diagnoses and gathered information about provider attitudes towards psychiatric patients. These pseudo patients observed that when nurses came upon a scene of a patient who went berserk due to unintentional or intentional provocative handling by a male aide, the nurses would rarely inquire into the environmental stimuli that caused the violent behavior and would accept the out-of-control behavior as part of the patient's pathology. These pseudo patients reported that the segregation of the staff in the nurse's "cage" (station) for long periods set an atmosphere for the patient that caused feelings of powerlessness, fear, mistrust, and horrible expectations. The pseudo patients also noted that nursing staff members contributed to their fears because of the lack of caring responses, such as eye contact and interpersonal contact that emphasized careful listening.

A former psychiatric patient suggests an approach that can help staff model nonconfrontive and caring responses for patients: "The staff must be an example of how to handle anger, mistrust, in other words, show patients how to handle their emotions. Indirect example, not a direct confrontation. This is the most comfortable and tolerant form of learning. . . . Non-verbal is far more powerful than verbal in its meaning. Most of the patients admitted to hospitals are frightened, very sick. . . . They express themselves in non-verbal ways. Verbal communication upsets them. It is the sound that upsets them most; words have lost their meaning. These patients need non-verbal support and communication." (Lunt, 1979).

A Model for Self-assessment When Working with the Violent Patient

As mentioned above, anger is a normal response to assaults on one's domain, and unfortunately, confrontation is the intervention of choice most frequently used. Figure 9-2 shows a working self-assessment model for staff caring for the assaultive or violent patient. The model summarizes Beck's theory that direct verbal, physical threats, or assaults on rights, standards, authority, or self-esteem cause anxiety and anger. All threats to the personal domain or self-space can cause anger, which in turn can bring about fight or flight reactions.

The flight reaction to the anxiety and anger experienced can be explained as automatic compensatory reactions to danger signals (Cannon, 1929), unconscious countertransference, or identification phenomena (Levy and Harticollis, 1976). Automatic compensatory responses and unconscious phenomena can cause the provider to become provocative and punitive, to identify with the assaultive behavior, to attempt to appease the patient because of empathy, or to reject the patient. Also, a hostile affect as well as a depressed affect can become contagious for the staff involved.

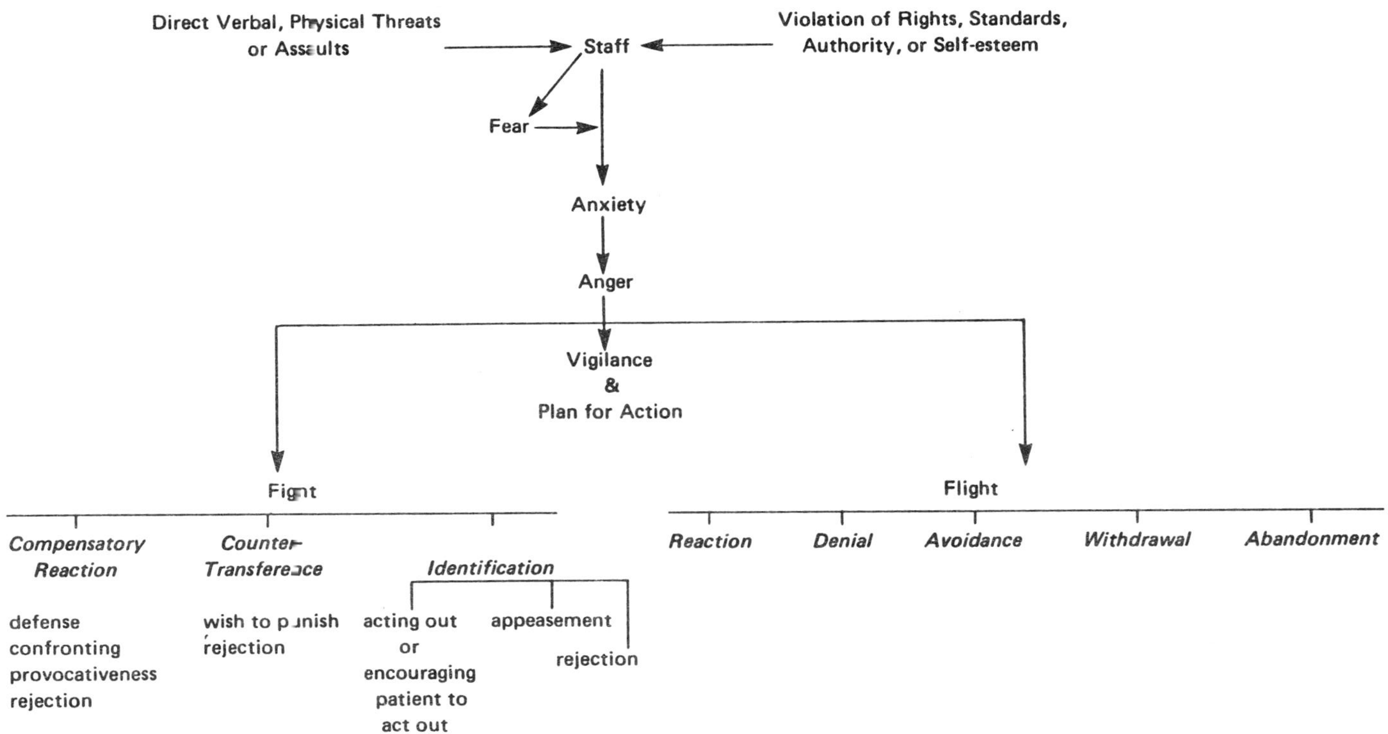

Figure 9-2. A Self-awareness Model when Working with the Assaultive Patient (Drawn from theories presented in A. Beck, *Cognitive Therapy and the Emotional Disorders*, New York, International University Press, 1976; and J. Haber et al., *Comprehensive Psychiatric Nursing*, New York, McGraw-Hill Book Co., 1978.)

Flight reactions are easily understandable responses to anger. Flight often results after the uncomfortable ego alien and physiological responses of anxiety and anger are experienced.

Defense mechanisms such as denial and reaction formation help the staff ignore potentially violent behavior and their own angry responses to it. Staff also can attempt to cope with violence by simple avoidance, withdrawal, and abandonment of the patient. Whitman (1976) found that psychotherapists believed that they were attacked by patients because they denied the clues to potential violence given by the patient or simply avoided hostile behavior of patients.

INTERVENTION WITH THE VIOLENT PATIENT

The ability of the nursing staff to intervene effectively with violent behavior is affected by the staff's awareness of what makes them afraid and angry and their response patterns to fear and anger. The basic assumptions used by the authors for preparing interventions are based on self-awareness of staff and the theory that aggressive responses are always psychologically, if not physically, damaging to both staff and patients. The major therapeutic approach to patients is to offer alternatives in order to assist them to deal more functionally with situations of helplessness and powerlessness.

Validation of feelings by the staff member at the outset of the encounter is essential. People who have low self-esteem and feelings of powerlessness will not listen to those in control until their feelings are confirmed. Acknowledgement of feelings by others symbolizes validation as a person (Ginnott, 1969; Glasser, 1967; Satir, 1967). Patients in an inpatient setting have lost their freedom and independence and need to have their feelings validated as a major part of their essential identity. Validation by the staff member also can communicate empathy, warmth, and genuineness, which are essential qualities for establishing a therapeutic relationship (Carkhuff, 1973). However, the first inroad to controlling violent behavior occurs when the staff member convinces the patient that he or she will be able to control the rage that the patient is experiencing (Haber, 1978).

The goals of prevention and management approaches with violent patients are (1) to protect the patient and staff member, (2) to assist the patient to gain control, (3) to help the patient focus more clearly on the source of the anger, and (4) to assist the patient to express anger verbally rather than in actions. When preparing interventions, it is important to remember that people are less likely to respond in relationships with anger if they judge those involved to be justified, nonarbitrary, and reasonable (Pastor, 1950; Ellis, 1962).

Crisis Approach to Prevention and Management of Violence

As demonstrated below, crisis interventions with potentially violent or violent situations on an inpatient unit can be organized as (1) maintaining territorial space, (2) developing a therapeutic environment and relationship, and (3) avoiding a power struggle.

MAINTAINING TERRITORIAL SPACE. A mandatory approach to the potentially violent or violent patients is to allow a territorial space that is five times greater than that of a person in control (Hildreth et al., 1971). Unless the patient has a trusting relationship with the staff member, he or she should not touch a patient in tenuous control. The patient usually distorts the gesture as a hostile act and it frightens the patient into a defensive combative behavior.

The staff also should heed the space around themselves in order to avoid physical entrapment if the patient loses control. Be sure at all times that there is access to an exit. For example, staff members who treat patients in rooms or offices should sit near the door. If the patient is in very tenuous control, the staff member should stand in the doorway.

DEVELOPING A THERAPEUTIC ENVIRONMENT AND RELATIONSHIP. Reduction of stimuli such as noise and multiple patient and staff contact with newly admitted, agitated, or potentially violent patients is essential. If the patient's hostile behavior is accelerating and threatening, the staff member will get the attention of the patient by addressing the patient by name in a respectful and nonauthoritarian manner. Other major initial interventions are to communicate empathy by validating the patient's feelings and appearing competent, nonarbitrary, and reasonable. The staff member can say, "You are having a rough time. You must feel angry enough to hurt someone. That is not necessary here. I will help you to get into control. Let's go to a quiet place to talk."

The staff member will assess his own fears and at this time assure the patient that the staff member will help the patient to stay in control of feelings and actions. In a caring manner the staff member can say, "I'm concerned about you. I will get more staff if I think I need to in order to keep you from doing anything impulsive or destructive. We will give you the care you need so that you do not have to lose control."

It is important for the staff to communicate empathy and an attitude of respect. A display of empathy at the outset of a threatening incident establishes the base for a therapeutic relationship. Empathy can best be conveyed by validating the patient's feelings here and now. The validation of feelings contributes to the patient's sense of identity by accepting a human feeling without a value judgment of approval or disapproval. Communication from staff to patient must be clear and free of jargon to reduce the risk of distortion by the patient.

Also, the staff establishes a therapeutic environment by offering hope and supportive actions. Instillation of hope is important because violence is inversely related to hope (Lion, 1975). Setting an expectation that the patient can control himself or herself begins to overcome feelings of powerlessness. Direct and frank language can communicate to the patient what is happening at the moment. For example, the staff member can interpret the hostility demonstrated by saying, "I can see you are mad enough to hit me. I will help you so that you can control yourself." Both the words and the tone used must avoid sounding derogatory and blaming or threatening to one's self-esteem and sense of power.

AVOIDING A POWER STRUGGLE. In order to develop a therapeutic culture, it is necessary to set limits for unacceptable behavior but without developing a power struggle. Also, self-awareness and vigilance frees the staff for care planning and offering choices of interventions to the patient. In order to mitigate a heightened sense of powerlessness and to avoid a power struggle, it will be necessary to present several suitable alternatives to uncontrolled behavior. To create a sense of sharing of power with the patient, the staff member will meet some of the patient's demands in one area in order to limit demands in others. For example the staff member can negotiate by saying, "The door can be left open if you stay in your room. I will visit every five minutes to check on how you are managing yourself."

Offering the patient alternative approaches to management is necessary because powerless people reject single demands. Alternative interventions with assaultive patients include providing more frequent contact with a trusted, familiar staff member of the opposite sex; if possible, helping the patient focus the anger felt on the precipitating factor and/or person; and verbalizing feelings regarding the event. If the patient is not too agitated, the staff member often can prevent assaultive behavior by offering patient physical activities such as walking, exercising, and playing at sports, which can diffuse anxiety. Expressing anger by acting out violent feelings is not an alternative approach to management.

Patients are not encouraged to "express" their anger by hitting a punching bag or pillow because working theories demonstrate that relieving anxiety and powerlessness through acting out anger with assaultive behavior actually reinforces the assaultive behavior (Lion, 1975; Mehr and Hollerauer, 1979). It is important to note that most patients have histories of acting out their feelings of powerlessness and frustrations by using assault as a coping mechanism. Therefore, the staff can concentrate on cognitive and supportive approaches that encourage talking out violent urges and feelings and taking medication when appropriate. These approaches can facilitate the development of a therapeutic relationship, which will enhance long-range interventions.

If a patient has experienced repeated episodes of violent outbursts, the staff member can ask the patient about the type and dosage of medications usually taken to help gain control. Patients often know what medications help and will recognize that they have some knowledge and are being given some negotiable power in the current situation. Patients are offered oral medications and are given medications intramuscularly only when they are clearly a danger to themselves and/or others and refuse oral medications. Giving intramuscular medications by force is to be avoided whenever possible because it is detrimental to the staff-patient relationship, reinforces powerless feelings, and models force as a therapeutic style.

When a patient is a danger to self and others, limits must be set, accompanied with empathy and an expectation that the patient will take responsibility for his or her behavior. The nurse can say, "Stop that. You cannot do that here. You are a danger to yourself and others. You can hurt someone with that chair. What do you usually do when you become so upset? Do it now. I want to help you now." Appendix A summarizes the above crisis interventions with the violent patient.

Violence Precautions

Violence precautions are another strategy for intervention with the potentially violent patient. As listed below, these precautions integrate crisis approaches to prevention and management of violent behavior. They include the following:

1. A minimum of fifteen-minute observations of the patient.
2. A twenty-four-hour care plan that includes specific approaches to decrease stimuli.
3. Detailed charting on each shift of an assessment of the patient's response to stimuli, violent and/or tenuous behavior, interventions, and the patient's response to them.
4. A discussion with the patient regarding staff's expectation that he or she remain in control and use staff as resources to bolster his or her control. Staff also convey that they will take over if the patient is in imminent danger of losing control.
5. Careful assessment of the patient's ability to tolerate off-unit tests, procedures, and activities, limiting these whenever necessary to promote the patient's well-being (If the patient is cleared for off-unit appointments, accompany the patient on a one-to-one basis or with an additional staff member if advisable.)
6. A thorough check of the patient's room and belongings for sharp and/or dangerous objects. Also, ensure that the milieu is as devoid as possible of articles that could be used as weapons.
7. Discussion with appropriate visitors about special precautions and careful inspection of items brought in. Only if necessary, limit either the number of visitors at a time or specific visitors if it is clear that their presence is highly likely to provoke a violent episode.
8. Refusal to meet with the patient alone in his room unless backup support is readily available and only if staff have free access to the door.
9. Implementation of time-outs, seclusion, or full-sheet restraint prior to a violent episode if the patient's behavior indicates that such an act is imminent.

The most effective implementation of violence precautions occurs when the staff in the emergency department determines that such an order should be instituted prior to transfer to an inpatient unit. A plan can be instituted prior to transfer easing inpatient admission and preventing an unexpected outburst during the transfer process or upon entry to the unit causing concern for other inpatients. Prior to transfer, the patient is searched for potential weapons. The emergency room staff then ascertain which unit is preferable for admission based on the number of patients on a unit who are on violence precautions. On the recommendation of the emergency room staff, the patient may be admitted directly to a seclusion room for a period of observation. The patient is also evaluated for the need for medication, and it is administered prior to transfer, whenever possible. Information about the patient's violence potential and the need for precautions is verbally conveyed by the emergency room staff to the charge nurse of the admitting unit. When planning such as this occurs for the potentially violent patient before admission to an inpatient unit, staff can prepare the milieu and reassign personnel in order to deal effectively with the acutely ill patient.

After patients are identified as being at risk for a violent episode, individualized approaches can be formulated to increase the possibility of preventing actual violence. One of the most effective approaches is to decrease stimulation and to decrease situations that may be frustrating to the patient. This necessitates close observation implemented in a manner that provides the patient with adequate space and privacy. For example, the patient who is suspicious and delusional generally is in need of room to move around the unit unencumbered. Such a patient is generally frightened of other patients and staff and is not receptive to having long or frequent verbal interchanges. Staff may elect to observe the patient at a distance, being readily available within the milieu to intervene in potentially troublesome situations. Staff can initiate occasional contact with the patient in order to meet basic needs, such as food, general comfort, and need for milieu information. In addition, staff can intervene with other patients who may be seen as intruders by the suspicious patient. Since the suspicious patient's perception of reality is distorted, behaviors by other patients may be misinterpreted as threatening or derogatory.

Seclusion

Because of its nature, patients and staff alike have strong feelings about seclusion. Since our society has experienced an increase in violence, and an inpatient psychiatric setting is a microcosm of the greater societal norms and behaviors, there will continue to be a need to use seclusion and to understand its potential therapeutic benefits, liabilities, and effective application.

Gair states "Seclusion is not a treatment policy, it is an implementation of the therapeutic necessity of limit-setting" (1980, p. 16). When patients cannot demonstrate an ability to internally control their behavior, which holds the potential for harm to themselves, others, or the environment, the staff is mandated to intervene for the safety of all involved. As mentioned earlier in this paper, there are other less restrictive methods than seclusion that need to be used first in potentially violent or violent situations, but when other approaches fail to produce the desired outcome, seclusion may be implemented.

Gutheil (1978) theorizes that seclusion rests on three interrelated principles: containment, isolation, and decreasing sensory input. Containment means restricting a patient's movement in a place that is both safe for the patient and others. Isolation is described as an oasis from interpersonal relationships; that is, patients who misinterpret the meanings of relationships are harassed by the misinformation and experience seclusion as an oasis. The seriously ill person is also vulnerable to sensory input, for example, sound, sight, smell, touch, and occasionally taste and vibration. Seclusion offers a means of decreasing this input.

Providing safety for the medication-free agitated patient is another distinct reason for seclusion (Schwab and Lahmeyr, 1979). Medication-free periods for the purposes of observation and assessment of symptomatology are particularly valuable during the initial phase of hospitalization.

When used with good clinical judgment, seclusion can be an effective therapeutic intervention. However, negative effects, such as regression, suicide attempts, and physical complications, have been identified (Greenblatt, 1980). Three major potentially negative effects were identified by Gutheil (1978): (1) an envy of the secluded patient by nonsecluded patients (seclusion in this instance symbolizes for the nonsecluded patient a caring by the staff); (2) a lasting anathema when patients who have been secluded hold a grudge against either those who placed them in seclusion, or against the person who ordered seclusion; (3) abandonment, when the secluded patient is forgotten by the staff, suggesting that staff attention may have been more effective than seclusion.

PLACING THE PATIENT IN SECLUSION. Although negative effects exist and the controversy continues, seclusion will remain as an approach for controlling the violent patient and needs to be effected in a skillful and humane manner. When a decision to seclude a patient has been made, sufficient numbers of staff should be organized with one nurse identified as leading the seclusion intervention. A clear plan should include designation of one nurse to talk with the patient and to explain available options. In some instances, the assignment of patient limbs to the staff for restraint may be done in advance if the patient is likely to resist. If medication is to be given after the patient is in seclusion, it should be prepared prior to or during the seclusion. Physical handling of the patient must be executed in a manner that prevents injury to both the patient and staff. Holding the patient's limbs next to major joints limits leverage and prevents dislocation or fracture.

An explanation as to why seclusion is being used, what will happen during the seclusion period, and behaviors expected before patients will be removed from seclusion is given to the patient as part of the seclusion process. Not all patients are able to comprehend the information during the initial seclusion process. Therefore, although the information is offered, it should be repeated upon subsequent visits. Often, the staff will request that patients contract to refrain from violent behavior as a condition for termination of seclusion. With some patients this can be very effective; with others it means a prolonging of seclusion unnecessarily. Some psychotic patients benefit from seclusion, but are not integrated sufficiently to make a rational agreement. A sensitivity to the patient's nonverbal behavior is required.

While in seclusion, the patient must be closely monitored and approached with the goal that seclusion will be terminated as quickly as possible. Fifteen-minute observations of the patient are necessary with hourly entry into the seclusion room by the staff to offer food, fluids, and bathroom facilities. Vital signs are monitored at these times, and an assessment is done of the effectiveness of medication or need for medication. Opportunities for interaction with the patient provide staff members with data necessary to evaluate the patient's progress—ability to handle stimuli and to control aggressive impulses. The patient is continually evaluated for potential or actual self-harm. In instances when the patient has scratched himself or herself, or is head-banging, a more restrictive approach such as full-sheet restraint may be necessary to safeguard the patient's physical well-being. In addition, some patients may become very intent on suicide while in seclusion, necessitating the staff's comprehensive inspection, during each observation period, of any alterations made in the room, such as dismantling light fixtures or heating equipment.

ENDING SECLUSION. When evaluation of the secluded patient warrants instituting a process of removing the patient from seclusion, a step-by-step plan should be formulated for the patient's reintegration into the milieu. Often limited therapeutic benefit is realized when the patient moves directly from seclusion into full milieu activities and stimuli. Therefore, the patient progresses from the room to access to limited areas of the unit and to small groups of patients.

Over the next twenty-four hours or longer if necessary, the patient is monitored closely to ensure continued progress or to intervene to prevent complete loss of control. The patient may be requested to return to his or her room to spend some quiet time if it is determined that he or she is having difficulty coping with the stimuli of the unit. Or, the staff may ask to spend some time with the patient apart from others, thus removing the patient from unit stimuli while affording him or her the opportunity to discuss feelings, to reflect on progress, and to plan for the next couple of hours.

SECLUSION AND OTHER PATIENTS. The seclusion experience can be frightening to patients, and so an opportunity to discuss perceptions and feelings associated with seclusion should be provided for each patient who is secluded. In addition, other patients who witness the seclusion process and/or are aware of the patient being in seclusion need an opportunity to discuss their perceptions and fears with staff. Generally, concerns about seclusion can be incorporated in a daily community meeting during which unit issues can be raised by both staff and patients, or an emergency community meeting can be convened. Some patients experience relief when patients who they fear could harm themselves or staff are secluded. If this response is not dealt with adequately, the secluded patient's reentry to the milieu may be more difficult. As well, patients may be angry that a violent patient was admitted to *their* unit and may desire that the patient be left in seclusion. In instances where staff members are injured, patients may express much anger toward the violent patient and fear that the staff cannot control him or her or may not be able to control one of them should they also become violent. Other patients also become concerned about their own violence potential and are in need of support and reality testing. Others may need additional limit-setting and a decrease in stimuli at these times. Lastly, patients may express anger towards the staff, feeling that their actions were abusive and unwarranted. Patients' anger may be motivated by fear that they too will be secluded without cause. Some patients, for a multiplicity of reasons, may fear that they will be secluded, and this fear will preclude active participation in a community discussion. Because of the complexity of feelings aroused by a patient's seclusion, the staff should facilitate an open discussion among patients and be receptive to varied opinions and feelings. Some patients may experience a one-to-one discussion with the staff as a more effective mode than the group meeting for expressing concerns and receiving reassurance.

In summary, seclusion is a restrictive therapeutic intervention, and when used with good clinical judgment and after other less restrictive measures have been tried, it can be effective in the prevention and control of violent patients. It is not always possible to prevent violence, but it is possible, based on a thorough assessment and implementation of violence precautions, to plan for the management of the potential and/or violent patient.

Long-range Interventions

As soon as possible after admission, the staff should plan long-range approaches with the patient who is prone to violence. Through discussions with the staff, the patient explores antecedents that lead to loss of control and identifies the sequel of learned, patterned behavior responses. Problems created by violent behavior are identified. Because patients prone to violence often have difficulty in communicating their needs and feelings clearly and directly, communication patterns of the patient are examined. It is important to point out the self-destructive aspects of acting-out and reasons new behaviors must be learned to handle the anger.

A primary focus both for the initial intervention and ongoing therapeutic intervention is to help the patient express anger and violent urges through words rather than actions. Lion (1972, p. 60) suggests a method for helping patients to learn how to identify and translate hostile feelings into words: (1) Recall and describe physical symptoms associated with anger, for example, tachycardia, flushed face, and muscle and stomach tension (these symptoms can warn the patient that he is feeling anger); (2) report incidents of violence in detail in order to recall affect as every detail is unfolded; and (3) help the patient fantasize about his or her feelings of wanting to harm or kill as a mechanism in order to get the patient to think of the consequences of impulsive actions and to motivate him or her to learn to control violent urges. Fantasy can help patients to understand what could happen after the violent act, for example, incarceration, loss of loved one, and alienation of family and friends.

Patients also can learn that anxiety resulting from feelings of powerlessness can be reduced by assertive rather than aggressive or assaultive behavior (Cotler and Guerra, 1976). Assertiveness training groups can be effective in helping patients to express their angry feelings in acceptable ways that do not infringe on the rights of others. Consequently, they develop self-respect, reduce anxiety, defuse potentially assaultive situations, and learn new social skills.

Outlined below are long-range preventive and management approaches to violent behavior. They emphasize helping the patient to express needs directly, to recognize feelings, and to actively try to meet needs with assertive behavior.

1. Contract with the patient to work to change learned assaultive behavior patterns.
2. Model caring and build trust.
3. Provide assertiveness training.
4. Develop communication skills to facilitate clear and direct communication.
5. Engage the patient in experiential learning on how to delay gratification, to negotiate, and to problem solve concerning alternatives to impulsive and assaultive behavior.
6. With the patient, develop specific plans to—

a) identify problems the client creates with assaultive behavior.
b) identify feelings of fear, anger, and powerlessness.
c) describe physiological states accompanying fear and anger in order to identify these feelings earlier and work on control.
d) fantasize the feelings and thoughts that accompany fear and anger as well as an anticipation of the consequences of acting out anger.
e) track stressful situations and antecedents leading to assaultive wishes and actions.
f) record patterns of acting out emotions.
g) identify transference errors in the hospital, at work, and in social situations.
h) recognize negative thinking errors associated with low self-esteem.
i) learn how to share power and negotiate with significant others and people in authority positions.
j) increase pleasure and recreation activities.
k) seek satisfying work situations.

Patterns of impulsive and violent behavior learned early and used over a long period of time often necessitate prolonged treatment with behavior modification, individual, or family therapy.

Other cognitive approaches also can be effective in changing violent interpersonal styles. The staff can help patients to recognize learned thinking patterns that contribute to low self-esteem and hopelessness (Beck, 1975). Hopelessness and self-hate can be countered by empirical demonstrations and reality testing of constant negative predictions and self-criticisms. The tyranny of the "shoulds and oughts" that build anger can be discussed, and problem-solving techniques can be explored (Coche and Flick, 1975).

The staff can discuss with patients the impact of strong feelings held towards significant others in relation to transference and displacement onto authority figures, for example nurses, doctors, bosses, and teachers. Frustration in the work or home situation should be evaluated with the patient to determine when these situations and individuals are provocative and reinforcing to assaultive behavior. For example, the patient may control the work group through the group's fear resulting from past violent outbursts. Also, the staff can model assertive behaviors as an alternative to confrontation.

Violent individuals have few sublimation outlets for their anger, such as being involved with sports and other pleasure activities. The staff and patients can explore leisure-time activities as possible therapeutic events. Efforts of patients to find appropriate and less frustrating work situations also can be supported by the staff.

CONCLUSIONS

Staff members assume a large responsibility for the prevention and management of violent behavior in emergency and inpatient psychiatric facilities. They can become more effective in handling this challenge when they (1) understand antecedent variables associated with violent behavior; (2) systematically assess patients regarding violence potential; (3) employ preventive strategies; (4) possess self-awareness and employ a self-assessment approach; and (5) intervene with strategies known for their effectiveness.

APPENDIX A

Crisis Approach to Prevention and Intervention with the Violent Patient

Goal: to protect self and patient and to assist patient to gain control

A. *Maintain Territorial Space for Patient and Self*
   1. Avoid physical entrapment.
   2. Maintain territorial space five times that of the patient in control.
   3. Do not touch the patient.
   4. Seek additional help if necessary and state, "I'm concerned about your condition and I'm going to have some other people here so that you will not do anything impulsive or destructive."

B. *Develop a Therapeutic Environment and Relationship*
   5. Remove stimuli.
   6. Call the person by name using an attitude of respect and

avoiding an authoritarian or punitive approach.

7. Reflect the patient's feelings of anger, fear of loss of control, and powerlessness. Validate feelings: "You sure are uptight. You must feel angry enough to hurt someone."
8. Be direct, frank, for example, "I can see you want to hit me. That is not necessary. I will help you control yourself."
9. Identify unmet needs: "What happened? Who's involved?"
10. Avoid contributing to feelings of low self-esteem and powerlessness. Do not use derogatory language or blaming statements. Provide hope and support.
11. Do not threaten. Keep words simple, concise, and clear, for example, "I'm concerned about you. I want to help you get control."

C. *Avoid a Power Struggle*

12. Give power by offering alternatives, for example, "What do you usually do to get control when you become so angry? How can we help? Does walking help? Talking? Talking in a quiet place?"
13. Set limits if threatening: "You are a danger to yourself and others. I will help you get into control. Stop that. I am going to have to help you stop that. You can hurt someone with that chair."
14. Discuss helpful interventions and give choices; single demands will be rejected:
    a. Time-outs and decreased stimuli: "This place is upsetting. Take some time out. Let's move to a quiet place to talk."
    b. Medications. Ask what has been helpful in the past: "Do you take medications when you think you are losing control? What helps most?"
    c. Activity helps when the patient is not too hyperactive or agitated.
    d. Offer frequent contact with a trusted, familiar person, usually of the opposite sex.
    e. Physical isolation (seclusion): "You will have to be in a room by yourself to help you stay in control of your actions."
    f. Physical restraint: "Do you think being covered with a heavy sheet would help you stay in control? Someone will

stay with you to take care of you until you can control yourself."

15. Determine cause of out-of-control feelings and antecedent events. Focus anger by talking about feelings, stressors, and antecedents.
16. Reality-test around antecedents: "Sometimes when people are under a lot of stress, they see situations in an exaggerated way."

REFERENCES

Anders, R.L.: When a patient becomes violent. *American Journal of Nursing, 77(7)*:1144-1149, July 1977.

Beck, A.T.: *Cognitive Therapy and the Emotional Disorders*. New York, International University-Press, 1976.

Berkowitz, L.: *Aggression: A Social Psychological Analysis*. New York, McGraw-Hill, 1962.

Block, B.: Preparing students for physical restraints. *Journal of Psychiatric Nursing and Mental Health Services*, October 1976, pp. 9-10.

Blout, A.R., et al.: Relationship between childhood abuse and assaultive behavior in adolescent male psych patients. *Psychological Reports, 44*:1223-1229, June 1979.

Cannon, W.B.: *Bodily Changes in Pain, Hunger, Fear, and Rage*. New York, Appleton, 1929.

Carkhuff, R.: *The Art of Helping*. Amherst, Mass., Human Resources Development Press, 1973.

Carney, M.W.P.: Management of the disturbed patient in a psychiatric hospital security unit. *Nursing Times, 75*:1896-1899, Nov. 1, 1979.

Clark, J.: Nursing intervention into the aggressive behavior of patients. In Burd, S.F., and Marshall, M.A. (Eds.): *Some Clinical Approaches to Psychiatric Nursing*. New York, MacMillan, 1963, pp. 199-236.

Cline, R.: The rageful patient. *Nurse Practice*, January-February, 1980.

Coche, E., and Flick, A.: Problem-solving training groups for hospitalized psychiatric patients. *Journal of Psychology*, 1975, p. 91.

Conference report: Handling the violent patient in the hospital. *Hospital and Community Psychiatry, 29(7)*:463-467, July 1978.

Cornfield, R., et al.: Impact of the threatening patient on ward communications. *American Journal of Psychiatry, 137(5)*:616-619, May 1980.

Danesh, H.B.: Anger and fear. *American Journal of Psychiatry*, October 1977, pp. 1109-1112.

DiBella, G.A.W.: Educating staff to manage threatening paranoid patients. *American Journal of Psychiatry, 136(3)*:333-335, March 1979.

Dollard, J., and Miller, N.E.: *Personality and Psychotherapy*. New York, McGraw-Hill, 1950.

Ellis, A.: *Reason and Emotion in Psychotherapy*. New York, Lyle Stewart, 1962.

Fauman, N.A., and Fauman, B.J.: Violence associated with phencyclidine abuse. *American Journal of Psychiatry, 136*:1584-1586, 1979.

Fottrell, E.: A study of violent behavior among patients in psychiatric hospitals. *British Journal of Psychiatry, 36*:211-221, March 1980.

Gair, D.S.: Limit-setting and seclusion in the psychiatric hospital. *Psychiatric Opinion, 17(2)*:15-19, February 1980.

Garfield, S.Q.: *An Exploratory Study of the Use of Seclusion*. Unpublished manuscript, New Haven, Conn., Yale University of Nursing, 1969.

Ginott, H.G.: *Between Parent and Child*. New York, Avon, 1979.

Glasser, W.: *Reality Therapy: A New Approach to Psychiatry*. New York, Harper and Row, 1965.

Goldstein, R.: Brain research and violent behavior. *Archives of Neurology, 30*:1-18, 1974.

Gorney, R., et al.: Cultural determinants of achievements, aggression, and psychological distress. *Archives of General Psychiatry, 37(4)*:452-459, April 1980.

Greenblatt, M.: Seclusion as a means of restraint. *Psychiatric Opinion, 17(2)*:13-14, February 1980.

Guenther, A.L.: Conference report on handling the violent patient in the hospital. *Hospital and Community Psychiatry, 29(7)*:463-467, July 1978.

Guirguis, E.: Management of disturbed patients: an alternative to the use of mechanical restraints. *Journal of Clinical Psychiatry, 39(4)*:295-303, April 1978.

Gutheil, T.: Observations on the theoretical bases for seclusion of the psychiatric inpatient. *American Journal of Psychiatry, 135(3)*:325-328, 1978.

Haber, J., et al.: *Comprehensive Psychiatric Nursing*. New York, McGraw-Hill, 1978, pp. 247-280.

Halleck, S.L.: Psychodynamic aspects of violence. *The Bulletin of the American Academy of Psychiatry and the Law, 4(4)*:328-335, 1976.

Hartocollis, P.: Aggressive behavior and the fear of violence. *Adolescence, 7*:479-490, 1972.

Hellman, D., and Blackman N.: Enuresis, firesetting and cruelty to animals: A triad predictive of adult crime. *American Journal of Psychiatry, 122*:1431-1435, 1966.

Hildreth, A.M., et al.: Body buffer zone and violence: A reassessment and confirmation. *American Journal of Psychiatry, 127(12)*:77-81, June 1971.

Hudgens, R.W.: Murder by a manic depressive. *International Journal of Neuropsychiatry, 1*:381-383, 1965.

Jasmin, S., and Trygstad, L.N.: *Behavioral Concepts and the Nursing Process*. St. Louis, C.V. Mosby Co., 1979.

Justice, B., Justice R., and Kraft, J.: Early warning sings of violence: is a triad enough?, *American Journal of Psychiatry, 131*:457-459, 1974.

Kalogerakis, M.G.: The assaultive psychiatric patient. *Psychiatric Quarterly, 45(3)*:372-381, 1971.

Krashmer, J.F.: The application of social learning theory to aggression. *Perspectives in Psychiatric Care, 16*:223-227, 1978.

Kilgalen, R.K.: The effective use of seclusion. *Journal of Psychiatric Nursing and Mental Health Services*. January 1977, pp.22-25.

Kinzel, A.F.: Body-buffer zone in violent prisoners. *American Journal of Psychiatry, 127*:1, July 1970.

Lange, S.: The "violent" patient: Approaches to coping with problematic patients. In *Scientific Bases for Therapeutic Nursing Practice*. San Francisco, ANA Clinical Sessions, 1966.

Lemmer, B.: A slap in the face. Violence in psychiatric hospitals. *Nursing Mirror, 149*:18-19, Aug. 30, 1979.

Levy, P., and Hartocollis, P.: Nursing aides and patient violence. *American Journal of Psychiatry, 133(4)*:429-431, April 1976.

Lion, J.R.: *Evaluation and Management of the Violent Patient*. Springfield, Ill., Charles C Thomas, Publisher, 1972.

Lion, J.R., Bach-Y-Rita, G., and Ervin, F.R.: Violent patients in the emergency room. *American Journal of Psychiatry, 125*:12, June 1969.

Lion, J.R., Madden, D.J., and Christopher, R.: A violence clinic: Three years' experience. *American Journal of Psychiatry, 133*:4, April 1976.

Lion, J.R., Snyder, W., and Merrill, G.L.: Under-reporting of assaults on staff in a state hospital. *Hospital and Community Psychiatry, 32*:497-498, July 1981.

Lunt, L.B.: *Walking Against the Wind*. Published by author, 1979.

Madden, D.J.: Assaults on psychiatrists by patients. *American Journal of Psychiatry, 133*:432-435, 1973.

Mark, V., and Ervin, F.R.: *Violence and the Brain*. New York, Harper and Row, 1970.

Medico-Psychological Association. *Manual for Mental Deficiency Nurses*. London, Bailliere, Tendall and Cox, 1931.

Mehr, J., and Hollerauer, T.: *Violence Workshop*. New York, October 1979.

Mikolejczak, J., and Hagen, D.Q.: Aggression in psychiatric patients in a VA hospital. *Military Medicine, 143(6)*, June 1978.

Mills, T.: *The Sociology of Small Groups*. Englewood Cliffs, N.J., Prentice Hall, 1967.

Montague, M.C.: Physiology of aggressive behavior. *Journal of Neurosurgery Nurse, 11*:1-5, March 1979.

Pastor, N.: The role of arbitrariness in the frustration-aggression hypothesis. *Journal of Abnormal Social Psychology, 47*:728-731, 1952.

Pennigroth, P.E.: Control of violence in a mental health setting. *American Journal of Nursing, 75*:606-609, April 1975.

Pilette, P.C.: The tyranny of seclusion: A brief essay. *Journal of Psychiatric Nursing and Mental Health Services*, October 1978, pp.19-21.

Prevention and Violence (Editorial). *British Medical Journal, 31*, March 1979.

Roche report. *Frontiers of Psychiatry, 10(1)*:12-13, 1980.

Rose, D.: The Palo Alto destructive content scale as a predictor of physical assaultiveness in men. *Journal of Personal Assessment, 44(3)*:228-233, June 1980.

Rosebaum, P., and Beebe, J.: *Psychiatric Treatment, Crisis, Clinic, Consultation*. New York, McGraw-Hill, 1975.

Ruben, I., et al.: Physical attacks on psychiatric residents by patients. *Journal of*

Nervous Mental Disorders, 168(4):243-245, April 1980.

Rumpler, C.H., et al.: A behavior modification approach to dealing with violent behavior in an intensive care unit. *Perspectives in Psychiatric Nursing, 16*:206-211, September-December 1978.

Satir, V.: *Conjoint Family Therapy*. Palo Alto, Calif., Science and Behavior Books, Inc., 1967.

Schwab, P., and Lahmeyer, C.: The uses of seclusion on a general psychiatric unit. *Journal of Clinical Psychiatry, 40(5)*:228-231, 1979.

Sears, R.R., Macoby, E., and Levin, H.: *Patterns of Child Rearing*. New York, Harper and Row, 1957.

Shah, S.A.: Dangerousness and mental illness: Some conceptual, prediction, and policy dilemmas. In *Dangerous Behavior: A Problem in Law and Mental Health*. Washington, D.C., NIMH, U.S. Department of Health, Education, and Welfare, 1978, p. 154.

Slaby, A., Lieb, J., and Tancredi, L.: *Handbook of Psychiatric Emergencies*. New York, Medical Examination Publishing, 1975.

Sosowsky, L.: Crime and violence among mental patients reconsidered in view of the new legal relationship between the state and the mentally ill. *American Journal of Psychiatry, 135(1)*:33-42, January 1978.

Stanton, A.H., and Schwartz, M.S.: *The Mental Hospital*. New York, Basic Books, 1954.

Steadman, H.J:., Coccozza, J.J., and Melick, M.: Explaining the increased arrest rate among mental patients: The changing clientele of state hospitals. *American Journal of Psychiatry, 135(7)*:816-820, July 1978.

Storr, A.: *Human Aggression*. New York, Atheneum, 1968.

Stuart, G.W., and Sundeen, S.J.: *Principles and Practice of Psychiatric Nursing*. St. Louis, C.V. Mosby, 1979.

Sullivan, H.S.: *The Interpersonal Theory of Psychiatry*. New York, W.W. Norton & Co., Inc., 1953.

Trincomi, B., et al.: Perspectus on the combative patient. *Journal of Nursing Care. 12*:15-24, November 1979.

West, L.J.: *The Biosocial Origins of Violence*. Address delivered at the University of Rochester Conference, Violence: Origins and Management, June 1979.

Whaley, M., and Pamirez, L.: The use of seclusion rooms and physical restraints in the treatment of psychiatric patients. *Journal of Psychiatric Nursing and Mental Health Services, 18(1)*:13-16, 1980.

Whitman, R.N., et al.: Assault on the therapist. *American Journal of Psychiatry. 133*:133:426-429, 1976.

Chapter 10

BEHAVIORAL TREATMENT FOR AGGRESSION IN RESIDENTS OF INSTITUTIONS FOR THE EMOTIONALLY DISTURBED AND THE MENTALLY RETARDED

JOSEPH J. MEHR AND TYRONE C. HOLLERAUER

THE need to treat individuals who are violent continues to be a significant problem for staff working in residential facilities for the emotionally disturbed and the mentally retarded. Disagreement exists regarding the proportion of such individuals who actually manifest behavior before, during, and after institutionalization (Rappaport and Lassen, 1965, 1966; Giovannoni and Gurel, 1967; Guze, Woodruff, and Clayton, 1974; Lagos, Perlmutter, and Saexinger, 1977; Zitrin et al., 1976). However, a number of studies have demonstrated that significant numbers of such individuals are present in human service delivery systems at any one time. Evenson and his colleagues (1974), for example, found that in a population of 1,004 inpatients at St. Louis State Hospital, there were 395 reported incidents of assault, property damage, or self-injury during 1969 and 1970. More recently in 1979, Mehr (1980*a*) surveyed twenty Illinois facilities for the mentally ill or the mentally retarded and found a very significant number of residents who engaged in chronically violent behavior (*see* Table 10-I).

Table 10-I

Residents manifesting repeated violent acts toward others, self, or property in facilities for the mentally ill or mentally retarded in Illinois.

	No. of Facilities Surveyed	Total No. of Residents	No. of Violent Repeaters	Percentage
M.I.	11	3648	436	9.9
M.R.	9	4845	408	8.4
Combined	20	8493	844	9.1

For some time, the authors have had the opportunity to examine this issue in Illinois and to have formal discussions on the topic with several hundred staff members from many other states. These contacts have highlighted a number of factors that may have enhanced the perceived significance of the problem. At the beginning of the deinstitutionalization movement in the late 1950s and early 1960s, many residents in such institutions were described as "model" patients, that is as manifesting little in the way of problem behaviors outside of a dependence on institutional life. Since that time, facility populations have decreased nationwide by approximately two-thirds, and it was the least problematic residents who were discharged.

During the two decades from 1960 to 1980, when mental hospital populations decreased from approximately 600,000 to less than 200,000 residents, however, those who manifested chronic aggression were unlikely to be discharged, or if discharged, were likely to be readmitted if the behavior occurred in the community. Institutional residents who have a *history* of aggressive behavior (even when that behavior is not currently being manifested) are extremely difficult to place in the community. Most community health care providers, such as sheltered care living facilities, are simply not willing to take the risk of recurrence of the aggressive behavior in their setting.

A concurrent development, which seems to have accentuated the problem for institutional staff, has been the national trend to limit involuntary hospitalization to persons who are a physical danger to themselves or to others. An involuntary patient is now simply more likely to be behaviorally dangerous than in the past. What is being suggested here is *not* that mentally ill and mentally retarded persons are *more* dangerous now than they were twenty years ago, but rather that staff in residential treatment programs encounter a greater *proportion* of individuals who manifest behavior dangerous to themselves or others. This appears to be particularly the case in settings in which longer-term treatment is required. The continued manifestation of physical violence is likely to lead to extrusion from short-term intensive programs to longer-term treatment programs in public mental hospitals or institutions for the retarded. In these settings, aggressive individuals reach the end of the line, so to speak, and become proportionately a problem of major significance for the staff involved in their treatment.

CHARACTERISTICS OF THE AGGRESSORS

Individuals in institutional residential settings for the emotionally disturbed (mental hospitals) and for the mentally retarded (state schools) who are chronically aggressive tend to share many characteristics (Mehr, 1980*b*). These characteristics are particularly apparent in individuals who have been called "under-controlled" aggressors.

LACK OF FRUSTRATION TOLERANCE. The chronic institutionalized aggressor appears to have an inability to tolerate frustration and delay. When he or she wants something, it is wanted *now*, not later. They seem relatively unable to postpone, to accept contingencies. The lack of frustration tolerance may in part be due to the *degree* of frustration we require them to tolerate. The institutional setting places many constraints on its residents that are not experienced, or at least not so acutely, in community life. An obvious example is in the regulation of sexual behavior: In most institutions, *any* sexual behavior is considered a violation of rules, and staff are expected to prevent it in some way.

PROBLEMS OF TRUST. The chronic aggressor is usually distrustful of both staff and other residents. Staff have made promises or agreements that they have broken (often for good, rational reasons, but that matters little to the patient). Other patients have perhaps physically attacked him or her, or have "squealed" to staff about events that have occurred. This lack of trust may also revolve around the hypervigilance and sensitivity of a paranoid life-style or transient paranoid ideation.

EXTERNALIZATION OF RESPONSIBILITY. The chronic aggressor typically places the responsibility for his or her behavior on the environment or on other persons. In a sense, they don't experience themselves as mediators of their own behavior: The chair is thrown because someone taunted them, the nurse is hit because she "tried to make me sit down," or another patient is beaten because the "voices told me to." One rarely hears the aggressor say, "I hit because I was angry."

LITTLE CAPACITY FOR SELF-OBSERVATION. Chronic aggressors are often "out of touch" with themselves in the sense that their motivations for aggressive behavior often evade them. Along with the externalization of responsibility described above, such individuals act out precipitously and often seem unaware of the feelings and cognitions leading up to the behavior. As the aggressive act draws near, they seem to have a sense of agitation, but often do not seem to feel anger or rage until the act is imminent.

LIFETIME HISTORY OF AGGRESSION. Most of our chronic adult aggressors have long histories of using aggressive acting-out as a response to frustration. The aggressive behavior is apparent in their histories far back into adolescence and childhood, usually long predating their first institutionalization. In those years, aggression was frequently an effective immediate coping mechanism, reinforced by its effects on those around them.

THE IMPACT OF CHRONIC AGGRESSORS ON RESIDENTIAL INSTITUTIONS: SYSTEMS IN CRISIS

The chronic aggressors, either in a treatment sense or a management sense, throw our systems into crisis, and the part of the system affected is the mental health worker, who by education, training, and experience is ill-prepared to deal effectively with the violent patient. Understanding, empathetic, and nonjudgmental, the worker is expected to deliver a valued service, to help those who need help, and to some extent to be appreciated by those who are helped. While the violent patient is not the only category that does not mesh with our own role definition and our expectations, it is a significant one.

In some conceptual systems, aggression is seen as the primary issue in both the patient violent toward others and the patient violent toward self (i.e. depressed). However, in terms of our feelings about such patients, we can usually empathize with the depressed patient, be nonjudgmental towards him or her, offer our help and be accepted, and usually maintain common goals. In contrast, while we may understand the violent patient, it is difficult to empathize except in the abstract and almost impossible to be nonjudgmental when the behavior endangers others, especially ourselves.

How we see ourselves (as helpers), how the violent patient sees us (as agents of the system and as obstacles to behavioral expression), and the broader social system's controls for deviant behavior have led to a situation in which *extrusion* is our crisis response to violence. Society extrudes violent persons to institutional units. As violence occurs on one unit, the patient is extruded to another. When the behavior becomes maximally intolerable that unit surrenders, and the facility extrudes to a more secure setting. Finally, the resident reaches the end of the line—a program whose staff has no option but to manage the resident as best they can.

The human service staff's concern for these patients is obvious in the large numbers of articles on the topic. Crain (1979), for example, surveys a wide variety of precipitating factors of aggression; Gutheil (1980) concerns himself with the legal issues of restraint versus treatment; Madden, Lion, and Penna (1976) have studied assaults on psychiatrists; and Whitman, Armao, and Dent (1976) have studied the incidents of assault on therapists in general. In addition, a number of recent programs that focus on the physical *management* of aggressive behavior have been developed (Blake and Taylor, 1977; Gold Award, 1976). These programs focus on training staff in physical containment strategies, that is, how to avoid a blow or kick, how to escort a physically combative patient, etc. Unfortunately, such approaches are primarily reactive management techniques, and treatment that will eliminate or decrease the chronically aggressive behavior in any way is not addressed.

The absence of effective treatment approaches for the chronically aggressive institutionalized individuals has presented treatment staff with a no-exit situation. Such individuals are usually frightening to deal with, and staff are (understandably) reluctant to work in situations that subject them to a heightened potential for physical harm. Often the staff who do end up working with such individuals see themselves as providing a last line of physical management services, since they think everything else has been tried. Aggressive patients are often considered untreatable by the staff who are supposed to work with them, *and* their long history of hospitalization and aggression prevents placement in community settings, even during periods when aggression is absent. The usual result is a history of being shunted from one group of staff to another, as each group becomes burnt out or reaches its limit in dealing with the behavior. In the final analysis, the chronically aggressive patient remains untreated because staff believe treatment doesn't help. A concern for the abandoning of these patients and for the dilemma of the staff responsible for them led the authors to become instrumental in the application of an approach that holds promise for resolving the aggressive behavior of many such chronically institutionalized individuals.

SPECIFIC APPROACHES TO AGGRESSIVE BEHAVIOR

From the early 1970s to the early 1980s, the authors were instrumental in developing, implementing, and operating a residential treatment program for aggressive mentally ill or mentally retarded individuals. The specific approaches that this program has applied to chronic aggressive behavior have been based on a particular paradigm. The assumption held is that the aggression has been learned. In some instances, there may be an underlying causal process. However, the particular manifestation of disordered behavior (in this case, the manifestation of aggression) is primarily due to the shaping of the behavior by the environmental contingencies in which the patient has existed. Aggressive behavior is seen as a function of an interaction of causal factors: physiological predisposing factors, psychodynamic factors, cognitive factors, and the environment. If any factor is changed, there is likely to be a behavioral change. The guiding principle has been that it is most effective to focus primarily on changing, in a very structured way, the contingencies that lead to or maintain aggressive behavior. This approach has been found to be objective, controllable, and measurable. In the sections to follow, the primary strategies used on this unit will each be described.

Positive Reinforcement

Among the positive reinforcement strategies utilized in the program has been a token economy system. In this system, the residents gain positive reinforcers in the form of points that can be redeemed for commodities, such as cigarettes, pop, toiletry articles, snack foods, watches, and jewelry (Ayllon and Azrin, 1968). Residents in the system are reinforced for a variety of positive behaviors, such as bed-making, appropriate dress, and good hygiene. In addition to this global program, each resident would have an individual treatment plan specifying the particular behavior for which the individual would receive additional reinforcers. As an example, an appropriate behavior might be walking away from a confrontation. Residents' individual treatment plans also contained consequences for failure to manifest appropriate behaviors. As in most token economy systems, this involved a system of fines for these behaviors.

The focus of this aspect of the program, however, was on the positive reinforcement approach. A wide variety of tasks were developed through which residents could obtain reinforcers. An example of one task is "nuts and bolts assembly." Residents take a box of assorted nuts, bolts, and washers and assemble them in units for reinforcement. At the end of the tasks, they would be disassembled and the client could begin again or move on to another task. The client is being reinforced for attending to a task and ignoring distractions, both internal and external.

Subsequent to these tasks, residents would move on to tasks more relevant to their problem areas (e.g. practicing reading for an individual with no recreational skills). With some "mute" patients, the focus would be on repeating speech sounds. Most of these tasks would involve a shaping procedure. In one case, for example, a twenty-year-old mentally retarded girl who had never used speech was taught a usable vocabulary of 300 words. In that particular case, the enhanced ability to communicate basic needs appeared to result in a reduction in frustration and a related reduction in aggression. These procedures enriched the environment so that more positive reinforcers were available. Periodic evaluations indicated that on the average, each resident was engaged in 350 task sessions per month that could gain reinforcement. While many of these task sessions were of short duration, approximately five minutes each, each patient had approximately ten to fifteen staff contacts per a sixteen-hour day.

Within this enriched base, a variety of techniques were used to deal with the specific manifestation of aggressive behavior.

Extinction

Extinction, withholding the reinforcer that has been sustaining behavior, was used initially as a consequence for aggression. However, it soon became obvious that this was simply not a usable procedure. When attention was withheld in response to an aggressive act, aggression increased in frequency and intensity, making intervention necessary and thus reinforcing the behavior. Extinction per se was abandoned as a viable alternative. One aspect of extinction has been retained, however. While the staff always intervenes using techniques to be described in the following material, they do so using "bland effect." No matter what happens during an aggressive incident, the intervening staff do not manifest any emotion; there is no expression of anger, shouting, scolding, or sympathy on the part of the staff. Although the staff are not *always* able to do this, it is a goal towards which they strive.

Withdrawal of Positive Reinforcement

An alternative to extinction, the withdrawal of positive reinforcement in the form of time-out, has become a major strategy in both managing and treating aggressive behavior. Time-out has been described by a variety of authors (e.g. Alevizos and Alevizos, 1975; Barstow and Bailey, 1969; Hobbs and Forehand, 1977). Time out from positive reinforcement is defined as a period of time during which the person is removed from the opportunity to acquire positive reinforcers from the usual environment on the treatment unit. Because a positive reinforcer increases or maintains the behavior it follows, removing the positive reinforcer(s) should decrease the behavior. When time-out is used following the occurrence of a problem behavior, the individual is removed to a nonstimulating and nonreinforcing environment, such as a separate room, a nonenclosed portion of the living area, or a chair, or even the staff member temporarily stops a training session by looking away from the resident and not speaking. The primary treatment approach used with aggressive behavior in our program is exclusionary time-out. Time-out would not be effective in reducing the frequency of the problem behavior if the resident (1) prefers the quiet time-out environment; (2) thinks the usual time-in environment is not reinforcing, or is even aversive; or (3) engages in self-reinforcing behavior during time-out.

In the program being described, two time-out rooms are available for use. These are bare rooms with comfortable temperature, ventilation, and lighting. The doors open outward and have external drop locks and visual access, which allows complete observation of all parts of the room.

When included in a treatment plan, time-out is specific to a particular behavior, such as throwing a chair or hitting another person, and is implemented only subsequent to the occurrence of the behavior.

Guidelines for the procedure are as follows:

1. Observe the resident exhibiting time-out specified behavior.
2. The staff agrees that observed behavior is time-out specified behavior. The staff agrees on a plan that ensures that the resident will get to the time-out room in the safest manner.
3. The resident is told in a calm, flat, unemotional tone of voice, "Go to the time-out room for (*defined time*) minutes of quiet, because you (*state the problem behavior*)." There is no attempt to counsel, to reason with, to reprimand, or in any way to give attention to the patient.
4. If the resident continues to engage in program-defined time-out behavior, he or she is taken to the time-out room.
5. There must be a body search to remove belts, shoes, matches and lighters, and all other potentially harmful objects from the resident.
6. The staff closes and locks the door; then obtains appropriate monitoring material, such as a session timer, a logbook, and the room-in-use signal. The time-out room should be occupied by one, and only one, resident at a given time.
7. Ensure constant and proper supervision of the client; closely

observe the time-out room, seeing that other residents do not congregate around the room and *checking on* the resident in the room *at least once every five minutes*.

All supervising persons should be familiar with all time-out procedures and the current treatment plan guidelines. It is critical to note that the amount of time a resident spends in the time-out room should be the program-specified number of minutes of continuous program compliance. *Two hours is the maximum period of time* a resident can spend consecutively in the time-out room. Therefore, if one hour and forty-five minutes has elapsed with the resident still in time-out, the program criterion may be decreased. This provides for additional opportunities before the two-hour deadline is up. This is a crucial point, since releasing the resident from time-out is likely to have a reinforcing effect. The resident will remain in the time-out room until he or she has complied with the requirements of the program. The compliance time may be as short as thirty seconds or as long as thirty minutes; however, times greater than fifteen minutes should be considered only in special cases.

Once placed in the time-out room, the patient is continuously monitored for compliance with the quiet time criterion. As soon as the patient reaches the quiet time criterion, he or she is released. Once released, the provoking incident is not discussed. No staff member will tell the patient that the aggression was bad or wrong.

A period of testing on the part of most residents follows the time-out. There is an initial increase in frequency of the aggressive behavior. This increase is usually followed by a decline in frequency (*see* Figure 10-1).

In the application of such a technique, accurate data collection is critical. Some patients are reinforced by the solitude and privacy that the time-out affords the patient. Other patients appear unaffected by it.

Required Relaxation

The second major procedure used to treat specific aggressive behavior is required relaxation (Foxx and Azrin, 1972; Webster and Azrin, 1973). The procedure was developed as an alternative to the use of a time-out for those residents who manifest a negative emotional state or negative behavioral reaction when placed in time-out.

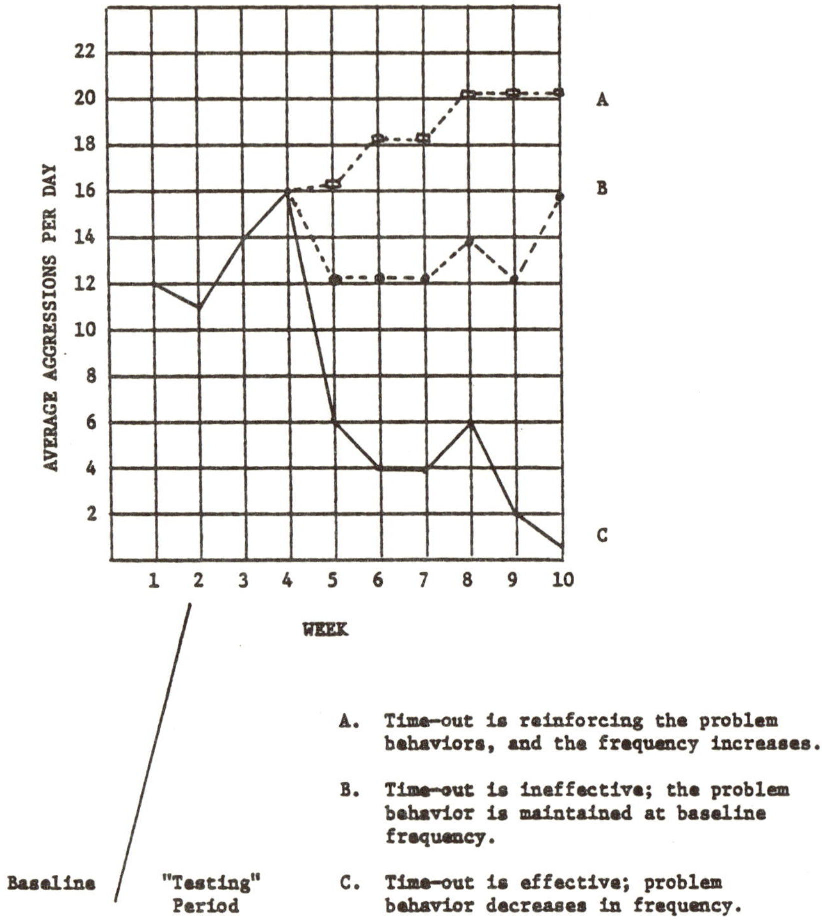

Figure 10-1. Typical Time-out Curve

Required relaxation is a treatment technique that teaches relaxation as an incompatible response to specific behaviors such as aggression, agitation, and disruptive verbalization. Sometimes there are specific behavior(s) that are precursors of the disruptive or aggressive behavior. When this pattern is observed, required relaxation should be implemented as soon as the first disruptive behavior in the pattern begins. The basic changes that this program has made to the original "Webster-Azrin" procedure are (1) the use of a mattress on the floor, as well as the use of a bed; (2) the use of an area other than the dorm for the procedure; and (3) requiring only a maximum of fifteen consecutive minutes of compliance. These changes were made in the interest of making it a safer, more easily observed and consistent procedure. The guidelines of the required relaxation procedure are as follows:

1. The resident is observed engaging in an aggressive behavior that may require relaxation, and staff members present are in agreement that the observed behavior was a required relaxation-specified behavior.
2. The staff present ensures that the resident gets to the relaxation mat (or bed) in the safest possible manner. The mat is located in an easily monitored "low traffic" area. A delay may negate the effectiveness of required relaxation or make its use inappropriate if longer than several minutes pass after the inappropriate behavior.
3. The resident is told in a calm, flat, unemotional tone of voice, "Go to the relaxation mat for (*defined time*) minutes of relaxation because you (*specify problem behavior*)."
4. Allow the residents all reasonable opportunity to go to the mat under their own power—thus reflecting a positive decision to comply with the procedure.
5. If a resident continues to engage in program-defined problem behavior, he or she should be taken to the relaxation mat physically, using no more force than necessary to effect compliance.
6. While taking the resident to the relaxation mat, staff members do not try to counsel, reason, reprimand, or in any way give attention. By providing attention at this point, a contingency may be established, and the inappropriate behavior that just occurred may be reinforced.
7. A body search is conducted to remove belts, shoes, matches and lighters, and all other potentially harmful objects.
8. The resident must be in and maintain a position that reflects relaxation (on stomach, face towards wall, arms by side). In case of resistance, the resident is held in an appropriate posture on a bed mattress with gentle firmness. The staff is not verbally argumentative and does not engage in discussion or debate. At any point the client relaxes, the physical maintenance is faded.
9. The staff monitors from increasing distance until out of the

area and until the client is self-maintaining. General observation of the resident is constant.

10. The length of time of relaxation procedure is based on the treatment needs of the individual patient. No period is scheduled for longer than fifteen consecutive minutes of compliance. Periods such as five or ten minutes are often used.
11. If the patient stops relaxing and becomes agitated or upset during the procedure, physical maintenance is instituted if necessary. After the resident becomes relaxed, the timing of the compliance begins again. The resident is told *once*, bland affect, why we have extended the procedure.
12. The relaxation procedure is ended when the patient has been relaxed for the number of consecutive minutes required in the treatment plan.
13. The behavior of the resident is monitored, making certain he or she is complying with the program. If a resident goes to sleep, that is considered relaxation and compliance.

As with time-out, accurate data collection and evaluation are critical. A technique is effective if the problem behavior, in this case, aggression, decreases. Figure 10-2 presents the typical data on residents when required relaxation is applied (*see* Webster and Azrin, 1973, p. 73 for similar data).

Residents may begin to initiate going to the mat or required relaxation about the fifth to seventh week of the program. This is viewed as a particularly positive sign that the resident has begun to develop an alternative to aggression. This behavior is heavily reinforced with both commodities and social reinforcement.

Frustration Response Event Training

The lack of alternatives for dealing with frustration is a major problem for aggressive residents. When frustrated, they act out in their characteristically maladaptive way. While the procedures so far described have been effective, one of the authors, Hollerauer, has developed a simple technique for dealing with agitated frustration responses that attempts to avoid hands-on procedures. We have called this process Frustration Response Event Training (FRET).

FRET training differs from many techniques used to treat ag-

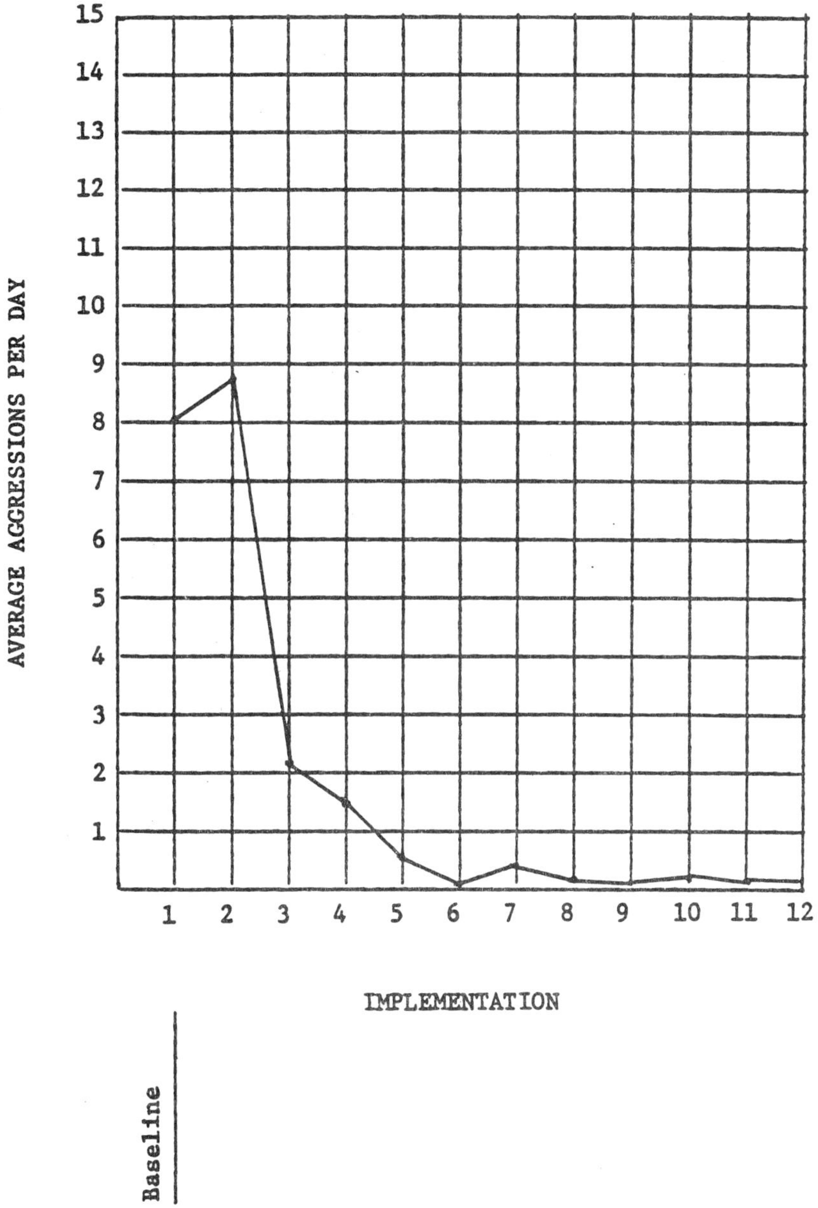

Figure 10-2. Typical Required Relaxation Curve

gressive residents in that it is not a reactive technique. In most other approaches the therapist waits until the aggressive behavior is emitted and then responds. In FRET, a relatively innocuous task is used to create a situation in which behaviors that are antecedents of violence can be emitted and to which the therapist can then respond, reinforcing the patient for appropriate compliance to the goal-oriented task. The focus of the technique is to teach the resident to recognize the onset of frustration and to defuse the situation. It also attempts to maximize the use of positive reinforcement. The following description is oriented around one case as an example.

The Case of Jane*

Jane is a thirty-two-year-old, mildly retarded woman with a long history of extreme acting-out behavior, including aggression to property, to others, and to herself. She has never spent a significant length of time outside of an institution and was transferred to the unit because of uncontrollable violence. Observation of Jane's behavior reveals that it is objectively at a level of extreme distress. It is explosive and frequent and escalates from pacing or fidgeting to running, yelling, and throwing followed by aggressive behavior toward staff or other patients. Jane, at this point in time, cannot sit through any therapeutic involvement without becoming frustrated and acting out by escape from the situation or aggression.

Jane externalizes the responsibility for her aggressive behavior to other patients, staff, and the hospital. Therapy therefore must create and recreate, over and over, the physical event until the response can be recognized and dealt with. Jane's experience with goal-oriented tasks often results in failure because of the frustration-reducing, maladaptive behavior she demonstrates. She views the staff (who are the initiators of tasks) as one source of frustration and the task itself as the other. She consequently cannot form interactions leading to basic trust of the staff. Therapy should be focused on completing a whole interaction without Jane acting out in order to

*Based on Hollerauer, T., *Institutional Aggression: Observation on Violence and the Case of Aggressive Patients in an Illinois Mental Health Center*. An unpublished dissertation in partial fulfillment of the requirments for the doctor of psychology degree at the Illinois School of Professional Psychology, Chicago, Illinois, 1979.

teach new responses to frustration and to identify the feeling of the frustration as an internal event rather than as an external object to be eliminated or avoided.

It is expected that recurring positive interactions will tend to enhance relationships between the patient and staff. As goals are achieved, the patient will learn a new response to frustration that will be faster and more effective. When the patient begins to attain goals easily and reinforcement is added, the definition of both task and staff changes from *sources of frustration* to *sources of gratification*. The feeling about staff and task will also change as the task and staff become gratifying.

In the therapeutic session proper, a task session is utilized to provide a means of training alternative behaviors. The task session is card sorting. This task is one that the therapist assumed would provoke characteristic responses (CR). The CRs for Jane are looking around, dawdling, escape, withdrawal, inappropriate verbalizations, and aggression. The program developed to deal with CRs follows below under the heading *FRET Session Procedure*. It was designed to be as simple and concrete as possible, while attempting to convey a sense of dynamics to the staff.

FRET Session Procedure

The purpose of task sessions is the eventual elimination of the characteristic response, which may be defined as the response likely to occur during task performance that is considered to be the problem behavior or in some way representative of the problem behavior. The objective is to place the maladaptive behavior under program control by placing the resident in a task situation where the behavior has a high probability of occurring and where environmental interruption of the behavior is relatively easy.

The rationale at the beginning is to teach the patient to suspend irrelevant stimulus and to attend to the task.

Procedure

I. Specific characteristic response (CR)
   A. Examples of CR are as follows:
      1. Nonprovoked laughing

2. Staring off into space
3. Talking to a wall or to empty space

[Apparently hallucinatory behavior]

4. Sitting with a blank stare
5. Looking up constantly from a task
6. Continuous mistakes in simple (baseline-determined) tasks
7. Fidgeting—standing up and sitting down, and squirming
8. Aggressive task avoidance (hitting, throwing, having tantrums, etc.)
9. Passive task avoidance (refusal to move or to do task correctly, walking away from task, etc.)
10. Involvement in anxiety-reducing behavior (leg swinging, babbling, tapping, shaking, etc.)

Numbers 5, 6, 7, 8, and 9 may be indicative of lack of attention span, low tolerance to frustration, inability to delay gratification, depression, paranoid affect, or delusional process.

B. Presentation of the task

1. Explain to the patient the following: "When you are given *X* (card sort) task to do, you often engage in (CR) behavior. I would like you to try to do the *X* task without (CR). If you do it without (CR), you will get (R +). If you don't do it, you have to start over again."
2. Establish a baseline for each task of difficulty and relative tolerance to frustration. This is the highest level of difficulty to be used in initiating training. For example, if the resident typically starts giggling (CR) after completing twenty or so cards, training should begin with twenty cards being the most extensive task he or she has to do.

The trainer's task is to encourage the client to complete the task without the CR occurring by prompt praise and positive reinforcement (R +) and at the same time eliciting internal responses of satisfaction, relaxation, control, visceral preoccupation (eating, smoking, etc.), and verbal-auditory preoccupation (processing our praise).

Task Introduction and Implementation

In Jane's case, the task was a card sort. The cards were color coded: blue, green, and yellow. Some of the cards were blank; others had the numbers 1, 2, or 3 and the letters A, B, or C on them. In the task session, numbers and letters followed normal sequence (A-B-C, 1-2-3). The originally presented task was to arrange the cards in the sequence in Figure 10-3. This was a predictably overwhelming task to the patient. Her reaction to being frustrated or overwhelmed was recorded as "her CR to frustration," the baseline data.

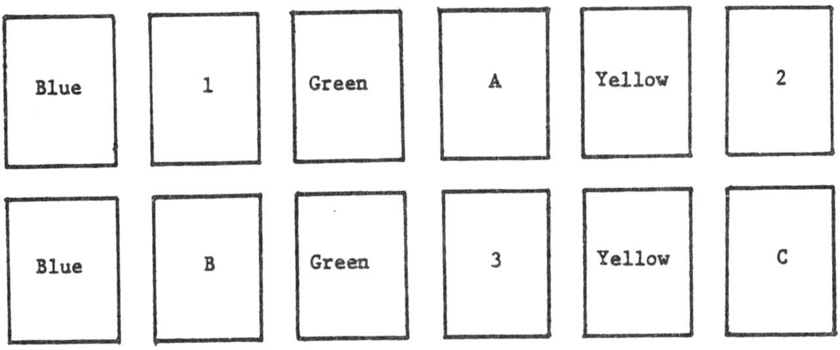

Figure 10-3. Required Card Arrangement in Jane's FRET Task

The task was then reintroduced, but the lettered cards were removed. This simpler task was not overwhelming but still was very frustrating. She was able to complete the "revised" task in approximately five minutes with help and encouragement. The next day, she was given the task again and she reacted with a considerable number of CR, but was maintained in the situation until completion, some forty-five minutes later, and she was reinforced.

There was a steady reduction of time and effort spent in the task over the next two days and little overt aggression. The weekend followed with no sessions taking place. On Monday, she had her tenth session. She was constantly looking around and complaining and had to spend a great deal of time in session. Her task performance that entire day, though improving, was poor.

The following days showed steady and dramatic improvement and aggression; escape behavior, withdrawal and dawdling ceased. "Inappropriate verbalizations" and "looking-up" behavior centered on jealous reactions to attention other patients were receiving while she was in task.

By the fortieth session, she had been able to consistently perform the task without CR. She was then reintroduced to the entire, more complex task with which she had little difficulty. Upon introduction of the whole task, she apparently didn't understand the arrangement. Her adaptive behavior was to figure out the proper sequence. She was praised heavily for this. The reinforcers used included cigarettes, pop, verbal praise, and hand-holding.

Prompting Level

The patient is instructed as follows at the beginning of each session: "Pay attention to what you are doing because you work faster and better when you look at what you are doing. Work quietly and quickly and tell me when you're done."

Some prompts were used to interfere with CR. They were either direct, such as, "Try to do it quietly," or indirect, such as, "Try to work as quickly as possible." Indirect prompts are intended to focus attention away from distraction. If the patient did not respond to prompts or had made more than three CR responses within the task, he or she was restarted.

The task was always concluded with successful completion, and reinforcement was always given at the end of a session. Praise was used when it was necessary during the task and at task completion.

The results of this procedure in regards to the reduction of aggressive behavior are shown in Figure 10-4. Results with Jane's other characteristic responses were as follows:

1. Looking up from task: eliminated in fourteen days.
2. Dawdling: eliminated in five days.
3. Escape: eliminated in three days.
4. Inappropriate verbalization: eliminated in fourteen days.
5. Withdrawal: eliminated in two days.

In observing Jane, the agitated level of her behavior substantially quieted. She entered a relaxation group, and the trainer reported, as did Jane, that she frequently became so relaxed that she fell asleep during relaxation exercises. Jane was subsequently transferred to a nonspecialized unit and continues to be able to avoid the character responses.

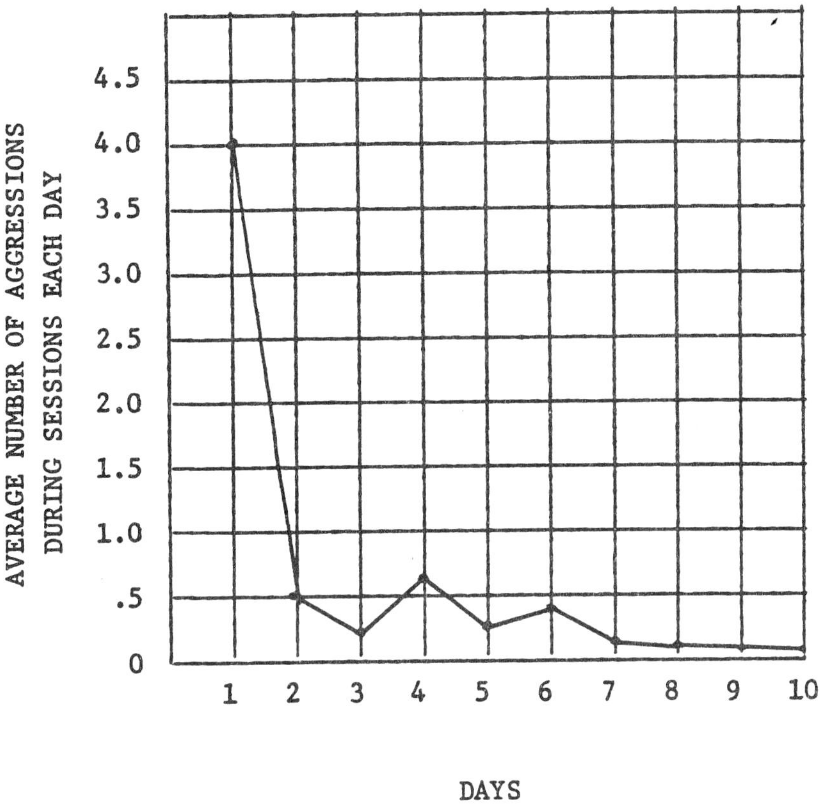

Figure 10-4. Aggression during FRET

TREATMENT OF SELF-INJURIOUS BEHAVIOR

So far, we have focused primarily on the treatment of aggression towards others. However, as we all know, aggression has another face: aggression towards self. Self-mutilation is a major problem for mental health providers. Frequently, aggressive persons are not only aggressive towards others, but they are *also* aggressive towards the self. Many approaches have been applied to this problem (*see* Bachman, 1972, for an extensive review of the problem). The use of extinction was ruled out because of the initial increase in the frequency and intensity of the behavior that results. The use of aversive stimulation was also ruled out due to the difficulty in obtaining approval for the use of such controversial techniques as painful electrical stimulation. The use of positive reinforcement of self-care skills has been found to be effective and easily applied. The following case illustrates the procedure.

A Case of Self-mutilation*

This twenty-three-year-old, moderately retarded (IQ 40) white female had been referred from a private institution where she had lived for many years. She adapted to the unit environment and received standard nursing care during her first nine days on the unit. During the seven-day baseline period, she was closely observed by a staff member for fifteen minutes out of every hour in the ward dayroom from 8 AM to 9 PM each day. The observer noted bizarre behavior, such as screaming, as well as self-injurious behavior, such as picking at sores on her face and hands during 50 percent of the observation periods.

Interestingly, she never was observed to scratch or pick or have any sores at all in areas that could not be observed and commented on by staff members and residents in other settings. She was examined by staff at shower time for concealed injuries. There were none. During this baseline period, the staff was careful not to attend to the injurious behavior nor to respond in a sympathetic way to her complaints regarding her sores.

Observations by trained unit staff of her behavior were continuous for her stay at the behavior modification unit. These observations were scheduled, as in the baseline review, for fifteen minutes out of each hour and made inconspicuous. Bizarre and disruptive behaviors also were recorded. Initially, she was prompted to do her premeal and postmeal grooming: (1) wash her face, (2) wash her hands, (3) comb her hair, (4) brush her teeth, and (5) make sure her clothes were neat both before and after meals. Staff members observed and recorded her completion of each of these steps.

This patient was extremely uncooperative in the initial stages. On the first day of the program, she required verbal prompts for all of the behaviors except one time. The staff was required to use

*Adapted from Knowlton, H., and Hollerauer, T., *Modifying Self-Injurious Behavior Through Reinforcement of Incompatible Self-Care Responses*. Unpublished paper, Elgin Mental Health Center, Elgin, Ill., 1975.

Graduated Guidance (GG) to get her to complete her cleanup session on first day of the unit. Simply defined, GG consisted of taking her hand and putting it on the soap or taking her hairbrush and going through the appropriate movements to accomplish the task. This was accompanied by much kicking and screaming on many occasions. In addition to performing all five behaviors both before and after meals, she was required to go through numerous between-meal and after-dinner sessions. On the first day of the program, the patient and the staff completed ten such sessions, the first five of which were accomplished with verbal prompts. Session six ended in repeated self-mutilations while session seven was conducted entirely with graduated guidance. By session nine in the evening, she initiated all five steps without prompting. Verbal praise was the prime reinforcer for her, since she was capable of understanding and quite receptive to praise except when she was agitated. Telling her how nice she looked and how each step was improving her appearance had a strong effect, as evidenced by the rapid change in behavior, and the more gradual, but ultimately dramatic change in her appearance. At the end of the cleanup sessions, she was also offered edibles. Initially, she was a problem eater and regularly refused meals as well as edible rewards. By the end of the treatment, however, her eating had increased to the point that she was verging on overweight.

As was the case with several other self-mutilators treated on the unit, this resident proved extremely responsive to verbal praise of her appearance. Once she began responding to verbal prompts to do her tasks, she began to show positive affect following praise for completing steps of her program. During this phase, a picture and word explanation of the steps was posted for her outside the washroom; if she missed any steps, these were pointed out to her on the drawings. In addition, staff supplied more and more praise and attention to her when her behavior outside of sessions was appropriate. The patient had a limited vocabulary and understanding of the working of her environment, but she seemed to clearly understand when she was told she looked pretty, that her hair looked nice, or that her clothes looked very neat.

It was assumed for the purpose of this approach that persons demonstrating severe abuse of their bodies are not overfond of their bodies and either have little concern for their appearance or are convinced of their ugliness and unacceptability. Working with this assumption led the therapists to explore praise as a useful tool for increasing the subject's sense of self-worth or, in behavioral terms, teaching her new verbal responses concerning personal appearance by supplying praise. From the behavioral point of view, taking care of one's appearance is incompatible with mutilation, for at exactly the same moment, one cannot both be mutilating and performing self-care tasks. Self-mutilation disfigures and detracts from the newly learned descriptive pattern of "pretty" and "neat and clean." One might expect rejection and bitterness from subjects who have primarily negative comment on their appearance over a period of years. However, with this severely retarded subject, praise seemed effective almost immediately, and other subjects in the treatment responded quickly to similar praise, including residents with normal intelligence. The praise followed grooming tasks and was given at other times when the patient was not involved in SM and had a neat appearance in comparison with her former norm. Of course, a face that is a mass of scabs is not what one normally would call pretty, but the praise offered was part of an overall program that proved quite effective. Staff members were quite enthusiastic in providing verbal reinforcement for the cleanup skills and neat appearance. Returning from a self-care session, two or more staff members would touch the subject and talk to her about how nice she looked. In the dayroom, she was prompted at least ten times per shift to straighten her clothes, for instance. During the first few days, when GG was used, she was so resistant that she seemed oblivious to the praises, but she became receptive to the praises as she became less involved in an adversary relationship with the staff. When credibility was established, that is to say, when she learned she must do the session without opportunity for refusal, she quickly fitted into a pattern of going through grooming tasks on cue or self-initiating responses. From the beginning, the staff demanded a high number of sessions. As the GG responses diminished, she responded willingly to suggestions and fell quickly into self-initiated responses (*see* Figure 10-5). In a one-year follow-up, the private institution where she had resided for the past year reported she continued to have some behavior problems but that self-mutilation was not a problem.

As Figure 10-5 illustrates, through the treatment period, a great deal of variability in self-mutilating behavior occurred. Note par-

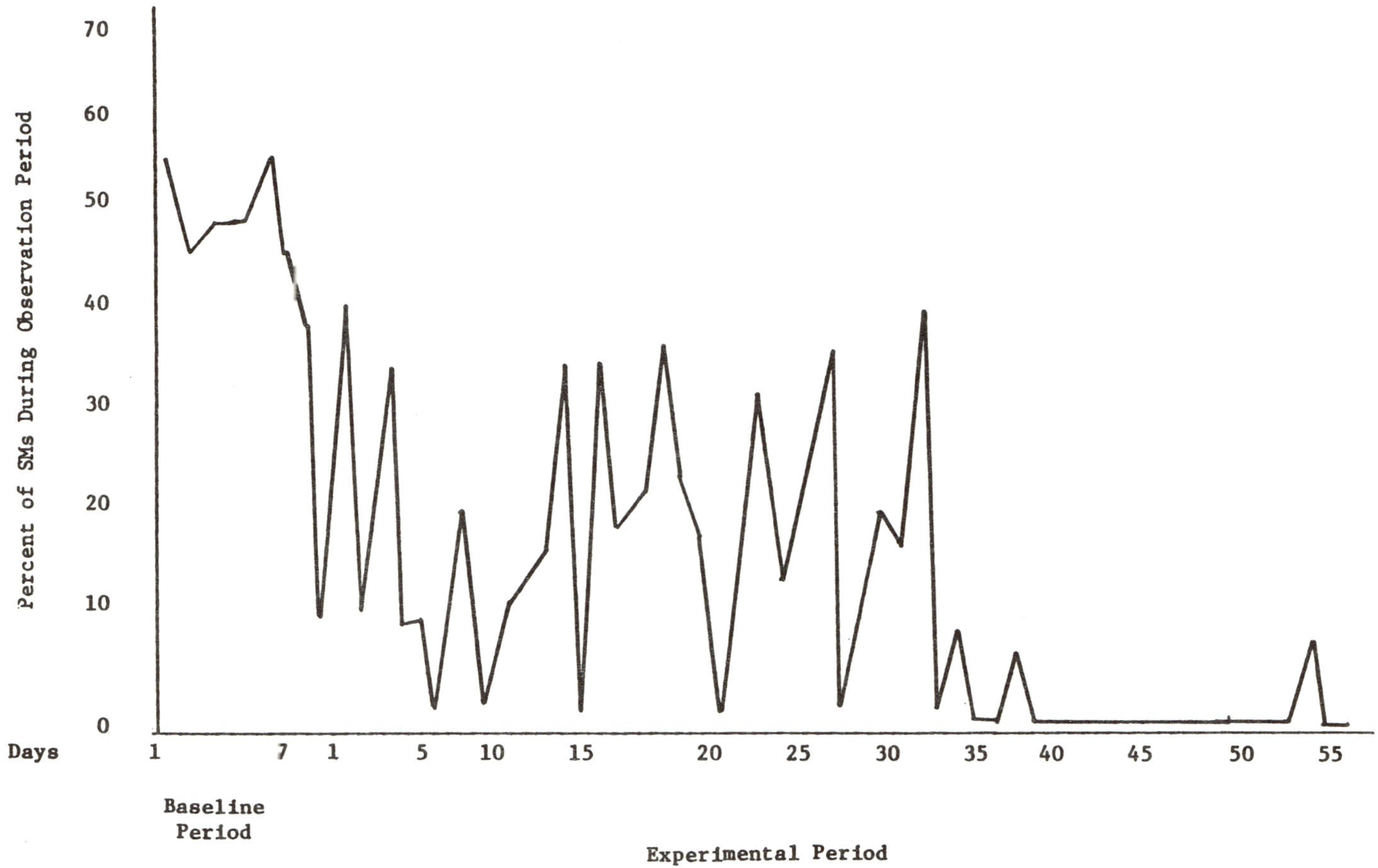
Percent of SMs During Observation Period
70
60
50
40
30
20
10
0
Days
1
7
1
5
10
15
20
25
30
35
40
45
50
55
Baseline
Period
Experimental Period

Figure 10-5.

ticularly the average decline around days five and ten and the major increases between day twenty and twenty-five and at day thirty before the behavior virtually disappeared. These peaks are not unusual in this approach to self-mutilative behavior, and the staff must guard against overresponding when these frequent increases appear.

CONSISTENCY AND THE TREATMENT OF AGGRESSION

In the preceding material, a number of behavioral approaches to the treatment of aggression have been described. The literature is replete with studies demonstrating that these approaches are very effective in the reduction or elimination of aggressive behaviors toward self or others. However, most of these studies report on the application of these techniques with single individuals or on small groups of patients. Usually, the procedures are applied by a number of extremely well-trained staff members who focus on one or a few patients in series, rather than on a large group of residents concurrently. The program that has been described is quite different. During a seven-year period, the program treated well over 300 extremely aggressive individuals within a typically resource-poor state hospital system. The success of the application of this approach was due to a number of factors:

1. Training
2. An egalitarian staff
3. Enhanced resources
4. Commitment
5. Consistency of treatment
6. Invested leadership

TRAINING. At the initiation of the program in 1973, the original staff members were extensively trained in a variety of techniques. A small handful of the staff already had a primitive level of understanding of these approaches and were able to make some contributions as trainers; however, the great majority of training consisted of reading a journal article and some of Skinner's works or Bandura's and the next day trying it out! The facility had few resources and was not able to bring in outside consultants to train the staff. The initial patients taught the staff as much as any trainer! As the program developed, the staff who had gained experience could provide more formal training for new employees.

AN EGALITARIAN STAFF. A unique feature of the program from its inception was that no distinction was made between so-called nonprofessionals and professionals. The only person with an office was the program director. All staff, including the "professionals," spent their total eight-hour workday in the dayroom with the residents. No one had an office to retreat to, and when an aggressive incident would occur, whoever was nearby would apply the contingency. Aides and professionals alike were required to physically intervene. A psychologist, for example, did not have the luxury of standing back and analyzing, while telling a nonprofessional to stop the patient from aggressing. The importance of this shared responsibility was very significant.

ENHANCED RESOURCES. As already noted, the program was well staffed. Its bed capacity was ten residents and twenty staff members; however, it ran at times with fourteen patients and eighteen staff members and had at times as few as fourteen staff members. During seven years of operation, there were twenty staff members and ten patients only during a period of two months. The physical plant was no better nor any more secure than any other typical state hospital ward.

COMMITMENT. From the beginning, an underlying philosophy was maintained in the program that this was a "last-resort" program. Staff members were committed to success. With the patients' reputations for violence, the staff members were aware that these patients would be consigned to a life in an institution if they could not change. The staff had a sense of pride in tackling a problem that most other people ignored.

CONSISTENCY. A major concept of the program was consistency. The treatments were behavioral, based on concepts of learning theory, and the language of the program reflected that philosophy. Although some staff members were and still are psychodynamically oriented, there was a consistent unit philosophy of a behavioral approach, thus avoiding the danger of reinforcing inappropriate behavior by applying a behavioral approach one moment and an insight-oriented approach the next. Within the behavioral paradigm itself, consistency was demanded. To the extent possible, aggression was always met with a response of time-out or required relaxation so that residents would be aware that if they acted out, they could be certain of the consequences.

INVESTED LEADERSHIP. The leadership of the program, from its inception, was invested in providing support, public relations, *and* contingencies for staff behavior. Staff members were reinforced for doing their best with verbal and social praise and the few monetary rewards available in a typical state bureaucracy.

OVERALL PROGRAM EFFECTIVENESS

The program described was funded out of a resource-poor state hospital budget for the immediate treatment of a patient management problem. The data presented is the result of day-to-day program data collection, an extra investment of time on the part of two staff members who were finishing advanced degrees. However, because of staff interest in the fate of residents who passed through the program, some gross effectiveness data is available on 297 patients. Of this group, 174 were transferred back to typical treatment units with an absence of aggressive behavior or with a significant decrease in frequency or intensity of aggression. Many of these persons have since been discharged, but not all. In addition to the 174, eighty-two of the 297 were discharged to less restrictive community settings, and an additional twenty-four were discharged independently to families or to self. During the course of the program, there were seventeen notable failures (6 percent of the total). These were patients on whom the program had either no impact or a negative impact. However, there were no identifiable individual characteristics that distinguished them from others who were more successful.

REFERENCES

Alevizos, K.J., and Alevizos, R.N.: The effects of verbalizing contingencies in timeout procedures. *Journal of Behavior Therapy and Experimental Psychiatry, 6*:253-255, 1975.

Ayllon, T., and Azrin, N.H.: *The Token Economy: A Motivational System for Therapy and Rehabilitation*. New York, Appleton-Century-Crofts, 1968.

Bachman, J.A.: Self-injurious behavior: A behavioral analysis. *Journal of Abnormal Psychology, (3)*:211-224, 1972.

Bandura, A.: *Principles of Behavior Modification*. New York, Holt, Rinehart and Winston, 1969.

Barstow, D.E., and Bailey, J.B.: Modification of severe disruptive and aggressive behavior using brief time-out and reinforcement procedures. *Journal of*

Applied Behavioral Analysis, 2(1):31-37, 1969.

Blake, K., and Taylor, C.E.: *The Prevention and Management of Aggressive Behavior*. Columbia, S.C., South Carolina Department of Mental Health, 1977.

Crain, P.M.: Clinical Approaches to assaultive behavior: I. Evaluation. *The Psychiatric Journal of the University of Ottawa, 4(3)*:224-232, 1979.

Evenson, R.C., Sletten, I.W., Altman, H., and Brown, M.L.: Disturbing behavior: A study of incident reports. *Psychiatric Quarterly, 48(2)*:266-275, 1974.

Foxx, R.M., and Azrin, N.H.: Restitution: A method of eliminating aggressive-disruptive behavior of mentally retarded and brain damaged patients. *Behavior, Research and Therapy, 10*:15-27, 1972.

Giovannoni, J.M., and Gurel, L.: Socially disruptive behavior of ex-mental patients. *Archives of General Psychiatry, 17*:146-153, 1967.

Gold Award. A program for the prevention and management of disturbed behavior. *Hospital and Community Psychiatry, 27(10)*:724-727, 1976.

Gutheil, T.G.: Restraint versus treatment: Seclusion as discussed in the Boston State Hospital case. *American Journal of Psychiatry, 137(6)*:718-719, 1980.

Guze, S.B., Woodruff, R.A., and Clayton, P.J.: Psychiatric disorders and criminality. *Journal of the American Medical Association, 228*:641-642, 1o74.

Hobbs, S.A., and Forehand, R.: Important parameters in the use of timeout with children: A re-examination. *Journal of Behavior Therapy and Experimental Psychiatry, 8*:365-370, 1977.

Lagos, J.M., Perlmutter, K., and Saexinger, H.: Fear of the mentally ill: Empirical support for the common man's response. *American Journal of Psychiatry, 134(10)*:1134-1137, 1977.

Madden, D.J., Lion, J.R., and Penna, M.W.: Assaults on psychiatrists by patients. *American Journal of Psychiatry, 133(4)*:422-425, 1976.

Mehr, J.: *A Survey of the Incidences of Aggressive Behavior in Illinois MH/MR Facilities*. Report to the State Task Force. Unpublished manuscript, 1980*a*.

Mehr, J.: Aggression and violence: A clinician/administrator's odyssey towards a treatment perspective. *The Ohio Forensic Reporter, 1(3)*:6-11, 1980*b*.

Rappeport, J.R., and Lassen, G.: Dangerousness-arrest rate comparisons of discharged patients and the general population. *American Journal of Psychiatry, 121*:776-783, 1965.

Skinner, B.F.: *Science and Human Behavior*. New York, Macmillan, 1953.

Webster, D.R., and Azrin, N.H.: Required relaxation: A method of inhibiting agitative-disruptive behavior of retardates. *Behavior Research and Therapy, 11(1)*:67-78, 1973.

Whitman, R.M., Armao, B.B., and Dent, O.B.: Assault on the therapist. *American Journal of Psychiatry, 133(4)*:426-428, 1976.

Zitrin, A., Hardesty, A., Burdock, E.I., and Drossman, A.K.: Crime and violence among mental patients. *American Journal of Psychiatry, 133(2)*:142-149, 1976.

Chapter 11

PHARMACOTHERAPY IN VIOLENT BEHAVIOR

David Barry

INTRODUCTION

VIOLENT behavior is the concern of clinicians when it comes about as a result of disease or disorder. Only a small fraction of such behavior is thus accounted for, and it should be noted at the outset that drug therapy is indicated in an even smaller subset of those appropriately referred for clinical assessment. Those whose disturbing behavior is not the product of illness are at times improperly directed to clinicians. In these instances, we must acknowledge the limitations of our art and decline to intervene.

Many of those referred will view their own behavior as troubling or ego dystonic. They make a genuine plea for assistance in eliminating or modifying behavior over which they have no control. It is with this group that a traditional clinician-patient therapeutic alliance can best be established. Other patients, by virtue of impaired judgment due to delirium or major mental disorder, may either express no interest in interventions proposed or may actively resist them. Here clinicians must carefully weigh the need of the patient for treatment against the basic right to determine his or her own course in life. The immediate concerns and interests of family members must be considered as well in arriving at a treatment decision. In this situation, the imminence of the violent behavior and its anticipated severity will be the primary factors in determining the course of intervention. The clinician may elect to manage the situation as an emergency, proceeding on the assumption that the patient would have consented if he or she was capable. If the patient's condition permits, the clinician may delay intervention until the patient's informed consent can be obtained or that of others on his or her behalf. To complete the spectrum, there will be patients whose behavior will indeed be attributable to disease or disorder, but who will either require no treatment at the time or competently withhold their consent for the appropriate interventions.

The ethical concerns raised by the use of drugs in the management of the violent patient deserve the clinician's most serious consideration. Whether the clinical situation is emergent or one in which the patient is being asked to make an indefinite commitment to a course of pharmacotherapy with potentially irreversible adverse effects, the issue of securing the patient's competent informed consent to the course of treatment is of paramount importance (Stone, 1975).

When a patient has the ability to understand the risks and benefits of the proposed course of treatment and to make a reasonable judgment based on that understanding (competent) and has been properly advised of these risks and benefits (informed), then treatment should proceed only with the patient's freely offered consent. When the patient is not competent, then immediate treatment can be given with the consent of family members (surrogate or proxy consent) or without consent if no family members are available and the need for treatment is clear and urgent. An example would be that of the paranoid patient who is convinced the medication offered is poison and who, at the same time, is prepared to inflict whatever injury on the "persecutors" as may be necessary to stop them from further harming him or her

A course of pharmacotherapy of indefinite duration should be suggested only after careful discussion of both the anticipated net effect of the treatment on the overall quality of the patient's life and the potential for irreversible adverse outcomes directly related to treatment. We have known for some time about the more common complaints associated with the long-term use of neuroleptics, such as uncontrollable weight gain, sexual dysfunction, and abnormal pigmentation of the skin. However, we have come only in recent years to recognize the potential of the neuroleptic or antipsychotic drugs for producing disfiguring and irreversible abnormal involuntary movements (tardive dyskinesia) over a period of time. In some instances, the benefit of neuroleptic use to the individual was marginal, if not negligible, and gained only at the cost of these significant, and sometimes hidden, risks. The clinician must not use authority to prevail on the reluctant patient to consume medication over a prolonged period in the presence of a decidedly unfavorable risk-benefit ratio. He or she should not encourage the patient who is a resident in a public facility for long-term care to continue taking potentially damaging medication when the major purpose served is that of easing the burden of those around him or her rather than benefitting the patient.

ASSESSMENT AND DIAGNOSIS

Most often the patient who is a candidate for pharmacotherapeutic management of violent behavior comes to our attention in a situation calling for immediate intervention. Under these circumstances rapid assessment of the situation is called for to determine what kind of intervention will defuse the crisis (Lion, 1972). Such assessment always includes gathering whatever history may be available from the patient or others, with particular attention to physical illnesses, recent exposure to toxins, or ingestion of psychoactive substances. The assessment continues with a physical examination including appropriate laboratory tests to augment the information pertaining to organic factors developed in the history. The clinician must always pay careful attention to the social context within which the symptoms have appeared since problems in the home or on the job, for example, may play a major part in determining the behavior. On the basis of this assessment, for which there may be no more than a few minutes available, a plan of intervention, which may or may not include the use of medication, is formulated. Diagnosis, a term suggesting greater precision in elucidating the specific underlying causes of the patient's symptoms, may require days or even weeks. Often the clinician is obliged to intervene long before arriving at the more thorough understanding implied by this term.

CONDITIONS REQUIRING IMMEDIATE PHARMACOTHERAPEUTIC INTERVENTION

Conditions underlying violent behavior can be separated into three general categories. The first of these is the group consisting of medical diseases, exposure to toxins, and ingestion of psychoactive drugs. The second group subsumes what are commonly referred to as the major mental disorders, including schizophrenia and bipolar affective disorder. The third group is the loosely defined collection of character and behavior disorders. Since many patients in this latter group are perceived by clinicians as simply reacting to adverse life circumstances in an anxiety-provoking, socially inappropriate way, rather than behaving as they do because of illness, evaluation here requires careful attention to the clinician's bias or negative countertransference (Lion and Pasternack, 1973). A number of these patients have treatable symptoms, respond quite positively to relief, and require our most objective and thoughtful consideration.

Medical Conditions

Medical conditions that have been reported to be associated with violent behavior include hypoglycemia, seizure disorders, central nervous system vasculitis, hyperthyroidism, infections, cardiopulmonary insufficiency, dehydration with resulting electrolyte imbalances, severe pain, and brain lesions, such as tumors, abscesses, and trauma-related conditions. These should be considered whenever a new patient presents with combative behavior. Routine medical assessment will quickly establish whether or not these conditions are present and point the way toward incisive therapeutic intervention. These patients often show signs of delirium, a syndrome of cerebral insufficiency, arising from the underlying medical disorder. Delirium has been described as a condition characterized by a reduction in clarity of awareness of the environment (*Diagnostic and Statistical Manual*, 1980). It is manifested through its classical signs of difficulty in sustaining attention, sensory misperception, and a disordered stream of thought. Judgment is impaired as a result of the cognitive impairment, and the diagnosis always bespeaks an underlying medical condition calling for immediate treatment.

Toxins that have been implicated include carbon monoxide, hydrocarbons (including halogenated derivatives), inorganic mercury, and boric acid. The treatment in all such cases, of course, is removal of the offending agents in addition to whatever other supportive measures, such as oxygen or intravenous fluids, may be needed.

A number of drugs have been mentioned in association with violent behavior. Some, such as alcohol, the sedative-hypnotic drugs including barbiturates, and others capable of producing physical dependence, may cause difficulties both when used as intoxicants as well as when the patient who has become dependent is withdrawing. When the history suggests physical dependence on alcohol or one of the sedative-hypnotic drugs, the diagnosis may be confirmed and a withdrawal schedule may be established by administering a 200 mg. test dose of pentobarbital (Nembutal®) given by mouth. The patient's response to the drug is evaluated within the hour and a withdrawal schedule established. Typically, the patient who is not dependent will be asleep, while those who are will show less pronounced signs of intoxication from the test dose, enabling one to estimate the amount of drug the patient has been using (Barry and Weintraub, 1978).

Some of the benzodiazapines, for example chlordiazepoxide (Librium®) and diazepam (Valium®), have been reported to cause paradoxical rage reactions in rare instances when used in appropriate doses by those vulnerable to this effect (Di Mascio, Shader, and Giller, 1970; Lion, Azcarte, and Koepke, 1975). Another drug in this class, oxazepam (Serax®), has been reported to be free of this effect (Kochansky, Salzman, et al., 1977). Violent behavior has also been reported in association with withdrawal from these drugs when the patient has become physically dependent.

The amphetamines have also been associated with violent behavior both during recreational use and the abstinence syndrome. Abuse of these drugs and other stimulants, such as methylphenidate (Ritalin®), can produce a paranoid psychosis closely resembling an acute schizophrenic episode.

Other common drugs of abuse (phencyclidine, LSD, marijuana, etc.) do not produce physical dependence and may be associated with violence only when used as intoxicants. Phencyclidine (PCP) is particularly troublesome in this regard because it is widely available and is often associated with serious medical complications (Showalter and Thornton, 1977).

Rapid withdrawal of high maintenance doses of corticosteroids has also been reported as a cause of seriously disruptive behavior. Tapering the dose more gradually or using neuroleptics during the phase of withdrawal is recommended in these cases. Digitalis preparations, lidocaine (Xylocaine®), pentazocine (Talwin®), and the narcotic analgesics, even when used in ordinary therapeutic doses, have been linked with violent behavior in susceptible subjects.

Another group of drugs sometimes associated with iatrogenic illness and violent behavior are those with anticholinergic effect. In addition to atropine, scopolamine, and the anti-Parkinson agents, many of the neuroleptics and tricyclic antidepressants have potent anticholinergic activity and can, either singly or in combination, produce the syndrome of atropinism. This is always associated with delirium and not infrequently with combative and even violent behavior. In addition to being "red as a beet and dry as a bone," these patients are typically "mad as a hatter." When suspected, the diagnosis can be readily confirmed by the injection of 1 mg. of physostigmine salicylate (Antilirium®), a cholinesterase inhibitor that traverses the blood brain barrier and rapidly, albeit transiently, relieves the symptoms. Withdrawal of the offending agent is the recommended treatment in conditions resulting from exposure to a drug.

Psychiatric Conditions

Major mental disorders may lie at the root of violent behavior that develops in interpersonal settings. Included here are patients suffering from acute episodes of schizophrenia and mania. When schizophrenic or manic patients are sufficiently decompensated, they may pose an immediate threat of violence and may require structured management by clinicians. Of particular importance in defusing the immediate potential for violence is the manner in which the clinician approaches such patients.

Typically, the thought processes of these patients are quite disorganized, and they are frightened. A low-keyed and brief initial encounter coupled with a simple and unambiguous plan for action will often relieve the patient's fear considerably and at the same time his potential for violence. It is important to convey to such patients our capacity to assist them in controlling their behavior, be it through explanation to the more rational patient or the use of restraints with the more disorganized patient. In some instances, assembling a significant number of staff when the patient's behavior gives rise to the belief that some form of violent behavior may be imminent will suffice to enable the patient to regain control. Rather than being designed to initimidate, this maneuver reassures the patient that the clinician is in charge of what may appear to him or her as a threatening, or even terrifying, situation and is prepared to take decisive action. These patients generally benefit as well from reduction in the stimuli impinging upon them. This may be accomplished through conducting the evaluation without interruption in a quiet area. Depending on the clinician's assessment of the urgency of the situation, medication may or may not be required from the outset.

The neuroleptic drugs are specific pharmacological agents in the treatment of these disorders and are almost always used further along to aid in the resolution of the more severe episodes of both schizophrenia and mania. When patients present with the clear potential for violent behavior, these agents should be used parenterally and in sufficiently large doses to enable the patient to bring his or her behavior under control rapidly.

Maladaptive Behavioral Conditions

Patients with personality disorders, ranging from the occasional histrionic or passive aggressive patient at one end of the characterological spectrum to those with severe antisocial personality disorders at the other, may respond to stress with angry, combative behavior. When the situation is of sufficient gravity to warrant intervention over and above interpersonal measures, including seclusion and physical restraint, parenteral neuroleptics may be employed to control the immediate threat of violent behavior. Once this is accomplished, the drug is no longer required, and strategies for resolving the difficulties leading to the outburst may then be considered. Such strategies generally are based on various combinations of psychotherapeutic interventions and alterations in life circumstances.

Small subgroups of this amorphous lot of patients, those who fall between the well-defined boundaries of organic CNS dysfunction and character pathology and who present a continuing risk for violent behavior, are best managed with a combination of the above mentioned therapeutic strategies plus pharmacotherapy. These subgroups of patients will be described in greater detail in the section on intermediate to long-term pharmacotherapeutic management.

PHARMACOTHERAPEUTIC INTERVENTION IN BEHAVIORAL EMERGENCIES

In some instances in all three of the aforementioned categories, the requirement for rapid control of threatening or combative behavior may call for the use of intramuscularly or intravenously administered medications to settle the patient, in addition to any specific treatment that may be indicated. The behavior referred to here consistently eludes definition, but is well known to any clinician with experience in acute care settings. It ranges from the terrified efforts of the acutely delirious patient in the intensive care unit to separate himself or herself from the life-sustaining tubes to the rage-fueled determination of the delusional paranoid patient to neutralize his or her "detractors." Even in the absence of disease or disorder, such behavior may be precipitated by extreme stress and may exhaust the most ingenious interpersonal skills of the clinician. These patients should be treated with parenteral drug therapy to forestall injury and restore equanimity, thus facilitating some resolution of the precipitating problem.

The drugs most commonly used in these situations are those in the neuroleptic or antipsychotic class (Itil and Mukhopadhyay, 1978). These drugs are safe and effective when used in the large and frequently administered doses called for in these situations (Donlon, Hopkin, and Tupin, 1979). They are discontinued when the immediate behavioral disturbance is under control, except in those instances when the patient suffers from a major mental disorder. In that situation, continued use of neuroleptics will most often be indicated.

The neuroleptic drugs available in this country fall into five separate chemical groups: phenothiazines, thioxanthenes, butryophenones, dibenzoxapines, and dihydroindolones. Drugs in each of these groups are available in parenteral form. Any of the higher potency, less sedating agents can be used to bring threatening behavior under rapid control (Guidelines, 1977).

These drugs must be administered in adequate amounts and with sufficient frequency to achieve the desired end point as quickly as possible. Most of the failures here come from insufficient doses given too infrequently. The troublesome extrapyramidal effects associated with these agents can be readily treated; also they occur less frequently when the drug is given in large doses and by the parenteral route.

The high-potency drugs most commonly used are haloperidol (Haldol®), fluphenazine (Prolixin®), trifluoperzine (Stelazine®), thiothixene (Navane®), perphenazine (Trilafon®). These drugs are preferred because they rarely cause hypotension, marked sedation, or pain at the site of the injection. This site should be the deltoid (shoulder) muscle because absorption here is more rapid than from the gluteus (buttock) muscle.

The initial dose for injection is on the order of 5 mg., except for trifluoperazine, where the dosage is 2 mg., and haloperidol, where it is 10 mg. The same dose is injected approximately every hour thereafter until agitation subsides and behavioral control is achieved; this almost always occurs within three hours. If suffering from a major mental disorder, the patient may still be psychotic at this point. Some of the symptoms of psychosis, such as delusions and hallucinations, may yield to medication only after weeks of continuous treatment.

Clearly, what is being described here is a technique for titration, rather than the more conventional determination of dose on a milligram per kilogram of body weight basis. With all these drugs, there is a tremendous range in blood levels achieved when a standard dose is given to different patients. In addition, the effective dose for an individual patient will vary markedly depending on his or her clinical state. The combative, frightened patient will rarely respond to the modest doses adequate for a patient in a state of early remission. The wide margin of safety associated with these compounds permits us to use this unconventional "loading" approach to dosing without subjecting the patient to undue risk.

When it is imperative to control the agitated patient in as short a time as possible, haloperidol can be given intravenously (Intravenous, 1978). The dosage may range from 2 to 25 mg. or more. This regimen has been employed safely in the presence of serious medical pathology, and the drug is even less likely to produce the characteristic extrapyramidal side effects when given by the IV route. Another butryophone, droperidol (Inapsine®), has been used for intravenous injection as well (Parenteral, 1980). It has greater sedative and hypotensive effect than haloperidol and has an added disadvantage in that the Food and Drug Administration has not approved psychosis as an indication for its use. However, it has a faster onset of action, a shorter duration of action, and a lower propensity to evoke extrapyramidal reactions than its congener, haloperidol.

There are other points to keep in mind once a rapid neuroleptization regimen is under way. The patient should be kept in a quiet room, preferably with an attendant to monitor the response to medication, to reassure the patient, and to check blood pressure. Secondly, the orders should include an as-needed injection of 2 mg. benztropine mesylate (Cogentin®) or 50 mg. diphenhydramine (Benadryl®) for those extrapyramidal reactions which are unsettling enough to the patient to warrant immediate response.

The most common of these extrapyramidal reactions, akinesia, is the least dramatic. This is manifested as drowsiness, lethargy, weakness, and fatigue. It is best managed by reducing the dose of the neuroleptic drug and prescribing an anti-Parkinson drug by mouth. More troublesome reactions are dystonia (involuntary sustained contraction of susceptible muscle groups) in its various forms and akathisia (extreme restlessness). The former presents more dramatically but fortunately is the more easily controlled. It responds well to the anti-Parkinson drugs administered intramuscularly or to 10 mg. of diazepam (Valium) intravenously. Diazepam is absorbed erratically from muscle tissue, and so the drug is often ineffective by this route. Akathisia is more difficult to control and has been suggested as a condition leading to violent behavior (Keckich, 1978). If standard doses of anti-Parkinson drugs are ineffective in managing akathisia, then one may add small doses of a barbiturate, a sedative phenothiazine such as chlorpromazine (Thorazine®), or an antihistamine such as diphenhydramine.

When a patient is under control, the neuroleptic medication can generally be stopped without further incident. In those patients with major mental disorders who will require continuing neuroleptic medication, the twenty-four-hour oral dose of medication required can be roughly calculated by doubling the total intramuscular dose given to achieve initial control. Some prefer to give one-third of the total dose in the morning and two-thirds at bedtime. Others switch immediately to giving the entire dose at bedtime. Whichever method is used, six to seven hours of uninterrupted sleep per night is the best sign that the patient is being adequately medicated. Gradually, the dose can be reduced to the smallest amount necessary to maintain sleep. It is worth underscoring that these drugs are not always reliably absorbed in tablet form. Chronic schizophrenics, for example, often achieve negligible serum concentrations with chlorpromazine tablets and can only be maintained on the liquid concentrate form (Rivera-Calimlim, Castaneda, and Lasagna, (1973; Rivera-Calimlim, Nasrallah, Strauss, et al., 1976).

When it seems as though the patient with the major mental disorder may be a candidate for long-acting injectable neuroleptic therapy, he or she may be initially brought under control with injections of fluphenazine hydrochloride. The dose is then converted to the tablet or liquid form as outlined above. When the patient is ready for injection of the depot form, the dosage may be estimated as follows: 20 mg. of fluphenazine per day given orally is roughly equivalent to 25 mg. or 1 cc. of the fluphenazine decanoate given every two weeks. For each additional 5 mg. required per day by the oral route, the biweekly dose of the decanoate should be increased by 12½ mg. or ½ cc.

LONGER-TERM PHARMACOTHERAPEUTIC MANAGEMENT OF REPETITIVE VIOLENT BEHAVIOR

At this point, we will consider those patients who suffer from a chronic, though often poorly defined, disease or disorder that predisposes them to repetitive acts of violence. Those who behave in this way as a result of uncomplicated major mental disorder are excluded from consideration here on the assumption that their behavior will be contained as well as it can be over time through use of the specific agents commonly employed in the treatment of these disorders, namely the neuroleptics and lithium carbonate. We also eliminate from consideration here those whose episodic violent behavior occurs primarily, or exclusively, as the result of clear external precipitants and whose overriding need, therefore, is for a change in life circumstances. The patients to be discussed often do not meet the standards for inclusion in a specific diagnostic category. They are characterized by sets of reliably observable clinical phenomena associated with clusters of medication responsive symptoms.

Episodic Dyscontrol

Monroe (1979) in his now classic work has offered a lucid outline for the classification of episodic behavioral disorders, which he describes as "any precipitously appearing maladaptive behavior, usually intermittent and recurrent, which interrupts the life style or the life flow of the individual (Monroe, 1981). In his comprehensive nosological scheme, he includes the subgroup of patients suffering from episodic dyscontrol, defined as "an abrupt single act or short series of acts with a common intention carried through to completion with at least partial relief of tension or at most an immediate gratification of a specific need." He separates these into patients suffering from primary dyscontrol, when behavior represents a true "short circuit" between stimulus and response, and secondary dyscontrol, when a delay occurs between stimulus and response reflecting either conscious or unconscious premeditation. Primary dyscontrol is further subdivided into behavior associated with seizures or the inability to control instinctual surges. Secondary dyscontrol includes the behavior of those who struggle for a time with an impulse they are ultimately unable to resist and of those who act out in the traditional psychoanalytic sense.

Of particular interest to us are his finding that a number of patients in the first category (primary dyscontrol) had signs of clouding of consciousness at the time of the behavior in question. He has referred to their behavior as epileptoid and has had gratifying results in these cases with a regimen of medications known to raise the seizure threshold, including phenytoin (Dilantin®), primidone (Mysoline®), and chlordiazepoxide (Librium). Because of the relative infrequency with which the seizure discharges can be demonstrated using surface electroencephalographic leads, the selection of patients for this regimen is made on clinical grounds, namely evidence for clouded sensorium at the time of the aberrant behavior. That there are indeed seizure discharges in subcortical, usually limbic, areas associated with the behavior in many of these patients is attested to by studies Monroe and others have done on the small numbers of patients in whom depth electrodes have been implanted for diagnostic purposes.

Many of the patients with whom this anticonvulsant regimen has been employed suffer from chronic major mental disorder in addition to the organic central nervous system dysfunction. Several of those treated by Monroe were housed in secure facilities at psychiatric centers because of their long-standing proclivity toward violent behavior. He suggests first adding chlordiazepoxide (40-200 mg. qd) to the neuroleptic drug already prescribed. Primidone may then be added (1 gram per day in divided doses) if the response to the first drug is inadequate. Monroe has generally withdrawn the chlordiazepoxide from those patients satisfactorily controlled on the three-drug regimen and has found that several of these patients could be maintained satisfactorily on the neuroleptic and primidone alone (Fields and Sweet, 1975). Covi (1970) has found a statistically significant reduction in the number of infraction reports made on a group of patients maintained on phenytoin (200 mg. qd) in a maximum security setting for defective delinquents. No effort was made here to select patients on the basis of clouded sensorium at the time of the aggressive behavior, suggesting that the phenytoin effect is potent enough (or the percentage of "epileptoid" patients in the sample was high enough) to overcome the lack of specificity in patient selection in this study. Bach-Y-Rita et al. (1971) call our attention to the multifactorial nature of the violent behavior of the episodic dyscontrol patient. They look upon violence "as a symptom not solely psychogenic in origin or due to brain dysfunction or a product of social disorganization, but as resulting from the interplay of all three factors."

Aggressive Behavior and Lithium

It has been suggested that the lithium ion has a specific antiaggressive effect (Sheard, Marini, Bridges, et al., 1976; Marini and Sheard, 1977). This is not a function of its well-documented effect on modulating affective swings in patients. Patients free from major mental disorder as well as organic brain disease have responded well to standard doses of lithium carbonate designed to maintain a serum level in the vicinity of 0.60 to 1.0 meq/L. Again, much of the work has been done on institutionalized populations, but the implications for compliant outpatients are promising. In the author's experience one patient reported, "I used to try to count to ten, but never got past two; now with this (lithium carbonate), some of the time I get all the way to ten." It is interesting to note in connection with Monroe's work that other authors have reported an anticonvulsant effect of the lithium ion (Erwin, Gerber, Morrison, and James, 1973).

Aggressive Sexual Behavior

Medroxyprogesterone acetate (Provera® or Depo-Provera®), a synthetic progestin that interrupts testicular synthesis of testosterone, has been reported anecdotally to curb compulsive-aggressive sexual behavior in males (Money, 1970; Barry and Ciccone, 1975). It has also been reported effective in controlling less aggressive sexually deviant behaviors, such as exhibitionism and pedophilia.

This drug has been given safely and quite effectively to a number of patients for periods of several years (Berlin and Meinecke, 1981; Gagne, 1981). Experience to date indicates that the effect is fully reversible and that the drug is without any long-term, adverse effects, although Walker has suggested the possibility of a heightened predisposition to adult onset diabetes mellitus (Walker and Meyer, 1979).

Medroxyprogesterone acetate is generally administered in the long-acting injectable form to meet the usual requirement of the courts in these cases for certainty that the full prescribed dose is received by the patient. The doses range from 250 mg. injected intramuscularly every two to three weeks to 400 mg. injected every week. Doses in this range effectively suppress the synthesis of testosterone with the effect of reducing the serum level from several hundred nanograms percent to less than 100 nanograms percent, the order of magnitude generally found in females and prepubescent boys. The most common side effects are mild lethargy and weight gain.

Medroxyprogesterone acetate practically eliminates vulnerability to aberrant sexual impulses, and this accounts for the rather surprising loyalty of the patients who choose to receive the medication. Those among this group who are able to maintain stable interpersonal relationships find that, for the most part, they are able to function sexually with a cooperative and willing partner. This is less true with increasing age.

The one flaw with the medroxyprogesterone acetate regimen is the relative lack of success of the psychotherapy and behavioral modification treatment programs undertaken during the medication-induced moratorium. Several investigators have followed patients on the medication for years with no sign of the unwanted sexual behavior, only to share with the patient the most disheartening experience of relapse once the drug is withdrawn.

Because of the highly controversial nature of hormonal treatment of the sexually deviant, it must be emphasized that medroxyprogesterone acetate is offered only to those who ask to be relieved of an otherwise uncontrollable compulsion to misbehave sexually. It is used to enable the patient to live his life under the least restriction consistent with the protection of others. It has little applicability in an institutional setting.

Aggressive Behavior in the Neurologically Impaired

Propranonol has been reported to be effective in the treatment of violent behavior in patients with chronic brain syndromes (Yudofsky, Williams, and Gorman, 1981). Propranonol, the first of the beta-adrenergic blocking drugs, has been used quite effectively over the last few years in the control of hypertension, angina pectoris, and certain cardiac arrythmias. It has been used in very high doses with limited success by various authors in the treatment of schizophrenic patients. It did not have a specific antipsychotic effect with this group but did show some effect in reducing the agitated and sometimes combative behavior of some of these patients. This prompted others to try the drug in the treatment of a group of neurologically impaired patients whose many symptoms included a tendency toward repeated, socially intolerable outbursts of anger and violent behavior. In the few initial case reports that have been published, the drug has been noted to be remarkably effective in the dosage range of 320 mg. to 520 mg. per day. While further investigation with this neuropsychiatrically impaired population is clearly indicated, the early results are promising, and the risk-benefit ratio clearly tilts in the direction of a trial of propranonol or one of the other beta blockers in violent patients with signs of CNS impairment.

CONCLUSION

The use of drugs in the management of violent behavior is a subject fraught with both conflict and promise. While only the most inexperienced among us would turn to drugs early or often in the care of these patients, there is a group for whom the drugs can provide a substantial improvement in the quality of life. Our responsibility as clinicians is to remain ever watchful for those who can benefit from a regimen that includes medication, while keeping in mind the importance of securing the understanding consent of the patient, our partner in treatment.

REFERENCES

Bach-Y-Rita, G., Lion, J.R., Climent, C.E., and Erwin, R.F.: Episodic dyscontrol: A study of 130 violent patients. *American Journal of Psychiatry, 127(11)*:1473-1478, May 1971.

Barry, D.J., and Ciccone, J.R.: Use of Depo-Provera in the treatment of aggressive sexual offenders: Preliminary report of three cases. *Bulletin of the American Academy of Psychiatry and the Law, 3*:179-184, 1975.

Barry, D.J., and Weintraub, M.: Barbiturate management of withdrawal syndromes. *Drug Therapy (Hosp.)*:46-49, 1978.

Berlin, F.S., and Meinecke, C.F.: Treatment of sexual offenders with antiandrogenic medication: Conceptualization, review of treatment modalities, and preliminary findings. *American Journal of Psychiatry, 138(5)*:601-607, 1981.

Covi, L.: *Effects of Dephenylhydantoin in Anti-social Personalities*. APA Annual Meeting, San Francisco, 1970.

Diagnostic and Statistical Manual of Mental Disorders, 3rd Ed. Washington, D.C., American Psychiatric Association, 1980, p. 104.

Di Mascio, A., Shader, R.I., and Giller, D.R.: Behavioral toxicity, Part III: Perceptual cognitive functioning, and Part IV: Emotional (mood) states. In Shader, R.I., and Di Mascio, A. (Eds.): *Psychotropic Drug Side Effects*. Baltimore, Williams and Wilkins, 1970.

Donlon, P.T., Hopkin, J., and Tupin, J.P.: Overview: Efficacy and safety of the rapid neuroleptization method with injectable haloperidol. *American Journal of Psychiatry, 136*:273-278, 1979.

Erwin, C.W., Gerber, C.J., Morrison, S.D., and James, J.F.: Lithium carbonate and convulsive disorders. *Archives of General Psychiatry, 28*:646-648, 1973.

Fields, W.S., and Sweet, W.H.: *Neural Bases of Violence and Aggression*. St. Louis, Warren H. Green Inc., 1975.

Gagne, P.: Treatment of sex offenders with medroxyprogesterone acetate. *American Journal of Psychiatry, 138(5)*:644-646, 1981.

Guidelines for using short-acting intramuscular neuroleptics for rapid nueroleptization. In Ayd, Frank J. Jr. (Ed.): *International Drug Therapy Newsletter, 12*:5-12, 1977.

Intravenous haloperidol therapy. In Ayd, Frank J. Jr. (Ed.): *International Drug*

Therapy Newsletter, 13:20-23, 1978.

Itil, T.M., and Mukhopadhyay, S.: Pharmacological management of human violence. In *Modern Problems of Pharmacopsychiatry*, Vol. 13. Kargil, Basil, 1978, pp.139-158.

Keckich, W.A.: Violence as a manifestation of akathisia. *JAMA, 240*:2185, 1978.

Kochansky, G., Salzman, R., et al.: Effects of chlordiazepoxide and oxazepam administration on verbal hostility. *Archives of General Psychiatry, 34*:1451-1459, 1977.

Lion, J.R.: *Evaluation and Management of the Violent Patient. Guidelines in the Hospital and Institution*. Springfield, Ill., Charles C Thomas, Publisher, 1972.

Lion, J.R., and Pasternack, S.A.: Countertransference reactions to violent patients. *American Journal of Psychiatry, 130*:207-210, 1973.

Lion, J.R., Azcarte, C.L., and Loepke, H.A.: "Paradoxical rage reactions" during psychotropic medication. *Diseases of the Nervous System*, October 1974, pp.557-558.

Marini, J.L., and Sheard, M.H.: Antiaggressive effect of lithium ion in man. *Acta Psychiatric Scandinavica, 55*:269-286, 1977.

Money, J.: Use of an androgen depleting hormone in the treatment of male sex offenders. *Journal of Sexual Research, 6*:165-172, 1970.

Monroe, R.R.: *Episodic Behavioral Disorders*. Cambridge, Mass., Harvard University Press, 1970.

Monroe, R.R.: The problem of impulsivity in personality disturbances. In Lion, J.R.: *Personality Disorders, Diagnosis and Management*, 2nd Ed. Baltimore, Williams and Wilkins, 1981.

Parenteral (IM/IV) droperidol for acutely disturbed behavior in psychotic and nonpsychotic individuals. In Ayd, Frank J., Jr. (Ed.): *International Drug Therapy Newsletter, 15*:13-16, 1980.

Rivera-Calimlim, L., Castaneda, L., and Lasagna, L.: Effects of mode of management on plasma chlorpromazine in psychotic patients. *Clinical Pharmacology and Therapeutics, 14*:978-986, 1973.

Rivera-Calimlim, L., Nasrallah, H., Strauss, J., et al.: Clinical response and plasma levels: Effect of dose, dosage schedules, and drug interactions on plasma chlorpromazine levels. *American Journal of Psychiatry, 133*:6, 1976.

Sheard, M.H., Marini, J.L., Bridges, C.I., et al.: The effect of lithium on impulsive aggressive behavior in man. *American Journal of Psychiatry, 1-3*:1409-1413, 1976.

Showalter, C.V., and Thornton, W.E.: Clinical pharmacology of phencyclidine toxicity. *American Journal of Psychiatry, 134*:1234-1237, 1977.

Stone, A.A.: *Mental Health and Law: A System in Transition*, DHEW Publication No. (ADM) 76-176, 1975, pp. 102-106.

Walker, P.A., and Meyer, W.J.: *Antiandrogen Treatment of the Sexual Offender*. Panel presentation at 10th annual meeting of American Academy of Psychiatry and the Law, Baltimore, 1979.

Yudofsky, S., Williams, D., and Gorman, J.: Propranolol and the treatment of rage and violent behavior in patients with chronic brain syndromes. *American Journal of Psychiatry, 138(2)*:218-220, 1981.

Chapter 12

TRAINING MENTAL HEALTH PROVIDERS TO WORK WITH VIOLENCE-PRONE PATIENTS

ROGER C. SIDER

IN a society where violent behavior is increasingly common and where mental health and human service professionals are frequently required to work with violent people, it is noteworthy that there are few settings in which specific professional training is intentionally conducted toward the acquisition of knowledge and skills necessary for effective intervention. Reasons for this neglect include ambivalence about the appropriateness of mental health professionals' involvement with violent persons, denial of the magnitude of the problem, the intensely uncomfortable countertransference affects of anxiety, fear, and anger that emerge when faced with violent persons, and, finally, the relative paucity of sound theoretical and empirical foundations upon which to construct a professional training program. Yet, clinical necessity requires the preparation of professionals to work with such patients, for they surely will find themselves in situations where intervention is required. The purpose of the chapter is to propose an approach to training that is appropriately staged and sequenced, encompassing both cognitive and experiential components. Essentially, this chapter provides a foundation for conceptualizing a structure for a training program for working with violence-prone clients. The specific content of such a program would need to be developed with the unique needs of each setting in mind.

THE COGNITIVE COMPONENT

Contrary to the impression of some professionals, there is by now a definable body of knowledge that is available to provide the cognitive foundation for clinical work with violence-prone clients (*Clinical Aspects*, 1974). This knowledge can be organized under three headings: theoretical foundations, clinical knowledge and methods, and intervention strategies and disposition resources.

Theoretical Foundations

There is no clinical science or professional practice without theory. Theory provides a conceptual model that orients observations, organizes and explains empirical data, and directs intervention. In the mental health disciplines, theory is especially crucial. Although the data with which professionals deal are inordinately complex and often incomplete, it is nevertheless imperative to think rationally and act wisely with those who are violence-prone.

To further complicate matters, two educational realities are important to consider at this point. The first is that all clinical trainees will bring with them assumptions, beliefs, and attitudes, which constitute a poorly articulated and perhaps only partially conscious theory of violence, to the study of the violent patient. Since this inchoate personal theory will have a decisive impact upon later learning and practice, it is wise to begin early to have them explore their own theory of violence. This is particularly effective when conducted in a nonjudgmental group discussion setting with a supportive and evocative group leader who is capable of stimulating students to share their thoughts and feelings about violence.

Secondly, the theoretical component of the educational program must of necessity be conducted in the absence of a single, comprehensive, unifying theory of violence. As in all other areas of human behavior, there are at least four major theoretical paradigms that have been applied to violent behavior: the social (family and social level systems), the psychodynamic, the behavioral, and the medical. Each approach views violent behavior from the perspective of its own vantage point, highlighting certain observations and correlations while neglecting others. Applied to an understanding of violence, each perspective provides valuable insight. It is important, therefore, that the basic principles of each model be taught as they relate to violent behavior so that sutdents can later utilize these paradigms in their clinical reasoning.

Unfortunately, a type of theoretical tunnel vision sometimes ensues, even among experienced professionals. In such cases, the explanatory framework for violence is confined almost entirely to one paradigm. There is a particularly strong temptation for trainees who, having become aware of the inadequacies of their personal idiosyncratic theory of violence, exchange it for uncritical acceptance of one of these major theoretical models. For a number of reasons, the social-family system model and the behavioral model are most often chosen. Fresh from an emergency room consultation with a violent patient in which the senior clinician has masterfully evoked the antecedent family dynamics, the novice is prone to a "eureka" experience as ignorance and fear give way to dynamic illumination. Henceforth, he or she may tend to see *only* family dynamics in *every* violent patient, negating the possibility of hormonal imbalances, temporal lobe disorders, or inadequate superego restraints. Conversely, the behavioral perspective is highly appealing. Its orderly scientific approach to antecedent variables and operant consequences quickly renders violent behavior understandable, but ignores some of the richness and potential usefulness of an approach balanced by the integration of other perspectives.

The desirable educational objective regarding theoretical understanding of violence is to assist the trainee in replacing his or her personal theory, not with dogmatic allegiance to any one established paradigm, but rather with a balanced, comprehensive, multifaceted theoretical understanding. Such understanding emerges through the application of a biopsychosocial model to violent behavior (Engel, 1977). Based upon general systems theory, this model enables the clinician to incorporate data from all levels of organismic function and to avoid simplistic either/or thinking. This model allows the clinican to consider simultaneously a variety of biological, psychodynamic, behavioral, family, and social factors in prevention, assessment, and intervention.

Clinical Knowledge and Methods

This section of the curriculum is designed to inform trainees about the relevant facts regarding violent behavior and the methods available to ascertain and order these facts. Such empirical information includes a knowledge of the risk factors in working with violent patients and methods of reducing such risk. It is reassuring to trainees to learn, for example, that the likelihood of lethal attack is extremely low and that such attacks rarely occur during the initial assessment (Madden, Lion, and Penna, 1976). Similarly, instruction in risk-reducing techniques enhances the student's sense of competence and mastery. In addition, the relevant epidemiologic, psychiatric, psychodynamic, behavioral, and familial correlates of violence need to be thoroughly examined. Specifically, trainees require instruction in the known psychiatric conditions that may give rise to violence, the demographic characteristics of persons who commit violence, and an informed understanding of intrapsychic and interpersonal dynamics that lead to violence. It will soon become obvious to trainees that, although there is substantial data of this type available, the application of this data to a particular case is notoriously difficult. Statistical correlation provides neither etiologic proof nor assured therapeutic strategies. Yet, it is only with knowledge of these data that sound hypotheses and treatment plans can be constructed.

Equally important is the mastery of a methodologic outline that will organize and direct clinical inquiry. The assessment of a violent patient is only a special case of the general approach to clinical assessment of any patient. Therefore, trainees from each mental health discipline will already have in mind a basic outline by which they organize their clinical inquiry. This can be readily modified to incorporate specific features relevant to the violent patient. For example, Rada (1981) has outlined a method for brief evaluation of the violent patient that focuses upon three themes: first, the issue of provocation in the preassault phase, then the question of goal-directedness in the assault phase, and, finally, the patient's response to the act in the postassault phase. To thoroughly evaluate a particular patient in regard to these three phases, trainees should be instructed in the common factors and dynamics operative in each.

Intervention Strategies and Disposition Resources

It is desirable during the cognitive part of the curriculum to provide a descriptive overview of intervention strategies and disposition resources. Regarding the former, several chapters in this book provide excellent guidance. Trainees need to be thoroughly familiar with the entire range of interventions available, from an interview approach designed to calm and restore control to the patient (Lion, 1972) to the use of physical and chemical restraints (Tupin, 1975). As these techniques are described, a thorough discussion of indications and contraindications for each intervention should be provided.

Disposition resources are an important but often underrated or overlooked aspect of the curriculum. When faced with a violent patient, the practitioner who needs to refer should be thoroughly familiar with the options available for both continuity of care and for the transfer of responsibility after an appropriate clinical intervention has been made. The nature of the disposition question is largely determined by the setting in which the patient is seen: for the inpatient psychiatric ward nurse, the issue may be whether to place the patient in seclusion; in a community agency, the question may concern referral to a child protective program; or in the community, the violent person might be incarcerated. A comprehensive knowledge of the disposition options, however, is insufficient by itself. There are many vicissitudes in the referral process, and when the patient has been identified as violent, many agencies are resistant to accepting referrals who may pose a danger to the staff or require special management. It comes as a disillusioning insight to trainees to learn that, in practice, helping agencies may be anything but helpful.

THE EXPERIENTIAL COMPONENT

Clinical training must ultimately be experiential since the professional role requires the ability to think and act appropriately in an intensely experiential context. Hence, the didactic, cognitive curriculum is necessary but of limited value. Four relevant features of the experiential component will be discussed.

The Setting

Violence-prone people may appear in virtually any mental health setting, but the frequency, severity, and type of violence varies widely with the context. In general, trainees should undergo their training in a variety of settings, thus exposing them to a wide range of challenges. Emphasis should be placed on the importance of the setting in defining the task, the risks, and the disposition options. Ideally, at least one of their placements should resemble their probably future professional venue.

Personal Security

Trainees need to be aware not only of the potential for violence in the patients they are assessing, but also of the methods by which risks to the professional can be reduced to the lowest possible level. Frequently beginning students, embarrassed to appear frightened, will atempt with mock courage to conduct their work under conditions requiring unwarranted personal risk. Such considerations as the presence of other professionals or, if necessary, of guards, the importance of an open setting where the professional can remove himself or herself if necessary, and explicit instructions to surrender weapons are all elementary but important pedagogical points. Moreover, Lion (1972) has suggested approaches to the interview that will reduce the patient's fear of loss of control while setting appropriate limits and respecting the patient's humanity. Obviously, in such a situation, the first few moments of the interview are particularly crucial, for they set the tone for the whole interaction. Specific instruction in the initial clinical approach to the violence-prone patient is, therefore, particularly important.

The Task

Appropriate clinical assessment and management of violent patients ranges across a wide spectrum of choices depending upon the task that requires addressing in a given situation. The nurse on an inpatient ward or the police officer on the street may face very different tasks than does the emergency room psychiatric resident when confronted with a violent person. Moreover, hidden agendas are often operative, particularly from referring agencies who may wish to be relieved of a disposition problem or from spouses or families who may have brought the patient to professional attention for purposes of labeling or punishment. A particularly difficult and unsatisfactory task is that of assessing dangerousness. The literature is replete with the difficulties in making this concept operational and in deriving clear guidelines for clinical assessment (Peszke, 1975, and Monahan, 1978). In general, trainees should be taught to avoid assuming responsibility for defining for other persons or agencies the level of dangerousness in any given client. Much more helpful is the student's ability to probe for the implicit agenda, to make it explicit, and to redefine the task, when necessary, to conform to appropriate professional role responsibilities.

Personal Reactions and Countertransference Issues

Clinical work with violent patients is certain to evoke intense emotional responses in trainees (Lion and Pasternak, 1973). An integral part of their experiential training, therefore, is the opportunity to express, understand, modify, and integrate the feelings so generated. Anxiety, fear, and anger are particularly common. Individual trainees will, of course, utilize their characteristic defensive devices to cope with these painful affects. Part of every clinical training exercise, therefore, should be devoted to discussion with the supervisor of these feelings and the defenses against them. Usually most trainees handle such supervision well. Occasionally, however, because of a personal history of violent trauma or intense intrapsychic conflicts around aggression, a trainee may be clearly unable to function professionally with such patients. This may become visible in maladaptive coping patterns with violent patients (e.g. excessive passivity or angry confrontation). As well, the trainee's anxiety level may rise so high as to render him or her unable to function. In these cases, referral for personal psychotherapy is an appropriate recommendation.

It should be noted that not every professional is personally equipped to work with violent patients. As with other diagnostic categories (e.g. alcoholism), professionals vary widely in their aptitude for and success with various groups. It is important, then, to assist trainees to become more fully aware of their limitations and, where these are not overcome by further experience, supervision, or therapy, to respect them and plan their professional careers accordingly.

CURRICULAR STAGING AND SEQUENCING

In the foregoing discussion, artificially divided as it is between the cognitive and experiential aspects of the curriculum, there has been no mention of how to stage and integrate these components. In general, because of the nature of clinical work with violent patients, trainees should have had general professional training and clinical experience with nonviolent clients prior to undertaking this aspect of their training. There has been needless controversy regarding the relative merits of extensive classroom preparation prior to clinical exposure compared to early clinical immersion in a "sink or swim" approach. Neither extreme is ideal; rather a phased cognitive and experiential approach is most effective in which basic didactic instruction is initially combined with observational opportunities for trainees in the clinical context. The premature assumption of clinical responsibility for violent clients before extensive learning and experience have been acquired is to be avoided. After basic instruction and observation, trainees require a period of apprenticeship during which they function professionally but under close supervision so that interventions are discussed and approved by their supervisor prior to implementation. Because of the risks and the emotional intensity inherent in the management of violent patients, this apprenticeship period is especially crucial. Ultimately, however, the well-trained professional must feel competent to stand on his or her own, relying upon accumulated knowledge and experience to render sound judgments in the clinical setting. Such is the goal of the program outlined above.

SUMMARY

Essentially, this chapter provides a foundation for conceptualizing a structure for a training program for professionals working with violence-prone clients. The specific content of such a program would need to be developed with the unique needs or specific settings in mind. Regardless of setting, any such program needs to include both cognitive and experiential components that are properly sequenced and staged.

REFERENCES

Clinical Aspects of the Violent Individual, Task Force Report 8, Washington, D.C., American Psychiatric Association, July 1974.

Engel, G.L.: The need for a new medical model: A challenge for biomedicine. *Science, 196*:129-136, 1977.

Lion, J.R.: *Evaluation and Management of the Violent Patient*. Springfield, Ill., Charles C Thomas, Publisher, 1972.

Lion, J.R., and Pasternak, S.: Countertransference reactions to violent patients. *American Journal of Psychiatry, 130(2)*:207-215, February 1973.

Madden, D., Lion, J., and Penna, M.: Assaults on psychiatrist by patients. *American Journal of Psychiatry, 133(4)*:422-425, April 1976.

Monahan, J.: Prediction research and the emergency commitment of dangerous mentally ill persons: A reconsideration. *American Journal of Psychiatry, 135(2)*:198-201, February 1978.

Peszke, M.: Is dangerousness an issue for physicians in emergency commitment? *American Journal of Psychiatry, 132(8)*:825-828, August 1975.

Rada, R.: The violent patient: Rapid assessment and management. *Psychosomatics, 22(2)*:101-109, February 1981.

Tupin, J.: Management of violent patients. In Shader, R. (Ed.): *Manual of Psychiatric Therapeutics*. Boston, Little, Brown & Company, 1975, pp. 125-136.

NAME INDEX

A

Alevizos, K.S., 205, 224
Alevizos, R.N., 205, 224
Allen, R.P., 80, 83
Altman, H., 198, 225
Anders, R.L., 194
Aragona, J., 94, 96, 97, 107, 111
Archbold, Patricia, 140, 161
Armao, B.B., 202, 225
Ayd, Frank J., Jr., 241, 242
Ayllon, T., 204, 224
Azar, S.T., 92, 110
Azcarte, C.L., 230, 242
Azrin, N.H., 204, 207, 210, 225

B

Bachman, J.A., 217, 224
Bach-Y-Rita, G., 75, 83, 167, 196, 238, 241
Bailey, J.B., 205, 224
Bakan, D., 116, 135
Bandura, A., 222, 224
Bard, M., 36, 54, 58, 59, 67
Barnhill, L.R., 112, 128
Barry, D.J., 239, 241
Barstow, D.E., 205, 224
Beck, A.T., 98, 109, 172, 174, 175, 170, 179, 191
Becker, Howard, 9
Beebe, J., 196
Bellak, L., 80, 85
Benson, F.D., 75, 83
Berkowitz, L., 194
Berlin, F.S., 239, 241
Bevins, L.W., 75, 84
Bion, W.R., 17
Birkman, R., 19, 33
Blackman, N., 73, 85, 168, 195
Blake, K., 202, 225
Blenker, Margaret, 202, 225
Block, B., 194
Block, Marilyn, 142, 143, 144, 145, 161
Blout, A.R., 194
Blumer, D., 75, 81, 83, 84
Boszormenyi-Nagy, Ivan, 10, 17, 141, 161
Boucher, R., 73, 84
Bousha, D.M., 91, 92, 95, 101, 109
Boyd, A., 96, 111
Breiner, S., 23, 33
Bridges, C.I., 238, 242
Brody, Elaine, 138, 139, 141, 142, 145, 161
Brown, B.S., 75, 84
Brown, M.L., 198, 225
Budman, S.H.J., 127, 136
Burd, S.F., 194
Burdock, E.I., 198, 225
Burgess, A., 47, 54, 60, 63, 68, 73, 84
Burgess, R.L., 96, 109
Burston, G.R., 161
Busse, Ewald W., 138, 161
Butler, Robert N., 138, 162

C

Cannon, W.B., 178, 194
Caplan, G., 65, 68, 109
Carkhuff, R., 180, 194
Carlson, B.E., 36, 54
Carney, M.W.P., 194
Castaneda, L., 236, 242

Christensen, 176
Christopher, R., 171, 196
Ciccone, J.R., 239, 241
Cicero, 9
Clangn, T.L., 79, 86
Clark, J., 166, 194
Clark, Robert, 138, 162
Clayton, P.J., 198, 225
Climent, C.E., 238, 241
Cline, R., 194
Coche, E., 191, 194
Coccozza, J.J., 197
Cocozza, J., 21, 33
Cohen, M.L., 73, 84
Cohen, Stephan A., 141, 146, 162
Conger, R.D., 96, 109
Conway, C., 23, 33
Cornfield, R., 194
Cotler, 190
Covi, L., 80, 83, 238, 241
Crain, P.M., 202, 225
Cutler, N., 84

D

D'Amico, S., 42, 54
Danesh, H.B., 194
Davidson, L.A., 76, 85
de Lissovoy, U., 101, 109
Denicola, J., 99, 109
Dent, O.B., 202, 225
de Reuck, A.V.S., 86
DeBella, G.A.W., 172, 194
Di Giacomo, J.N., 78, 85
Di Mascio, A., 230, 241
Dodge, D., 111
Dollarel, J., 194
Donlon, P.T., 78, 84, 233, 241
Douglas, Richard, 142, 162
Drossman, A.K., 198, 225
Duncan, D., 110
D'Zurilla, T.J., 95, 110

E

Elliott, F.A., 115, 135
Ellis, A., 175, 181, 195
Elmer, E., 110
Engel, G.L., 245, 251
Ervin, F.R., 73, 75, 76, 81, 83, 84, 85, 86, 167, 196
Erwin, C.W., 239, 241
Erwin, R.F., 238, 241
Evenson, R.C., 198, 225

F

Farina, 176
Farrar, Marcella, 142, 162
Fauman, B.J., 167, 195
Fauman, N.A., 167, 195
Fields, W.S., 238, 241
Fishman, H.C., 135
Flick, A., 191, 194
Flitcraft, A., 38, 54
Forehand, R., 205, 225
Foster, 177
Fottrell, E., 195
Foulke, Sarah R., 142, 145, 162
Foxx, R.M., 207, 225
Frazier, S.H., 86
Freedman, A., 84

G

Gagne, P., 239, 241
Gair, D.S., 186, 195
Galston, R., 110
Gans, Bruce Michael, 141, 146, 162
Garattini, S., 86
Garfield, S.Q., 195
Gayford, J.J., 36, 54
Gelles, R.J., 36, 54, 55, 112, 115, 119, 135
George, C., 101, 110
Gerber, C.J., 239, 241
Gilbert, M.T., 99, 110
Gilles, D.R., 230, 241
Giovannoni, J.M., 198, 225
Ginnott, H.G., 180, 195
Glasser, W., 180, 195
Goldfried, M.R., 95, 110
Goldstein, R., 168, 195
Gordon, T., 99, 110
Gorman, J., 239, 242
Gorney, R., 195
Gould, R.W., 110
Gouldner, Alvin W., 9, 17
Green, A.H., 70, 84
Greenblatt, M., 186, 195
Grofalo, R., 73, 84
Groth, N., 73, 84

Guenther, A.L., 168, 169, 172, 195
Guerra, 190
Guirguis, E., 195
Guirguis, F.F., 78, 84
Gurell, L., 198, 225
Gurewitz, H., 69, 84
Gutheil, T., 186, 195
Gutheil, T.C., 84
Gutheil, T.G., 202, 225
Guze, S.B., 198, 225

H
Haber, J., 172, 179, 180, 195
Haberland, C., 73, 84
Haley, J., 82, 84
Halleck, S.L., 167, 168
Hanks, S.E., 70, 84
Harbin, H.T., 4, 17, 82, 84, 135
Hartocollis, P., 177, 178, 195, 196
Heiser, J.F., 84
Helfer, R.E., 99, 110, 111
Hellman, D.S., 73, 85, 168, 195
Herjanic, B., 40, 54
Herman, J.L., 41, 54
Hess, Beth, 142, 162
Hickey, T., 142, 165
Hilberman, E., 44, 54, 64, 68
Hildreth, A.M., 181, 195
Hill, J., 79, 85
Hitler, Adolf, 4
Hobbs, S.A., 202, 225
Hoffman-Plotkin, D., 101, 110
Hollerauer, T., 212, 218
Hollon, S.D., 110
Holstrom, L., 60, 63, 68, 73, 84
Holstrum, L., 47, 55
Hooker, Susan, 141, 142, 162
Hopkin, J., 78, 84, 233, 244
Hopkins, J., 110
Horowitz, M.J., 58, 61, 68
Howells, J.G., 17
Hudgens, R.Q., 167, 195
Huggins, M.A., 55
Hyman, Helen Kardell, 140, 141, 146, 163

I
Inhelder, B., 7-8, 17
Itil, T.M., 233, 242

J
Jacobson, G.F., 58, 59, 68
James, J.F., 239, 241
Jasmin, S., 195
Jervis, G.S., 73, 85
Johnson, Elizabeth, 142, 162
Jones, James, 4
Justice, B., 19, 21, 33, 99, 107, 110, 168, 195
Justice, R., 21, 33, 99, 107, 110, 168, 195

K
Kalish, Richard, 161
Kalogerakis, M.G., 169, 170, 195
Kaplan, M., 84
Katz, S., 68
Kaufman, K., 94, 96, 97, 107, 111
Kekich, W.A., 235, 242
Kempe, C.H., 36, 55, 110
Kempe, G.H., 110
Kempe, L., 111
Kempe, R.S., 110
Kendall, P.L., 110
Kern, S., 72, 86
Kihlstrom, J.F., 110
Kilgalen, R.K, 196
Kinzel, A.F., 196
Kirschner, Charlotte, 141, 162
Klein, D.F., 12, 18
Knopf, Olga, 141, 142, 162
Knowlton, H., 218
Kochansky, G., 230, 242
Kohnberg, L., 7, 17
Kosberg, Jordan I., 144, 162, 163
Kozol, H., 22-23, 33, 72, 85
Kraft, I., 21, 33
Kraft, J., 168, 195
Krashner, J.F., 195
Krupnich, J., 68
Kryso, J. 36, 56

L
Lagos, J.M., 198, 225
Lahmeyer, C., 186
Langdon, Bruce, 143, 162
Lange, S., 172, 196
Larrance, D.L., 91, 110

Lasagna, L., 236, 242
Lassen, G., 198, 225
Lazarus, A., 57, 68
Law, Elizabeth, 144, 162
Lemmer, B., 196
Levin, H., 197
Levy, P., 177, 178, 196
Lewis, Myrna, 138, 162
Lieb, J., 197
Lifton, R.J., 68
Likona, T., 18
Lion, J.R., 70, 73, 75, 76, 79, 80, 81, 82, 83, 84, 85, 165, 167, 168, 171, 182, 190, 196, 202, 225, 228, 229, 230, 238, 241, 242, 246, 247, 248, 249, 251
Loepke, H.A., 230, 242
Lunt, L.B., 178, 196
Lustig, N., 55
Lystad, M.H., 114, 135

M

McKay, L., 12, 18
Macoby, E., 197
Madden, D.J., 171, 176, 196, 202, 225, 246, 251
Main, M., 101, 110
Malamud, N., 85
Marcus, A., 23, 33
Maria, Roy, 55
Marinacci, A.A., 75, 85
Marini, J.L., 238, 242
Mark, V.H., 73, 81, 85, 86, 196
Marshall, M.A., 194
Maslach, C., 52, 55
Mazur, M., 68
Mehr, J., 182, 196, 198, 200, 226
Merchenbaum, D.H., 93, 98, 110
Meinecke, C.F., 239, 241
Meisel, A., 69, 86
Melick, M., 197
Menkes, J.H., 85
Menkes, M.M., 85
Merrill, G.L., 196
Meyer, W.J., 239, 242
Migeon, C., 75, 84
Mikolejczak, J., 168, 196
Milhoun, M., 99, 111
Miller, N.E., 194
Mills, T., 196
Milton, John, 15
Minuchin, S., 116, 135
Monahan, J., 23, 24, 27, 34, 249, 251
Money, J., 81, 85, 239, 242
Monroe, R.R., 4, 18, 75, 80, 85
Montague, M.C., 196
Morgan, Mildred, 142, 162
Morley, W., 58, 59, 68
Morris, M.G., 110
Morrison, S.D., 239, 241
Mukhopadhvav, S., 233, 242

N

Nadelson, C., 63, 64, 68
Nagi, 36
Nasby, W., 110
Nasrallah, H., 236, 242
Nelso, D., 43, 55
Neugarten, Bernice L., 163
Nichols, B.B., 36, 55
Noel, C., 142, 162
Notman, M., 63, 64, 68

O

Ochberg, F., 64, 68
O'Leary, K.D., 112, 135
O'Malley, Helen, 143, 145, 162

P

Pagelow, M., 119, 135
Pamirez, L., 197
Parker, B., 36, 55
Pasterna, 172
Pasternak, S.A., 82, 84, 85, 229, 242, 249, 251
Pastor, N., 181, 196
Paul, Saint, 10
Penna, M.W., 202, 225, 246, 251
Pennigroth, P.E., 196
Perlmutter, K., 198, 225
Perri, M.P., 92, 110
Peszke, M., 249, 251
Peterson, R.C., 79, 85
Pfeiffer, Eric, 161
Piaget, J., 7-8, 17
Pilette, P.C., 196
Pinderhughes, C., 115, 135
Pines, A., 52, 55
Pizzey, E., 36, 55

Platt, J.J., 95, 111
Plotkin, R., 90, 91, 92, 110, 111
Pollock, C.B., 111
Pope, Alexander, 7
Porter, R.A., 86

Q

Quitkin, F., 12, 18

R

Rada, R., 246, 251
Rathbone-McCuan, Eloise, 141, 162
Rappeport, J.R., 198, 225
Reitan, R.M., 76, 85
Renvoize, J., 162
Rigler, D., 88, 111, 115, 135
Rivera-Calimlim, L., 236, 242
Rodin, E.A., 86
Rogers, J.E., 72, 86
Rohrbeck, C.A., 111
Rose, D., 196
Rosebaum, P., 196
Rosen, H., 78, 85
Rosenbaum, A., 112, 135
Rosenhan, 177
Rounsaville, B.J., 55
Rowe, J.S., 85
Roy, M., 36, 55, 115, 135, 136
Ruben, E., 196
Rubin, B., 24, 34
Rumpler, C.H., 197
Ryan, W., 50, 55, 62, 68

S

Saexinger, H., 198, 225
Safer, D., 80, 83
Salasin, S., 59, 68
Salzman, R., 230, 242
Samuelson, Robert J., 138, 163
Sandler, J., 94, 96, 97, 99, 104, 109, 111
Sangrey, D., 58, 59, 67
Sarles, R.M., 36, 55
Satten, J., 24, 34
Satir, V., 180, 197
Saunders, D.G., 112, 135
Scherl, D., 61, 63, 68
Schmitt, B., 38, 39, 41, 45, 55
Schumacher, D.N., 36, 55
Schwab, P., 186, 197
Searles, H.F., 10, 14, 18
Sears, R.R., 197
Segal, J., 135
Seghorn, T., 73, 84
Seligman, 115
Selzer, M.L., 72, 86
Shader, R.I., 230, 241
Shah, S.A., 25, 34, 197
Shakespeare, William, 3
Shanas, Ethel, 140, 161, 163
Shapiro, R.J., 115, 127, 136
Sheard, M.H., 73, 79, 86, 238, 242
Sherman, S., 42, 54
Shorkey, C.T., 88, 111
Showalter, C.V., 230, 242
Shure, M.B., 95, 111
Siggs, E.B., 86
Silverman, 147
Silverstone, Barbara, 140, 141, 146, 163
Sinnet, Jan P., 142, 143, 144, 145, 161
Skinner, B.F., 222, 225
Slaby, A., 197
Sletten, I.W., 198, 225
Smith, D.B., 79, 86
Smith, S., 24, 34
Snyder, W., 196
Sosowsky, L., 197
Spark, Geraldine M., 10, 17, 141, 161
Spates, R., 64, 68
Spengler, Joseph, 138, 162
Spinetta, J.J., 88, 111, 115, 135
Spivak, G., 95, 111
Stanton, A.H., 171, 197
Steadman, H.J., 21, 25, 36, 197
Steele, B.F., 111
Steinmetz, Suzanne K., 36, 55, 112, 114, 136, 140, 141, 142, 144, 145, 146, 148, 149, 150, 151, 155, 163
Stillman, R.C., 79, 85
Stinnet, 163
Storlie, F.J., 52, 55
Storr, A., 197
Straus, J., 236, 242
Straus, M.A., 36, 51, 54, 55, 112, 113, 114, 115, 117, 119, 136
Streib, G., 161
Strickler, M., 58, 59, 68
Stuart, G.W., 197
Sullivan, H.S., 165, 174, 197

Summit, R., 36, 56
Sundeen, S.J., 197
Sutherland, S., 61, 63, 68
Sweet, W.H., 81, 85, 238, 241
Sweitzer, M., 96, 111
Symonds, M., 62, 63, 64, 68, 82, 86, 136

T

Tanay, E., 25, 27, 34
Tancredi, L., 197
Taylor, C.E., 202, 225
Thornton, W.E., 231, 242
Tinklenberg, J.R., 86
Tobin, Sheldon S., 138, 163
Townsend, Peter, 138, 139, 163
Treas, J., 139, 163
Trincome, B., 197
Trystad, L.N., 195
Tupin, J.P., 78, 79, 84, 86, 233, 241, 247, 251
Twentyman, C.T., 90, 91, 92, 95, 101, 109, 110, 111

V

Van Dercas, L., 99, 111
Viano, E., 68

W

Walker, L., 115, 136
Walker, P.A., 239, 242
Warner, C.G., 55
Wasserman, S., 88, 111
Webster, D.R., 207, 210, 225
Weintraub, M., 241
Wenk, E., 20, 34
West, L.J., 197
Whaley, M., 197
Whitman, R.M., 202, 225
Whitman, R.N., 172, 177, 180, 197
Wienchiwski, L.A., 75, 84
Wilbois, R.P., 40, 54
Williams, D., 239, 242
Wolfe, D.A., 94, 96, 97, 99, 107, 111
Woodrow, K.M., 86
Woodruff, R.A., 198, 225

Y

Yudofsky, S., 239, 242

Z

Zacker, J., 36, 54
Zitrin, A., 198, 225

SUBJECT INDEX

A

Abuse
 of alcohol (*see* Alcohol abuse)
 of child (*see* Child abuse, Family violence)
 of drugs (*see* Drugs, abuse of)
 of elderly (*see* Elder abuse, Family violence)
 of sibling, 113
 of spouse (*see* Spouse, abuse, Family violence)
Acts, violent, 35-36
 as crimes, 35
 definition of, 24
 minor, 113
 severe, 113, 114
Adolescence
 cult susceptibility during, 8-9
 delinquency during, 23
 fairness concepts of, 7-8
 episodic dyscontrol during, 82
 rebellion during, 70, 77
 scapegoating during, 5, 12
Adolescent parents
 and child abuse (*see* Child Abuse)
Age
 dangerousness and, 22, 168
 guilt feelings and, 63
Alcohol abuse
 epilepsy and, 75
 violence and, 4-5, 23, 31, 70, 72, 77, 79, 82, 167
Alcoholics Anonymous, 31
American Psychological Task Force on Clinical Aspects of the Violent Individual, 69
Amphetamines (*see* Drugs, abuse of)
Anger, 64, 95, 174-175
Antilirium (physostigmine salicylate), 231
Anxiety, 174, 178
Assault, 24
 victims of
  emergency medical assistance to, 43
Assaultive behavior
 definition of, 164, 166
 environmental variables causing, 169-170
 types of, 175-176
Assessment
 of dangerousness, 19-34, 69-86, 165-171, 172-173, 178-180, 249
  Birkman Method, 19-20
  Legal Dangerousness Scale, 21-22
 of family members, 115-116
 of neurological dysfunction, 75-75 (*see also* Electroencephalography, Epilepsy)
 of parental cognitive structures, 93-95
 of parenting behaviors, 95-96
 of pharmacotherapy candidates, 226-228
 of social interactional systems, 95-96
 psychological tests in (*see specific tests*)
 written reports of, 23-24
Availability
 of victim, 30, 72, 76
 of weapon, 23, 72, 76

B

Baxstrom v. Herold, 21
Benadril (diphenhydramine), 235
Bender Gestalt Test, 23
Benzotropine mesylate (Cogentin), 235

Bible, 6 (*see also* Mosaic Law, New Testament, Old Testament)
Birkman Method, 19-20
Blaming of victim, 46, 47, 49, 50, 62, 101, 123, 130
Blue Cross, 150
Boredom, 169
Burnout, 52, 53, 65

C

Carbamezepine (Tegretol), 80
Care giver(s)
- adequacy of, 169
- burnout of, 52, 53, 65
- characteristics of, 164, 165
- dangerousness of self-assessment of, 171, 173-180
- insensitivity of, 52-54
- objectivity of, 118-119
- reaction to violence of, 14, 35-36, 81-82, 119-127, 171-180, 243, 249-250
- responsibilities of, 36
- role of, 13-17, 46-47, 49-53, 118-127
- sensitivity of
  - factors affecting, 65
- training of, 243-251
  - cognitive component of, 244-247
  - experiential component of, 247-251

Catharsis, 15 (*see also* Ventilation)
Child Abuse, 24 (*see also* Cognitive-behavioral approach, Incest)
- adolescent parents and, 11, 105
- care givers' reaction to, 122-127
- *case history, 125-127*
- identification of, 38-40
- incidence of, 36, 38, 113
- interventions into, 104-109
- prevention of, 104-109
- relationship between abuser and victim in, 38, 117
- reporting of
  - legal requirements for, 41-42
- treatment of, 45, 97-102
  - involuntary, 97-98
- victims of
  - ages of, 38
  - characteristics of, 91, 101-102, 115-116, 123-124
  - emergency medical assistance to, 45
  - identification of, 38-40
  - role of, 91, 101

Chlordiazepoxide (Librium), 230, 237, 238
Chlorpromazine (Thorazine), 78, 235
Clinical Aspects of Violent Individuals, 23, 69
Clinician (*see* Care giver)
Cogentin (benzotropine mesylate), 235
Cognitive-behavioral approach, 87-110
- assessment according to, 93-96
- *case history, 89-90*
- implications of
  - for psychological assessment, 93-96
  - for treatment, 97
- parental expectations in, 87-88, 90-91
- research supporting, 89-93
- stages in, 87-89

Collective violence
- of cults, 3-4, 8-9
- group dynamics and, 4
- righteousness as a cause of, 6-8
- in terrorism, 3, 57
- warfare as, 3-4, 35

Community services, 48-49
Confidentiality
- reporting and, 70

Countertransference, 82, 119-120, 172, 243, 249-250 (*see also* Reaction to violence, *specific emotions*)
CPI, 21
Crisis approach, 181-183, 192-194
Crisis intervention, 45-47, 57-67
- objectives of, 60
- strategies for, 57-59

Cruelty to animals, 21, 23, 73, 168
Cults, 3-4, 8-9

D

Dangerousness, 27
- assessment of, 19-34, 69-86, 165-171, 172-173, 178-180, 249
- definition of, 23, 25

Death penalty, 35
Delinquency, 23
Dependency, 141-142
Depo-Provera (Provera, medroxyprogesterone acetate), 81, 239-240
Depression, 70
Deuteronomy, 6

Developmental Expectations Questionnaire, 90-91
Dexedrine (dextroamphetamine), 80
Diagnostic and Statistical Manual of Mental Disorders, III, 75, 239
Diagnosis
 categories of associated with violence, 166-168 (*see also* Inpatient violence)
Diazepam (Valium), 78, 79, 230, 235
Dilantin (diphenylhydantoin, phenytoin), 80, 237, 238
Diphenhydramine (Benadril), 235
Draw-A-Person Test, 23
Droperidol (Inapsine), 235
Drugs
 abuse of, 4, 20, 23, 71-72, 115, 167, 230-231
 case history, 31
 use in treatment of (*see* Pharmacotherapy, *specific drugs*)

E

Elder abuse, 117-118, 137-163
 causes of, 137-142
 incidence of, 113, 142-144
 interventions in, 113, 148-161
  checklist, 151-153
  counseling, 158-159
  role playing, 153-158
 as method of control, 146-147
 prevention of, 148-161
 role reversal in, 140-141, 147-148
 stigma of, 144
 victims of, 143-145
  characteristics of, 144
Electroencephalography, 4, 75, 76
Emergency medical assistance, 42-45, 77-82
Enuresis, 21, 23, 73, 168
Environment
 variables in, and inpatient violence, 30-31, 169-170
Epilepsy
 pharmacotherapy for, 80
 surgery for, 81
 of temporal lobe
  alcohol and, 75
Episodic dyscontrol
 definition of, 237
 during adolescence, 82
 episodic violence and, 4
 pharmacotherapy for, 237-238
Episodic violence, 4, 82, 237-238
Exhibitionism, 74
Extrusion, 202-203

F

Family and Marriage Clinic, 112, 113, 116, 117, 119, 123, 129, 133
Family Violence, 112-136 (*see also* Child abuse, Elder abuse, Spouse abuse)
 areas of, 116-117
 causes of, 114-116
 definition of, 113
 incidence of, 35
 stigma associated with, 116
 targets of, 117-118
 treatment of, 127-132
Fear, 60-61, 71, 81-82, 173-174
 of retribution, 129
Fluphenazine (Prolixin), 234, 236
Frustration Response Event Training (FRET), 210-216
 case history, 212-216
 prompting in, 216
 session procedure for, 213-214
 task introduction and implementation in, 214-216

G

Group dynamics, 4
Guilt, 62-64, 148, 157

H

Haldol (haloperidol), 78-79, 234, 235
Hatfields and McCoys, 7
Helplessness (*see* Powerlessness)
Holtsman Ink Blot Test, 23
Homicide, 22, 23, 24, 25, 70, 71-72
Homosexuality, 20
Hospitalization, involuntary
 for violent patients, 200
Hypnosis, 99

I

Inapsine (droperidol), 235
Incest, 36, 40-41 (*see also* Child abuse)
 family referral to treatment for, 48

reporting of
legal requirements for, 41
victims of
emergency medical assistance to, 44-45
identification of
Individual violence, 4-13, 19
Inpatient violence, 69-86, 164-197, 243-252
behavioral treatment of, 198-223
care givers' reaction to, 164
diagnostic categories associated with, 166-168
factors exacerbating, 198-200
impact on institutions of, 201-203
intervention in, 180-192, 247 (*see also* Crisis approach, Seclusion)
precautions against, 184
as response to therapy, 171-172
Insensitivity, 52-54
Intervention (*see also* Crisis Intervention)
in child abuse, 105-109
educational, 105-106
media, 105, 108-109
supportive, 105, 106-108
in family violence, 127-136
with violent inpatients, 180-192, 247
long-range, 189-192
strategies for, 247
Invisible Loyalties, 10

L

Legal Dangerousness Scale (LSD), 21-22
Librium (chlordiazepoxide), 230, 237, 238
Lidocaine (Xylocaine), 231
Lithium, 79, 236, 238-239

M

McCoys, Hatfields and, 7
Mania, 70, 231-232
Medicaid, 149, 150, 160
Medicare, 150, 160
Medroxyprogesterone acetate (Depo-Provera, Provera), 81, 239-240
Mental health facility
victim referral to, 46-47
violence in (*see* Inpatient violence)
Mental health practitioner (*see* Care giver)
Methylphenidate (Ritalin), 80, 230
Minnesota Multiphasic Personality Inventory (MMPI), 21, 23
Modeling, 99, 100
Mosaic Law, 10
Mount Hope Family Center
description of, 102
services provided by, 102
treatment model of, 102-104
case history, 103
Murder (*see* homicide)
Mysoline (primidone), 80, 237, 238

N

National Symposium on Child Abuse, 36, 55
Naziism, 6-7
Navane (thiothixene), 234
Nembutal (pentobarbital), 230
Neurological dysfunction, 74-75 (*see also* Epilepsy)
New Testament, 10
"Norm of Reciprocity," 9
Norms, cultural
for violence, 35-36, 114

O

Old Testament, 10
Oxazepam (Serax), 230

P

Paradise Lost, 15
Paranoia, 17, 70, 72, 166-167, 171, 230
Parental brutality, 23, 118
Parental Opinion Questionnaire, 94
Parent-Child Interaction Form (PCIF), 96
Parent Performance Checklist, 96
Parents Anonymous, 45, 49
Pathological intoxication (*see also* Alcohol abuse)
definition of, 75
Patients, violent
assessment of, 69-86
characteristics of, 168-169, 200-201
definition of, 69-70, 82-83
Pedophilia, 74
Pentobarbital (Nembutal), 230
Pentazocine (Talwin), 231
Pemphenazine (Trilafon), 234
Personality
of violence-prone, 168
Pharmacotherapy, 78-83, 226-242

candidate assessment for, 226-228
emergency use of, 77-79, 229-233
ethical consideration in, 227
in behavioral emergencies, 233-236
limitations of, 226-227
long-term use of, 77-80, 236-241
for sexual aggression, 239-240
side effects of, 227-228, 235
techniques for, 78-79, 234-235
Phencyclidine (PCP), 79 (*see also* Drugs, abuse of)
Phenytoin (Dilantin), 237, 238
Physostigmine salicylate (Antilirium), 231
Potential for violence (*see* Dangerousness)
Powerlessness, 61-62, 73, 180
Practitioner (*see* Care giver)
Prevention
of child abuse, 104-109
of inpatient violence, 180-194
Primidone (Mysoline), 80, 237, 238
Prolixin (fluphenzine), 234, 236
Propranolol, 240
Provera (Depo-Provera, medroxyprogesterone acetate), 81, 239-240
"Psychodynamics of Vengefulness," 12
Pyromania, 21, 23, 73, 168

R

Rage, persisting retaliatory, 5, 6, (*see also* Anger)
Rape, 22, 23, 24, 36, 41, 44-45, 74
consequences of, 57
emergency medical assistance to victims of, 44-45
intervention strategies for, 57-60
Rape crisis center, 43, 49, 65
Reaction to violence (*see also specific emotions*)
of care giver, 14, 35-56, 81-82, 119-127, 171-180, 243, 249-250 (*see also* Countertransference)
case history, 120-122, 125-127
of victim, 60-64, 130
Rebellion, 70, 77
Reciprocity, relational, 9-16, 73
definition of, 9-10
Reeducation, 99
Rehearsal, 102
Referral
to community services, 46-48
to psychotherapy, 81, 112
Reinforcement, 204-207
Reitan-Halstead Battery, 76
Relaxation, required, 207-210
Religion,7
Reporting
legal requirements for
of dangerousness, 69-70
of violence, 41-42
Resistance to treatment, 128-129
Restraint, physical, 78, 184
Retribution, fear of, 129
Righteousness, 6-8
Ritalin (methylphenidate), 80, 230
Role playing, 96, 153-158
Role reversal, 140-141, 147-148
Romans, 10
Rorschach Ink Blot Test, 23, 24, 76

S

Sadism, 74
Saint Louis State Hospital, 198
Scapegoating, 5, 12
Seclusion, 184, 186-189
Self-esteem, 19-20, 23, 24, 46, 73, 180
Self-mutilation, 217-222
case history, 218-222
Serax (oxazepam), 230
Sexual assault (*see* Rape)
Shipley Test, 95
Shaping, 101
Sibling abuse, 113
Social Security, 149, 160
Spouse abuse, 24, 36-38, 42-44, 53, 70
care givers' reaction to, 118-122
case history, 120-122
cultural norms for, 119
incidence of, 113
reporting of
legal requirements for, 41-42
victims of
characteristics of, 115
identification of, 37-38, 44, 117
emergency medical assistance to, 43-44
referral to community services of, 47
Staff, (*see* Care giver)
Stereotyping, sex-role, 36, 49, 50, 51, 54
Stelazine (trifluoperzine), 234
Stress, 30-31, 141-142, 161

Suicide, 4, 20, 24, 70, 71
Support systems, 106-108, 159, 161 (*see also* Alcoholics Anonymous, Parents Anonymous)
Symptoms of abuse, 37-41

T

Talwin (pentazocine), 231
Tarasoff decision, 69
Tegretol (carbamazepine), 80
Terrorism, 3, 57 (*see also* Collective violence)
Tests, psychological, 19-24, 76, 95 (*see also specific tests*)
Thematic Apperception Test, 23, 24, 76
Therapist (*see* Care giver)
Therapy (*see also* Treatment)
  behavioral, 98-99
  cognitive, 98-99
  family, 13-17, 82, 99, 103, 112-136
  group, 81, 100, 103
  individual, 13-17
Thiothixene (Navane), 234
Thorazine (chlorpromazine), 78, 235
Time-out, 184, 205-207
Titus Andronicus, 3
Treatment, 77-82 (*see also* Emergency medical assistance, Intervention, Therapy, Pharmacotherapy)
  behavioral, 205-223
  of child abuse, 97-110, 127-135
  cognitive-behavioral, 97-110
  of family violence, 102-104, 127-135
  goals of, 132-135
  of inpatient violence, 83, 205-223
  involuntary, 97-98, 119
  Mount Hope Family Center model of, 102-104
  required relaxation as, 207-210
  resistance to, 127, 128-129
  of self-mutilation, 217-222
  strategies for, 49-54
  of vengefulness, 13-17
  ventilation as, 15, 60-61, 64
Trifluoperzine (Stelazine), 234
Truancy, 21, 73

V

Validation, 180-182
Valium (diazepam), 78, 79, 230, 235
Venereal disease, 40-41
Vengeance, 3-18
  affective component of, 7
  Biblical concept of, 10
  case history, 5, 12-13
  cognitive aspect of, 5-6
  definition of, 6
  psychology of, 5-12
  religion and, 7
  treatment of, 13-17
Ventilation, 15, 60-61, 64 (*see also* Catharsis)
Victim, 36-56
  age of, and guilt, 63
  availability of, 30, 72, 76
  characteristics of, 101-102, 115-116
  emergency medical assistance to, 42-45
  identification of, 37-41, 44, 74
  legal rights of, 41-42
  reaction of, 60-64, 130 (*see also* Reaction to violence, *specific emotions*)
  role of, 115
Victimization, 57-67
  case history, 65-67
Victim response syndrome, 58-59
Vindication, 6
Vineland Social Maturity Scale, 90, 94
Violence
  acts of, 35-36
    as crimes, 35
    definition of, 24
    minor, 113
    severe, 113-114
  as defense, 12
  alcohol and (*see* Alcohol abuse)
  causes of, 4-5, 114-116
  cultural norms for, 35, 71, 119
  drugs and (*see* Drugs, abuse of)
  definition of, 24-25, 70, 113-114
  episodic, (*see* Episodic violence)
  family (*see* Family violence; *see also* Child abuse, Elder abuse, Sibling abuse, Spouse abuse)
  history of, 20, 22, 27-28, 71-72, 76, 115, 134, 170-171, 201
  individual (*see* Individual violence)
  inpatient (*see* Inpatient violence)
  nonphysical, 114

paranoia and, 5, 7
potential for (*see* Dangerousness)
predictors of, 10, 12, 21, 24, 27, 28, 73, 77, 167-171
prevention of, 23
reaction to (*see also specific emotions*)
of care givers, 14, 35-56, 81-82, 119-121, 171-180, 243, 247-250 (*see also* Countertransference)
of victims, 60-64, 130
Voyeurism

W

Warfare, 3-4, 35 (*see also* Collective violence)
Weapon availability, 23, 72, 76
Webster-Azrin procedure, 208-209
Wechsler Adult Intelligence Scale (WAIS), 23, 95
Wechsler Memory Scale, 23
Wife beating (*see* Spouse abuse)

X

Xylocaine (lidocaine), 231